Music in Korea

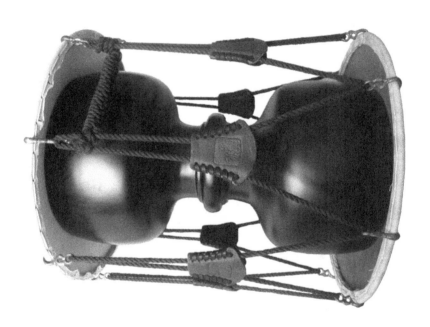

Music in Korea

∞

EXPERIENCING MUSIC, EXPRESSING CULTURE

∞

DONNA LEE KWON

New York   Oxford

OXFORD UNIVERSITY PRESS

Oxford University Press, Inc., publishes works that further Oxford University's
objective of excellence in research, scholarship, and education.

Oxford   New York
Auckland   Cape Town   Dar es Salaam   Hong Kong   Karachi
Kuala Lumpur   Madrid   Melbourne   Mexico City   Nairobi
New Delhi   Shanghai   Taipei   Toronto

With offices in
Argentina   Austria   Brazil   Chile   Czech Republic   France   Greece
Guatemala   Hungary   Italy   Japan   Poland   Portugal   Singapore
South Korea   Switzerland   Thailand   Turkey   Ukraine   Vietnam

For titles covered by Section 112 of the US Higher Education
Opportunity Act, please visit www.oup.com/us/he for the
latest information about pricing and alternate formats.

Published by Oxford University Press, Inc.
198 Madison Avenue, New York, New York 10016
http://www.oup.com

Oxford is a registered trademark of Oxford University Press

Library of Congress Cataloging-in-Publication Data
Kwon, Donna Lee.
   Music in Korea : experiencing music, expressing culture / Donna Lee Kwon.
      p. cm.—(Global music series)
   Includes bibliographical references and index.
   ISBN 978–0–19–536827–7
   1. Music—Korea—History and criticism.   I. Title.
   ML342.K867 2012
   780.9519—dc23   2011032313

Printing number: 9 8 7 6 5 4 3

Printed in the United States of America
on acid-free paper

GLOBAL MUSIC SERIES

General Editors: Bonnie C. Wade and Patricia Shehan Campbell

Music in East Africa, Gregory Barz
Music in Turkey, Eliot Bates
Music in Central Java, Benjamin Brinner
Teaching Music Globally, Patricia Shehan Campbell
Native American Music in Eastern North America, Beverley Diamond
Music in Pacific Island Cultures, Brian Diettrich, Jane Freeman Moulin, and Michael Webb
Music in Mainland Southeast Asia, Gavin Douglas
Carnival Music in Trinidad, Shannon Dudley
Music in Bali, Lisa Gold
Music in Ireland, Dorothea E. Hast and Stanley Scott
Music in Korea, Donna Lee Kwon
Music in China, Frederick Lau
Music in Mexico, Alejandro L. Madrid
Music in Egypt, Scott L. Marcus
Music in the Hispanic Caribbean, Robin Moore
Music in Brazil, John Patrick Murphy
Intertribal Native American Music in the United States, John-Carlos Perea
Music in America, Adelaida Reyes
Music in Bulgaria, Timothy Rice
Music in North India, George E. Ruckert
Mariachi Music in America, Daniel Sheehy
Music in West Africa, Ruth M. Stone
Music in the Andes, Thomas Turino
Music in South India, T. Viswanathan and Matthew Harp Allen
Music in Japan, Bonnie C. Wade
Thinking Musically, Bonnie C. Wade

Contents

∾

Moving Beyond "Tradition" in the Music of Jang
        Goon   171

Foreword

∞

In the past three decades, interest in music around the world has surged, as evidenced in the proliferation of courses at the college level, the burgeoning "world music" market in the recording business, and the extent to which musical performance is evoked as a lure in the international tourism industry. This heightened interest has encouraged an explosion in ethnomusicological research and publication, including production of reference works and textbooks. The original model for the "world music" course—if this is Tuesday, this must be Japan—has grown old, as has the format of textbooks for it, whether a series of articles in single multiauthored volumes that subscribe to the idea of "a survey" and have created a canon of cultures for study, or single-authored studies purporting to cover world musics or ethnomusicology. The time has come for a change.

This Global Music Series offers a new paradigm. Instructors can now design their own courses; choosing from a set of case-study volumes, they can decide which music they will teach and how much. The series also does something else; rather than uniformly taking a large region and giving superficial examples from several countries within it, case studies offer two formats: some focused on a specific culture, some on a discrete geographical area. In either case, each volume offers greater depth than the usual survey. Themes significant in each instance guide the choice of music that is discussed. The contemporary musical situation is the point of departure in all the volumes, with historical information and traditions covered as they elucidate the present. In addition, a set of unifying topics such as gender, globalization, and authenticity occur throughout the series. These are addressed in the framing volume, *Thinking Musically* (Wade), which sets the stage for the case studies by introducing those topics and other ways to think about how people make music meaningful and useful in their lives. *Thinking Musically* also presents the basic elements of music as they are practiced in musical systems around the world so that authors of each case study do not have to spend time explaining them and can delve immediately into the particular music. A second framing volume, *Teaching Music Globally* (Campbell), guides teachers in the use of *Thinking Musically* and the case studies.

The series subtitle, "Experiencing Music, Expressing Culture," also puts in the forefront the people who make music or in some other way experience it and also through it express shared culture. This resonance with global studies in such disciplines as history and anthropology, with their focus on processes and themes that permit cross-study, occasions the title of this Global Music Series.

Bonnie C. Wade
Patricia Shehan Campbell
General Editors

Preface

∞

Although I grew up with some familiarity with Korean culture as a second-generation Korean American, little did I know that becoming more deeply involved with Korean music would be such a transformative journey. Ever since I took my first lesson on the *changgo* drum (ubiquitous in Korean music and dance) more than two decades ago, I knew I was hooked. Apparently, I am not the only one. Over the years, I have heard countless stories of people becoming captivated with Korean culture. Whether it is the spicy and piquant food, intense films, infectious pop, addictive television melodramas, political displays or deeply rooted music, Korean culture has a way of being both engaging and elusive at the same time. With its complicated divisional politics and intermediary location, Korea has shown this duality over the course of its history. My goal in this book is to illuminate what makes Korean culture so distinctive, especially as it applies to Korean music making.

Korea's uniqueness in the world has much to do with its current state of division. Well into the 21st century, Korea remains one of the few divided countries that still harbor tensions left over from the Cold War. Given that North Korea (Democratic People's Republic of Korea) and South Korea (Republic of Korea) never signed a peace treaty at the close of the Korean War (1950–1953), the two countries are still technically at war. Despite this complex state of affairs, the division of Korea—not to mention North Korea in general—is minimally addressed in the literature on Korean music. In many of the texts that focus on Korean traditional music, time seems to end with the Chosŏn dynasty (1392–1910), as if the division never happened. Much of this has to do with the limited accessibility of North Korea. Scholars have shown some reluctance to conduct research or even write about North Korea because of the sensitivity and constantly shifting relationships among the DPRK, the ROK, and the rest of the world. For example, in the early stages of writing this book, the DPRK was showing significant signs of opening up to cultural diplomacy, even inviting the New York Philharmonic to perform in Pyongyang in February 2008. Since then, however, international engagement with the DPRK has become more challenging, and it is difficult to say where things will go in the near future.

In light of the contemporary focus of the Global Music Series, I feel strongly about addressing music and culture in *both* North and South Korea. North Koreans, in particular, are usually portrayed in negative and dehumanizing ways, and part of what I seek to do here is to provide a more balanced view of North Korean expressive culture. Although more of the volume is informed by my knowledge and experiences in South Korea, I have incorporated North Korean examples consistently throughout the text. In this endeavor, I have done my best to specify which "Korea" I am talking about in the text. Too often, when someone says "Korea" they really mean "South Korea." Generally speaking, I reserved the use of "Korea" to refer to the whole peninsula as a coherent region, especially when speaking about traditional genres that developed prior to division.

In deciding what to include in this book, I was guided by the notion of highlighting those genres that are still practiced or appreciated today, as well as those that are most representative. Like other volumes in the Global Music Series, this book is thematically organized and not intended to be a comprehensive or historical genre survey. I deliberately chose themes that applied meaningfully to Korea as a historical entity as well as to *both* North and South Korea in the contemporary context. In short, the three themes are transnationalism, cultural continuity and music and cultural politics. Throughout the volume, these themes act as conceptual frames to encourage the reader to go beyond just the learning of genres and think through them to understand their implications and cultural resonances.

Because of the limitations of the format of this book, there are many areas I could not cover. In particular, I did not delve into the rich religious musical traditions of Korea as much as I would have liked. In particular, Buddhist and Christian musical practices do not receive as much attention as they deserve. Although there is not a lot written in English on South Korean Christian music practices, there is a good deal of excellent scholarship already written on Confucian, Buddhist and Shamanist traditions (see the Resources section at the back of the book). Another area that could have been explored further is the issue of gender in musical expression. Given Korea's Confucianist leanings, there is much that could be explored here. I hope that this volume acts as a starting point about these matters and many other thought-provoking topics.

May this journey into the music and culture of Korea expand your musical horizons and challenge you to think about music and culture in new ways.

NOTES ON ROMANIZATION

The two most widely used Korean romanization systems are the McCune-Reischauer and the Revised Romanization of Korean; the latter was officially put into use in 2000 by South Korea's Ministry of Culture and Tourism (sometimes referred to as MCT). Although the MCT system is more straightforward and does not require diacritical marks or extra symbols such as apostrophes, the Revised Romanization system does lead to more problems in pronunciation for new readers. With this in mind, I have taken the almost unanimous advice of the reviewers of this book and chosen to follow the McCune-Reischauer system (hereafter referred to as MR). Please keep in mind, however, that when conducting research or looking for additional resources (especially online), you may want to try multiple spellings (especially those that follow MCT).

Several situations come up in the text that are occasions for exception, modification or further comment:

1. I have chosen to keep the spelling of some words, such as *kut* (ritual or performance), consistent throughout the text. Normally, when this word is combined with other words, the spelling should be changed to reflect pronunciation according to the rules of MR. For example, the word *p'ungmulgut* (*p'ungmul* ritual) has been spelled *p'ungmul-kut* where the *kut* is separated by a hyphen.
2. Hyphens and apostrophes are used abundantly and sometimes interchangeably in romanization of Korean. Generally speaking, hyphens are used to separate morphemes in a larger compound word, as in the word *ssikim-kut*. Apostrophes are used most often to differentiate the less aspirated consonants such as *p, t, ch* and *k* (pronounced more like *b, d, j* and *g*) from their more aspirated counterparts *p', t', ch'* and *k'* (pronounced closer to *p, t, ch* and *k* in English). Occasionally an apostrophe will be used to separate morphemes in larger words, especially between the letters *n* and *g* to prevent those letters from being pronounced with a soft *ng* as in the word "ringer." A good example would be the word for the Korean alphabet, *han'gŭl*, which should be pronounced with a harder *g*.

3. In general, I have made exceptions for cities, organizations, figures, musicians, authors, terms and titles of works that are better known by their non-MR spellings. These include the South Korean capital of Seoul (Soŭl in MR), the former president Park Chung-hee (Pak Chŏng-hŭi in MR), the rapper-musician Seo Taiji (Sŏ Taeji in MR), and the author Lee Young Mee (Yi Yŏng-mi in MR). Terms or titles of works with which I have chosen to use non-MR spellings include the North Korean concept of *juche* or "self-reliance" (*chuch'e* in MR) and the Korean national anthem, "*Aegukga*" (*Aegukka* in MR).
4. Another special case has to do with the word for Korean music, or *kugak*. In the text, I spell it this way according to MR, but when referring to the National Gugak Center (the premier South Korean organization, previously known as the National Center for Korean Traditional Performing Arts), I follow the MCT romanization.

Korean name order generally follows Korean practice, with the "family name" first and "given name" last (in other words, the name order is the reverse of Western practice). I have made a few exceptions to this in situations where the person is better known for putting the "given name" first, as with the first Korean president Syngman Rhee and the international composer Unsuk Chin. Foreign terms are italicized throughout, with the exception of proper nouns and government organizations.

NOTES ON PRONUNCIATION

The vowels *a, e, i, o* and *u* in the Korean language are pronounced roughly as they would be in Italian or Spanish. *Ŭ* is pronounced similarly to the *ou* in "could." *Ŏ* is pronounced as the *o* in "won" or "some."

Consonants are generally pronounced as they would be in English, with an apostrophe (') indicating a greater degree of aspiration (with consonants *p, t, ch,* and *k* being less aspirated than *p', t', ch'* and *k',* see exception 2 above). When *p, t, ch,* and *k* are surrounded by vowels or voiced continuant consonants such as *l, n, ng* or *w,* they are spelled and pronounced more like *b, d, j* and *g* in a softer, less aspirated fashion (such as *kayagŭm and kŏmungo*). The consonant *r* is always "flipped" or briefly rolled with the tongue.

S is usually pronounced as it is in the word "*sonic.*" When *s* is followed by an *i,* however, it is always pronounced as a *sh* sound; for example, the terms *sijo, sin minyo,* and *sinawi* are pronounced *shijo, shin minyo* and *shinawi.*

INSTRUCTIONAL AIDS AND RESOURCES

I have provided listening guides and activities throughout the text to help readers make meaningful links between the material in the text and the listening examples provided on the accompanying CD. Additional ideas and resources for classroom instruction are found on the Global Music Series website: www.oup.com/us/globalmusic. You will also find a list of other multimedia resources in the back of this volume to aid in exploring Korean music and culture.

ACKNOWLEDGMENTS

I have many people to thank for supporting me in my ongoing exploration of Korean music, culture and dance and for helping me in some way to complete this book. First of all, my thanks go to the Higher Education division of Oxford University Press; it has been a true honor and a tremendous opportunity. In particular, I would like to thank Janet M. Beatty (Executive Editor), Lauren Mine (Associate Editor), Talia Benamy and Cory Schneider for their patience and grace in shepherding this book to completion. Special thanks go to Bonnie C. Wade and Patricia Shehan Campbell. I am in awe of all that they have done to develop this series. In particular, I appreciate Patricia Campbell's editorial support and gentle hand in enlisting C. Victor Fung to write the instructional guide for this volume. In Bonnie Wade, I could not have asked for a more meticulous, astute, and generous editor. I also would like to thank the reviewers of this volume for sharing their knowledge, time and effort in commenting on my manuscript: Nathan Hesselink, the University of British Columbia; YouYoung Kang, Scripps College; Jonathan Kramer, Duke University; Fred Lau, University of Hawai'i at Manoa; Tong Soon Lee, Emory University; Chan E. Park, the Ohio State University; George Ruckert, Massachusetts Institute of Technology; Roger Vetter, Grinnell College; and Heather Willoughby, Ewha University. This book has benefited immeasurably from their input.

I would also like to thank the Korea Foundation for an Instructional Materials Development grant to prepare the audio and visual materials for this book. They lent much-needed support during a transitional time in my career, and for that I will be forever grateful. In addition, I would like to thank the Friends of Music at the University of Kentucky for funding my travel to Korea to continue to conduct research and work on obtaining permissions during the summer of 2009. In addition, thanks go to Elisa Gahng, Katherine Lee, Kyung Jin Lee and Linda Kwon for allowing me to include their wonderful photos in this book.

Going back to my childhood, I would to thank my grandmother for instilling in all of us a love for the arts. Cheers to my Aunt (Kyu Wha Lee) for teaching us how to perform Korean dance and proving to us early in life that there is a place for Korean music and dance in the United States. Thanks also to Jang Woo Nam, for being the first to teach me *p'ungmul* on the *changgo* drum and for introducing me to the Korean Youth Cultural Center in Oakland, California. There, I met numerous people who shared a passion for Korean culture, with whom I learned so much. In particular, I would like to thank Hojung Choi, Ann Kwon, Ko Mesook, Amber Heaton, Patrick Chew, Minjoon Kouh, Jongsuk Lee, Jenny Cho, Helen Min, Eunice Kwon and John Kim. Special thanks to Bonhae Ku for helping me secure music permissions in Korea and for introducing me to prominent artists such as Joung Taechoon and the current members of *Seulgidoong*. I also want to thank Michael Hurt for sharing photo tips and furnishing inexpensive housing in the heart of Seoul. Thank you also to Yi Boram for teaching us so many wonderful *minyo*.

In Korea, I have had the privilege of meeting and interacting with numerous artists and scholars to whom "thank you" cannot even begin to express my gratitude for sharing so much with me. To my teachers from the Imsil P'ilbong Nongak Preservation Society (Important Intangible Cultural Asset No. 11-5), I would like to thank Yang Chin-sŏng, Yang Chin-hwan, Oh Mi-hae, Ch'oe Ho-in and Han Jae-hun. Thanks also to Yang Ok-ran for teaching me *p'ansori* and *minyo*. I would also like to thank the members of *Kutsarang*, who practiced at the Seoul P'ilbong transmission center. In particular, special thanks to Cho Ch'unyong, who took great interest in my work and shared many invaluable insights with me over the years. I also want to thank Yi Chong-jin for his insights on P'ilbong *p'ungmul* as well as other Korean expressive folk culture forms.

I spent considerable time with the Kosŏng *Ogwangdae* mask dance drama group, and my work is very much informed by their spirit, philosophy, integrity and wisdom. In particular, I want to thank their managing director, Hwang Chong-uk; their president, Yi Yun-sŏk; and Han Man-ho for welcoming me into their world. Additionally, I want to thank Yun Hyŏn-ho for his friendship and willingness to teach me how to play the conical double reed or *t'aep'yŏngso*. Other groups or individuals I would like to acknowledge are Kim Chi-suk, Moon Hyun, Hwang Byung-ki, Wŏn Il, members of the National Gugak Center *samulnori* team, and Kim Duk-soo's *Hanullim* organization. I am indebted to Korean scholars Lee Young Mee, Park Mikyung and Song Hye-jin for their support and assistance in this project. I would also like to thank Joung Taechoon, members of Kkottaji, Jang Goon and Lee Chang-Eui at Master Plan Production.

This book is informed and inspired by the stimulating research of Korean music scholars who are working all across the globe. In this regard, I would like to thank Song Bang-song, Lee Byong Won, Keith Howard, Nathan Hesselink, Robert Provine, Lee Bo-hyung, Cho Chae-sŏn, Heather Willoughby, Chae Hyun Kyung, Hilary Finchum-Sung and Roald Maliangkay. In Korean studies, I would like acknowledge my debt to Chan E. Park, Namhee Lee, Jong Bum Kwon and Jae Chung.

Traveling to North Korea is no easy task, and I would like to thank all of those who made this trip possible (who I will leave anonymous). I would also like to thank my companions, organizers, and translators who provided such an unexpected mixture of humor, intellectual engagement, sensitivity and compassion. Heartfelt thanks go to my parents, O Kuk and Kyumeen Kwon, for their understanding and unwavering love. On a personal note, I would like to thank Robert Hackworth for making the maps for this volume and more importantly, mapping a new and amazing life together. Although she cannot read this yet, thanks to Sophie Lee Hackworth for being such a constant source of joy in my life. At the University of Kentucky, I could not ask for more stimulating colleagues than in Ben Arnold, Ron Pen, Jonathan and Beth Glixon, Lance Brunner and Diana Hallman; I thank them for their collegial support. I also want to thank graduate students Adam Sovkoplas, for his assistance with the musical examples; Melinda Lio, Erin Walker and Brad Meyer for always being so helpful and reliable; and Jennifer Tullmann for being an excellent childcare provider. Thanks as well to my former professors at the University of California, Berkeley, and Wesleyan University: Jocelyne Guilbault, Benjamin Brinner, Su Zheng and Mark Slobin. Lastly, I would like to make a dedication to three special individuals who no longer walk this earth but continue to inspire. Thanks to Margaret Dilling, whose courage, integrity and activism have made the path easier to trod. To Peter Kim, who always had a twinkle in his eye, a spring in his step and the ability to make everyone laugh. To Mirjana Lauševic, thank you for being such an incredible human being, scholar, teacher, storyteller and friend.

CD Track List

1. *"Pan'gapsŭmnida"* ("Glad to Meet You"). North Korean song excerpt. Kimch'ek University members of the youth league. Recording by the author in Pyongyang, July 2007.
2. *"Arirang."* Korean folksong excerpt in orchestral format. Pyongyang Conservatory Orchestra. Recording by the author in Pyongyang, July 2007.
3. *"Arirang"* (special track). Korean folksong excerpt in a rock format. From *Live 2: Live Is Life.* Yoon Do-hyun Band. Seoul Records: SRCD 3644A. 2002. Courtesy of Seoul Records.
4. *"Kunbam T'aryŏng"* ("Roast Chestnut Song"). Korean folksong excerpt in contemporary format. Kimch'ek University members of the youth league. Recording by the author in Pyongyang, July 2007.
5. *"Kunbam T'aryŏng"* ("Roast Chestnut Song"). Korean folksong excerpt in contemporary format. From *Kwenari.* Kim Yong-u. Samsung Music AK: SCO-165KYW. 2001. Used with permission.
6. *"Tasi Mannapsida"* (Let's Meet Again"). North Korean song excerpt. Kimch'ek University members of the youth league. Recording by the author in Pyongyang, July 2007.
7. *"Ch'unhyang-ga Sarangga"* ("Love Song" from *The Song of Ch'unhyang*). *P'ansori* excerpt. From *Saenghwal Kugak Taejŏnjip 7 (Haehakkwa Pungjalŭl Kyohunŭro).* Jŏng Hoe-sŏk (vocal), Kim Chŏng-man (*puk*). Seoul Records: SRCD-1217. 2003. Courtesy of Seoul Records and the National Gugak Center.
8. *"Seoulesŏ Pyongyangkkaji"* ("From Seoul to Pyongyang"). From *Kkottaji 1. Kkottaji. Kkottaji* HKC 145. Used with permission.
9. *"Munmyo Cheryeak: Hwangjongkung"* ("Sacrifice to Confucius: Hwangjongkung"). Confucian ritual court music. From *Saenghwal Kugak Taejŏnjip 9 (Ch'umowa Kiwonŭi Ŭmak).* Seoul Records SRCD-1219. 2003. Courtesy of Seoul Records and the National Gugak Center.

10. *"Chongmyo Cheryeak: Pot'aep'yŏng Hŭimun"* ("Sacrifice to the Royal Ancestors: *Pot'aep'yŏng Hŭimun"*). Royal Ancestral ritual court music. From *Saenghwal Kugak Taejŏnjip 1 (Yet Kungjungŭi Saenghwal Ŭmak).* Seoul Records SRCD-1219. 2003. Courtesy of Seoul Records and the National Gugak Center.

11. *"Sujech'ŏn"* ("Long Life Everlasting as the Sky"). *Hyangak* excerpt. From *Saenghwal Kugak Taejŏnjip 1 (Yaet Kungjungui Saenghwal Ŭmak).* Seoul Records SRCD-1219. 2003. Courtesy of Seoul Records and the National Gugak Center.

12. *"Kayagŭm Sanjo: Chungjungmori, Kutkori, Chajinmori."* Sanjo on the *kayagŭm* zither. From *Saenghwal Kugak Taejŏnjip 8 (Mŏtkwa Hŭngŭl Yŏkk-ko P'urŏsŏ).* Ji Ae-ri *(kayagŭm)*; Kim Chŏng-man *(changgo).* Seoul Records: SRCD-1218. 2003. Courtesy of Seoul Records and the National Gugak Center.

13. *"Kŏmungo Sanjo: Chinyangjo, Chungmori, Chungjungmori."* Sanjo on the *kŏmungo* zither. Han Kap-dŭk *(kŏmungo)*; Hwang Dŏk-chu, *(changgo).* Courtesy of the National Gugak Center.

14. *"Taegŭm Sanjo: Chungmori."* Sanjo excerpt on the *taegŭm* flute. From *Saenghwal Kugak Taejŏnjip 8 (Mŏtkwa Hŭngŭl Yŏkk-ko P'urŏsŏ).* Sŏ Yong-sŏk *(taegŭm)*; Kim Chŏng-man *(changgo).* Seoul Records: SRCD-1218. 2003. Courtesy of Seoul Records and the National Gugak Center.

15. *"Norae-kut"* ("Song Ceremony"). *P'ungmul excerpt. Honam Chwado Imshil P'ilbong Nongak Preservation Society,* Important Intangible Cultural Asset No. 11-5. Recording by the author in P'ilbong, South Korea, February 2002.

16. "North Korean 21-String *Kayagŭm* Excerpt with *Changgo* Accompaniment." Recording by the author at the Pyongyang Conservatory of Music, July 2007.

17. *"Ajaeng Sanjo: Chinyangjo."* Sanjo excerpt on the *ajaeng* zither. From *Saenghwal Kugak Taejŏnjip 8 (Mŏtkwa Hŭngŭl Yŏkk-ko P'urŏsŏ).* Pak Chong-sŏn *(ajaeng)*; Chang Tŏk-hwa *(changgo).* Seoul Records: SRCD-1218. 2003. Courtesy of Seoul Records and the National Gugak Center.

18. *"Basic Changdan."* Recorded and performed by the author.

19. *"Uddhari Poongmul."* Samulnori excerpt. From *Samul-Nori: Drums and Voices of Korea.* Nonesuch/WEA Japan 72093-1. 2001 [1984].

20. *"Chindo Ssikkimkut: Chogamangsŏk—Salp'uri"* ("Cleansing Ritual from Chindo: Invitation Ritual—Salp'uri"). Shaman music from Chindo. From *Music and Shamanism in Korea: A Study of Selected*

Ssikkum-kut Rituals for the Dead. Kim Tae-rye (vocals). Jigu Records: CSY 96071. 1996. Used with permission.
21. *"Sinawi." Sinawi* ensemble form. From *Saenghwal Kugak Taejŏnjip 9 (Chumowa Kiwonŭi Ŭmak).* Seoul Records SRCD-1219. 2003. Courtesy of Seoul Records and the National Gugak Center.
22. *"Chindo Arirang."* Korean folksong excerpt. From CD accompanying the book *Uriŭi Sorirŭl Chajasŏ* Vol. 2. Cho Kong-nye (vocals). MBC: 2002. Used with permission.
23. *"Sŏdosori Ipchang Yŏngbyŏn-ga."* ("Standing Songs from the Seodo Region: Nollyang"). From *Saenghwal Kugak Taejŏnjip 6 (Hŭngyoun Soripanesŏ).* Sŏdosori singers. Seoul Records: SRCD-1216. 2003. Courtesy of Seoul Records and the National Gugak Center.
24. *"P'yŏngsijo: Ch'ŏngsanri Pyŏkkyesuya"* (*"P'yŏngsijo:* Green Mountains"). From *Sŏn'ga Kim Wŏl-ha Chŏngga Vol. 1: Ch'ŏngsanri Pyŏkkyesuya.* Kim Wŏl-ha (vocals). Synnara: NSC-089. 2005. Used with permission.
25. *"Sach'ŏlga"* ("Song of Four Seasons"). *Tan'ga* excerpt. From *Kim Su-yŏn Chang Hŭngboga.* Kim Su-yŏn (vocals); Kim Chŏng-man *(puk).* Synnara/King Records: SYNCD-084~5. 1995. Used with permission.
26. *"Nunmul Chŏjŭn Tuman-gang"* ("Tear-Drenched Tuman River"). *Ppongtchak* excerpt. From *Kim Jŏng-gu Original Hit Song Chong Gyŏlsanjip.* Kim Jŏng-gu (vocals). Oasis Records: ORC-1148. 1991.
27. *"Kkolmangtae Arirang." Sin minyo* excerpt. From *30 Nyŏndae Sin minyo.* Kim Yong-hwan (vocals). Seoul Records: SRCD-1232. 1995. Courtesy of Seoul Records.
28. "Gagok for Voice, Guitar and Percussion." Contemporary composition excerpt by Isang Yun. From *Isang Yun: Chamber Music L'Art Pour Art.* L'Art Pour Art ensemble. Classic Produktion Osnabruck: 999 118-2. 1993. © Copyright 1972 by Bote & Bock Musik- Und Buhnenverlag GMBH & Co. Used with permission.
29. *"Double Concerto"* for piano, percussion and ensemble. Contemporary composition excerpt by Unsuk Chin. From *Unsuk Chin: Akrostichon-Wortspiel.* Ensemble Intercontemporain. Deutsche Grammophon/Universal Music DG7140/477 511-8. 2005. © Copyright 2003 by Boosey & Hawkes Music Publishers Ltd. Used with permission.
30. *"Ch'unsŏl: 3. Sinbisŭlŏpke"* ("Spring Snow: 3 Mysteriously"). *Kayagŭm* composition by Hwang Byung-ki. From *Byungki Hwang: Kayagum Masterpieces Vol. 4 Spring Snow.* Hwang Byung-ki *(kayagŭm);* Kim Chung-su *(changgo).* C & L Music Inc./EMI: CNLR 0106-2. 2001. Courtesy of Hwang Byung-ki.

31. "Moonlight Dance." Composition by Wŏn Il. From *Asura. Ene Media SCO-144WIN. 2003.* Courtesy of Won-Il.
32. *"Sahyangga"* ("Song of Nostalgia"). Excerpt for marimba and piano. Recording by the author in Pyongyang, July 2007.
33. *"Sora Sora Pururŭn Sora"* ("Pine Tree, Pine Tree, Green Pine Tree"). Korean hip-hop version of a song movement song, excerpt. From *So Sniper.* MC Sniper. Pony Canyon: 00019. 2002. Courtesy of Pony Canyon.
34. *"Kohyangjip Kasae"* ("Going Home to My Hometown"). Song movement excerpt. From *Joung Taechoon Pak Ŭn-ok 20nyŏn Best.* Joung Taechoon. Universal Music. Courtesy of Joung Taechoon.
35. *"Aradiho."* Korean hip-hop excerpt. From *Drunken Tiger 4: Ppuri [Foundation].* Drunken Tiger. Doremi Media Co., Ltd. DRMCD 1907. 2003.
36. *"Hangugin"* ("Korean Person"). Korean hip-hop excerpt. From *MC Sniper Chohaeng.* MC Sniper. Pony Canyon: PCLD 00023. 2003. Courtesy of Pony Canyon.
37. *"Sŏsa"* ("Written Word"). Korean hip-hop excerpt. From *MP Hip-Hop 2001 Taepak.* One Sun. MP Production: DBKPD 0036. 2001. Used with permission.
38. *"Ninano."* Korean contemporary pop fusion excerpt. From *Jang-Goon First Album Ninano. Jang-Goon.* EMI: EKLD 0801. 2007. Courtesy of Jang Goon.

CHAPTER 1

Korea from Both Sides
of the Border

Peering over the border of North and South Korea at the Joint Security Area of the Demilitarized Zone is like glimpsing a real-life alternate universe. Although the two Koreas share the same language, history and culture, they have become polar opposites in many ways since their separation in 1948. Even so, as I prepared to go on my first trip to North Korea in 2007, I was surprised to hear the same advice I was given when going to South Korea: "Prepare to sing at least one song from memory." These words served me well on both sides of the border. In both countries, the act of singing seems to transcend differences in governmental ideology and constitutes a basic form of introduction and interpersonal exchange. To get a better sense of the human face of musical exchange in North and South Korea, I offer some descriptions of everyday singing from the field.

TRAVELING TO PYONGYANG, NORTH KOREA

In July 2007, I was granted permission to visit North Korea as part of a delegation of Koreans from the United States. One of our first meetings was with the Youth League at Kimch'ek Industrial Polytechnic University. Both of our meetings with them were punctuated with song. On the first day, we met in a school gymnasium so that we could play a "friendly" game of volleyball. In anticipation of playing sports, we arrived wearing t-shirts and loose pants. In contrast, the North Korean students greeted us in formal college wear; this meant that the men wore dark slacks and white dress shirts while the women wore traditional *hanbok* or Korean-style dress with sloping white tops that fastened with long sashes over long, full skirts in dark navy. As soon as we were seated, short introductions were made, and soon we could hear the sounds of well-coordinated voices accompanied by a robust accordion played by a slender young woman. The songs proceeded in a predetermined order and were clearly arranged to highlight the ranges of the female and male lead voices. The accordion provided musical accompaniment throughout, transitions between the songs, and a seamless background to the performance. The singers also incorporated stylistic hand gestures, which helped convey a unified style and polish to the overall presentation.

In what we soon learned would become a very common gesture of welcome, the youths began with a group rendition of "Glad to Meet You" or *"Pan'gapsŭmnida"* (CD track 1). With its catchy diatonic melody and simple words, "Glad to Meet You" is one of North Korea's most recognized songs on the peninsula. With a rousing energy that matched the suggestive phrase printed on the sheet music ("overflowing with happiness, passionate"), the group sang the easy-to-follow words:

Tongpo yŏrŏbun, hyŏngje yŏrŏbun	*Fellow comrades, fellow brethren*
Irŏke mannani, Pan'gapsŭmnida	*Meeting like this, welcome*
Ŏlssa an-go chowa ussŭmiyo	*Oh, these smiles that I love and embrace*
Chŏlssa an-go chowa nunmurilse	*Oh, these tears that I love and embrace*
Ŏ, hŏ hŏ, Ŏ, hŏ hŏ hŏ hŏ nilliriya	*Oh, ho, ho, oh, ho, ho, ho, ho nilliriya*
Pan'gapsŭmnida, Pan'gapsŭmnida	*Welcome, welcome*
Pan'gapsŭmnida, Pan'gapsŭmnida	*Welcome, welcome*
Tongpo yŏrŏbun, hyŏngje yŏrŏbun	*Fellow comrades, fellow brethren*
Chŏngdaun kŭ sonmok chababopsida	*Let's shake hands with heartfelt love*
Choguk wihan maŭm ttŭgŏ-uni	*There's a warm feeling for our homeland in our soul*
T'ongil chanch'i-naldo mŏlchi annae	*The festive time of reunification is not far.*

In the context of Korea's turbulent history of division, the optimism and "passionate" tone of the lyrics can be read as somewhat defiant, or at least a little out of place. It is no wonder that this song has been interpreted in South Korea as subversive, in a country where it is still considered illegal to promote North Korean culture. For the Kimch'ek college youths, the upbeat tempo, coordinated togetherness and bright voices certainly conveyed an "overflowing happiness," but also a steely (and perhaps compulsory) strength of will that we were to encounter time and again during our trip.

Currently, Korea is divided into two nations: officially, the DPRK or Democratic People's Republic of Korea in the north, and the ROK or Republic of Korea in the south. There is no natural border between North Korea and South Korea; the division was based entirely on politics. Prior to World War II, Korea had long since become a casualty of Japan's colonial ambitions (1910–1945). In negotiating the release of Korean territory by Japan at the close of the war in 1945, the Soviet Union and the United States stepped in to help shepherd Korea's transition from colonial rule. Deciding arbitrarily to divide the peninsula at the 38th parallel, Soviet forces occupied the north while U.S. forces occupied the south. At the end of the Korean War (1950–1953), a new border was created along cease-fire lines, now known as the Demilitarized Zone. The relatively untrammeled nature of the DMZ lends a sense of increased distance between the two Koreas, but in truth the two capitals of Pyongyang and Seoul are less than three hours apart by car or train (Figure 1.1).

Despite all of the conflict and change, both North and South Korea have demonstrated remarkable cultural resilience. Today, the population of South Korea is over 49 million. North Korea is less than half this number, at about 23 million. Since the time of division, the people of both countries have been active in developing Korean music and culture in ways that are politically distinct and historically specific. This has resulted in dramatic musical, cultural and aesthetic differences that will continue to have a long-lasting impact. Even so, one cannot deny that North and South Koreans draw from several shared sources or "streams" of culture. For example, both countries draw actively from a repertoire of folksongs that were popular in the early twentieth century and before. They both continue to gain inspiration from these songs to create new arrangements, popular "covers" and compositions. For example, compare the DPRK and ROK versions of the same popular folksong, "*Arirang*," on CD tracks 2 and 3.

FIGURE 1.1 *Map of North Korea and South Korea.* *(Adapted from the CIA Worldbook.)*

During my trip to North Korea, we heard a combination of old and new songs. The Kimch'ek youths continued to present seven more solo songs. The majority that are presented here fit within the state-sanctioned anthem or lyric song styles that characterize much of the modern North Korean song repertoire. Thanks to the predominant use of duple rhythms, major/minor harmony and classically trained vocal style, it is easy to hear a dominant Western influence.

An exception to this was the inclusion of traditional Korean folksongs, notably one that is well known throughout the peninsula as the "Roast Chestnut Song" or *"Kunbam T'aryŏng"* (CD track 4). In fact, most recently it was made popular in South Korea in an *a cappella* version by Kim Yong-u (CD track 5). In contrast to the other songs, the folksongs featured medium-fast compound meters, modal harmony and a more highly ornamented vocal style. Although the accordion still supplied accompaniment, these folksongs added musical variety to the presentation. In addition, the inclusion of something as recognizable throughout the peninsula as the "Roast Chestnut Song" could be interpreted as a gesture of outreach.

In addition to the "Roast Chestnut Song," they also sang another song that dates back to pre-division Korea, entitled "Spring in My Hometown" (*"Kohyangŭi Bom"*). Written in the early 20th century by Hong Nan-p'a, who was in Korea's first wave of modern nationalist composers, "Spring in My Hometown" is a much beloved children's song. Full of longing sentiments to see one's mountain village or hometown abloom with azalea and peach blossoms in spring, this song draws on a nostalgia born from the changes wrought by the increased mobility and urbanization of the early modern era. Although we are well into the 21st century, it seems that this nationalist nostalgia for an idealized village or hometown still carries some currency on both sides of the border. This was followed with the group-sung finale of a well-known North Korean anthem called "We Like Our Country the Best" (*"Nae Nara Chaeillo Chowa"*).

Since the 15th century, Korea's borders have remained relatively stable, perhaps because they are so easily demarcated by geographical features (Figure 1.1). In the northwest, the Amnok (Yalu) River serves as the border with China, while the Tuman River marks the border with China and Russia to the northeast. The western, southern and eastern borders are all defined by bodies of water: the Korean Bay and the Yellow Sea to the west, the East China Sea (South Sea) to the south and the East Sea (Sea of Japan) to the east. Given that the period since division is relatively short, it is common to use the term "Korea" to refer to a former state and geographic area that produced a civilization with a shared history, people, culture, language and love of the land. Korea is situated on a peninsula that juts down from Northeast Asia, uniquely located among China, Russia and the islands of Japan. Roughly the size of Britain, Korea also includes more than 3,000 islands, among them the "honeymoon" destination of Chejudo and the culturally rich Chindo.

Following this presentation, a number of our members stood up to sing a few songs. Interestingly, as soon as we started singing one of the North Korean songs that we had prepared, the accordionist immediately caught on and was able to accompany us without any sheet music—demonstrating her ability to accompany well-known songs in any key while also improvising lively melodic fills and transitional melodies. Despite our best efforts to be prepared for such an occasion, our presentation paled in comparison to theirs.

After several hours of games, we took our leave as the North Korean youths stood outside waving. They began to sing (complete with accordion accompaniment) "Let's Meet Again" ("*Tasi Mannapsida*"), another well-known North Korean song (Figure 1.2). As we waved back and sang along with them, many of us could not help but be moved by the bittersweet irony of the words (CD track 6):

From Mt. Paektu to Mt. Halla, we are one people
How long has it been since separating,
How many tears have been shed
But go well, we will meet again
While crying one's voice out
Farewell, we will meet again

Although not the region's highest in elevation, Korea's mountains are numerous and well-loved, some to mythic proportions. For example, Mt. Paektu, which borders China in the north, is regarded as the birthplace of the Korean people; Mt. Halla continues to enjoy an aura of mystery as Korea's southernmost mountain, on the island of Chejudo. The two mountains are located on the opposite ends of the country, but they share the geographical feature of possessing distinctive volcanic peaks with stunning crater lakes nestled within. Uttered in the same breath, the phrase "from Mt. Paektu to Mt. Halla" often turns up in poems and songs to capture a sense of the dramatic span and continuity of the peninsula.

FIGURE 1.2 *Kimch'ek University students waving good-bye after the volleyball game. By the doorway, an accordion player accompanies them as they sing their farewells.* (*Photo courtesy of Elisa Gahng.*)

VISITING KOSŎNG, SOUTH KOREA

As is evident in the popularity of karaoke rooms or *noraebang*, singing is just as important to the social fabric of everyday life in South Korea as it is in the North. In the folk expressive culture circles that I became familiar with, the expectation was so high that having to sing a song by heart at the drop of a hat was a tacit given. This occurred frequently during instructional sessions at folk performing arts centers. A unique aspect of these sessions is that they often involved traveling to government-supported "transmission centers" that are located in a region where a given practice is believed to have been developed. Although singing plays some role at most transmission centers, I found it to be an entirely pivotal part of the program at the Kosŏng *Ogwangdae* mask dance drama transmission center.

Although Kosŏng is only about a four-hour drive from Seoul, it can feel more like a world away in terms of its culture, pace, people and dialect. Geographically speaking, Kosŏng is a small township located on a craggy stretch of serpentine coastline on the southwestern edge of the peninsula. Because of the natural beauty of this area, the Kosŏng *Ogwangdae* practitioners are particularly proud to call this place their home. *Ogwangdae*, meaning "five entertainers," is the regional term for the mask dance form for which Kosŏng is known. With its characteristic combination of strong stances and fluid movements, Kosŏng *Ogwangdae* is one of approximately 12 mask dance drama styles that have received from the government the status of Intangible Cultural Asset. The Kosŏng *Ogwangdae* center organizes weeklong training sessions every winter and summer. In addition to conveying expressive content, the purpose of the training session is to transmit a full experience by encouraging students to immerse themselves in the landscape, sights, sounds and tastes of the regional locale.

I began visiting the Kosŏng *Ogwangdae* transmission center in 1999 and have continued to visit regularly. From the very beginning, I was struck by how they schedule singing into their regular program, even though the bulk of the instructional content is focused on dance and character play. Dubbed the "open *madang*," singing takes place during the first 10–20 minutes of each morning and afternoon session, for the first two days. Fluid in expression, the *madang* is a spatial, temporal and aesthetic concept referring respectively to an open courtyard or field, an occasion in time, or a shared space of embodied participation. This open *madang* begins after each group has gathered to sit on the floor in parallel lines, with representatives of the group taking a place at the front of each line. The teachers face the students, sitting on chairs in the front of the classroom. After greetings and announcements are made, group representatives are asked to come up at random, introduce themselves and sing a song. In reciprocal fashion, teachers can also be called up to sing.

During one cold week in February 2002, I attended an especially lively series of open *madangs* at the Kosŏng *Ogwangdae* transmission center. This was due in part to several groups being in attendance that had significant training in Korean folk arts. Relishing the role of selecting his "victims" at random, Mr. Hwang, the center director, decided to call up one of the female *p'ansori* students. *P'ansori* is a narrative story-singing genre that is especially beloved among the teachers and was a sure way of getting things going. Sporting loose clothing and her hair in a casual ponytail, a petite young woman in glasses stood up and walked over to one side of the classroom. With only a simple fan as a prop, she sang one of the most well-known excerpts from *The Song of Ch'unhyang*, called "*Sarangga*" or simply "Love Song" (CD track 7), her husky voice booming out into the reverberant dance studio with ease.

From here, Mr. Hwang invited one of the elder mask dance teachers, named Hŏ Chong-wŏn. Standing up in the front of the class with his hands clasped behind his back, Mr. Hŏ announced that he would sing "Mother's Song." The accompanist then got up and made a big show of tying his *changgo* drum into a vertical position so he could accompany in a more pop-oriented style. As soon as the drum was secure, the accompanist began tapping out the characteristic "*ppong tchak-tchak ppong tchak!*" rhythms of *trot*, an oldies genre also known onomatopoetically as *ppongtchak*. Controversial in Korea for being derivative of Japanese *enka* and reminiscent of the Japanese colonial period, *ppongtchak* is just as passionately derided for being unsophisticated and maudlin, as it is beloved for its nostalgic expression by the over-60 set.

At the transmission center, elder teachers are sometimes jokingly referred to as the *ppongtchak* generation, while the younger students are routinely chastised for putting too much purchase in modern Western trappings such as bleached hair and brand-name blue jeans. In the open *madang*, however, I have observed an effort on the part of the younger students to suspend these differences. For example, as soon as Mr. Hŏ started to sing, the students were so eager to voice their support that you could barely hear the time-worn subtleties of his voice. Though they might not be caught dead doing so elsewhere, here the students were not afraid to fully embody their enjoyment of *ppongtchak*, clapping and shouting words of encouragement. This energy culminated as the teacher broke from his staid stance, making sweeping gestures with his arms and ending the song with the kind of panache that only an older dancer could pull off (Figure 1.3). In this context, the "openness" of the setting blurs the boundaries of genre between what is considered "folk" and "popular," and in the process it helps to bridge differences between generations.

To wrap up the session, Mr. Hwang called on Mr. Yi Yun-sŏk, the president of the mask dance organization. Standing up to the occasion, Mr. Yi began by narrating and singing the famous *p'ansori* work *The Song*

FIGURE 1.3 *Mr. Hŏ Chong-wŏn singing a* ppongtchak *song in front of the students at the Kosŏng Ogwangdae Transmission Center.* (Photo courtesy of Elisa Gahng.)

of the Underwater Palace, a tale about how a rabbit outwits the King of the Underwater Palace and a turtle servant. In a clever play on genre and theme, Mr. Yi soon switched gears and transitioned into a popular children's song called *"San Tokki"* or "Mountain Rabbit" all with his characteristic deadpan style. This move played on the audience's expectations associated with a given genre. *P'ansori* normally commands a degree of respect given its high level of difficulty, so when Mr. Yi started to sing the first notes of "Mountain Rabbit," it was all the more surprising to witness one of the most respected teachers of the organization sing an endearing children's song in public.

The message here is freeing. The boundaries that define and divide genres, and generations, can be crossed, and what is considered as "tradition" need not always be taken so seriously. In this way, a dialogue of genres is encouraged in the open *madang* and is indicative of how the generations freely negotiate their roles in the intertextual transmission of expressive culture in South Korea.

ACTIVITY 1.1 *Ethnomusicologists often seek to understand musical practices through careful observation, participation and fieldnote taking, all of which are ideally conducted "in the field." One common way in which this activity is processed and presented is through ethnographic description. Initial descriptions often engender further questions and open up areas for a deeper level of interpretation and analysis. In reading these ethnographic descriptions of music making in North and South Korea, please reflect upon these questions for discussion in class.*

- *What is the role of singing in North and South Korea, as represented in these two ethnographic descriptions? How is this role similar or different in both of the situations described?*
- *What kinds of musical repertoire are favored in each example? Why do you think these repertoires were favored in each situation, and do you think these tendencies have any cultural significance?*
- *Do these descriptions resonate with any of your own experiences?*

INTERSECTING THEMES

I have opened with these scenes to demonstrate that singing in everyday life stands as one of the more striking areas of expressive common ground between the two Koreas. Moreover, these scenes are suggestive of other common thematic areas that will be developed throughout this volume. I selected themes that apply to a notion of Korea both before and after the division as well as to the postdivision states of the DPRK and ROK. With this in mind, the themes presented here should aid in understanding the peninsula as a coherent region, as well as help stimulate thinking on the differences that have been wrought since the division.

Theme 1: Transnationalism. From cultural conduit in premodern times to influential media force in the recent "Korean wave," the Korean peninsula has played an important transnational role in East

Asia. Through this process, Korea has been subject to transnational influences.

Theme 2: Cultural continuity. Korea has crafted a distinctive cultural identity by maintaining a strong sense of musical and aesthetic continuity.

Theme 3: Music and cultural politics. Throughout Korean history, musical practices were often enmeshed in the cultural politics of various groups and interests.

All of these themes are perceptible in the opening scenes of this chapter. For example, transnationalism (theme 1) is evident in how Western musical forms and instruments are incorporated in several of the North Korean songs (CD tracks 1, 2 and 6). In the South Korean *trot* example, you encountered the lingering nostalgia for Japanese-influenced popular songs among the older generation. However, the struggle for cultural continuity (theme 2) persists in the strong presence of folksongs in both North and South Korea (CD tracks 2, 3, 4 and 5). This promotion of traditional forms of song and dance at folk transmission centers can also

THREE KINGDOMS

Koguryŏ	? B.C.E.–668 C.E.
Paekche	? B.C.E.–660 C.E.
Silla	57 B.C.E.–668 C.E.

DYNASTIES OF ROYAL KOREA

Unified Silla	668–935
Koryŏ	918–1392
Chosŏn	1392–1910

MODERN KOREA

(Korean Empire)	(1897–1910)
Japanese colonial period	1910–1945
Republic of Korea (South)	1948–
Democratic People's Republic of Korea (North)	1948–
Korean War	1950–1953

FIGURE 1.4   *Korean Historical Periodicity*

be seen as the work of cultural politics (theme 3). Lastly, the predomi-
nance of state-sanctioned songs in North Korea is a testament to the to
the close connection between music and politics in the DPRK (theme 3).
In the next sections, I further discuss these themes with the goal of
providing some history and cultural context that will give you a better
sense of Korea, before and after the division. To assist you with Korean
historical periodicity, Figure 1.4 gives you a timeline for reference.

Transnationalism in Flux: From the "Hermit Kingdom"
to the "Korean Wave"
Because of Korea's distinct geography and peninsular location, issues of
space and territory have often been of central concern. This may explain
in part why the peninsula has been variously imagined and geographically lived in ways that have had a definite impact on Korean expressive practices. For example, Korea has been dubbed variously a cultural
conduit, an isolated "hermit kingdom," an occupied colony, a divided
nation, an Asian tiger and more amorphously as a "Korean wave" of
culture emanating outward into the reaches of East, Southeast, Central
and South Asia. Although none of these designations tells the whole
story, each sheds some light on some of the driving forces at play in
Korea at various times.

Of all these designations, perhaps none have had as much power over
the imagination as the hermit kingdom. This popular appellation began
to gain currency in the West during the 19th century and is now used to
characterize the self-reliant or "isolationist" tendencies of North Korea.
To some degree, the term registers frustration with Korea's particular brand of stubborn resistance to opening itself up to things foreign.
One might be hard-pressed to find many traces of this attitude left in
South Korea today, but the opposite may be true in Pyongyang. On my
trip to North Korea in 2007, when a Pyongyang Conservatory teacher
was asked whether she would be open to programs in world music and
dance, she replied, "Why would we want to learn other forms of music
when we have all that we need?"

During the late 19th century, Westerners viewed the hermit kingdom metaphor as especially apt because Korea was the last of the East
Asian countries to submit to being "opened" by imperialist powers.
For China, increased contact with the West was spurred by the Opium
Wars of 1839–1842; by the 1930s, Shanghai was known as a hotspot of
cosmopolitanism, an Asian "jazz mecca" and the "Paris of the East"
(see Lau, *Music in China*, in this series). Japan's opening is usually

marked by the arrival of the U.S. Navy ships of Commodore Matthew Perry arriving in Tokyo Bay in 1853. In response to increased international contact, Japan launched the successful Meiji restoration, consisting of sweeping reforms designed to strengthen Japan and make it more competitive with the West (see Wade, *Music in Japan*, in this series).

In contrast, Korea did not participate in an international treaty with a Western power until 1882, when it signed with the United States at the urging of China. Prior to this, Korea had responded to Western foreigners with less-than-welcoming reactions. On the milder end of the spectrum, the Koreans simply turned away the *Lord Amherst*, a ship sent by the British East India Company in 1832, on the grounds of forbidding foreign commerce. More brutally, Korea's practice of slaughtering French and Korean Catholics from the early 1800s forward extended to the entire mixed crew (Americans, Chinese and British) of the U.S. merchant schooner *General Sherman* in 1866.

Korea's reclusive impulses make more sense when you take into consideration its history of invasion, from forces as formidable as the Mongols in 1231 and 1254 to the Japanese from 1592 to 1598 (led by the infamous Toyotomi Hideyoshi) and the Manchus in 1627 and 1636. In response to the Mongolian campaigns, Korea sought to fortify its northern border in an attempt to define Korea more as a protected island than a peninsula. After the Japanese invasions, they shunned contact with neighbors to the East as well, thus sealing their fate as a hermetic nation.

Running contrary to its legendary reputation as a reclusive hermit kingdom, Korea's peninsular positioning within East Asia has been pivotal in an intermediary role between the Asian continent and Japan. Korean contact with China can be traced back more than 2,300 years. By the time the tribal states active on the Korean peninsula were consolidated into three realms, during what became known as the Three Kingdoms period (? to 668 C.E.), Korean rulers were in regular contact with both China and Japan. Although Korea sent maritime envoys to Japan, it sustained the most consistent relations with China. Diplomats were regularly dispatched among the ruling courts of the Three Kingdoms, China and Japan. Official Korean envoys and missions traveled to China for special events such as the birthday of an emperor or crown prince. Within this context, goods and cultural artifacts were exchanged. When these exchanges included musical instruments and texts, they had a significant impact on musical practice, especially within the court.

Given its location, it is only natural that Korea played an intermediary role in transporting goods and other continental cultural exports to Japan, such as Confucianism and the Chinese character-based writing system. Although Buddhism originated in India in 483 B.C.E., it was exported through East Asia in a similar fashion. Interestingly, the Paekche court (of the Three Kingdoms) was especially important in transmitting Buddhist culture to Japan. For example, they sent several volumes of sutra texts there in 522 C.E (Lee Byong Won 1987). In another example, a Paekche man known as Mimashi moved to Japan in 612 C.E. and taught a style of mask dance drama that he had previously learned in Southern China (Lee Byong Won 1987). Inflected with Buddhist themes and characters, vestiges of this dance are believed to have survived in both Korea and Japan today.

In addition to China and Japan, Korea was connected to other cultures through the Silk Road, an extensive network of trade routes that flourished between the Mediterranean and the Pacific primarily between 100 B.C.E. and 1500 C.E. Although Korea was not situated near any of its major crossroads, it did serve as an instrumental outpost along the northern and southern routes that connected China and Japan (Figure 1.1). The Silk Road contributed greatly to the flourishing of the Silla kingdom (57 B.C.E.–668 C.E.), and its capital of Kyŏngju was hailed from afar as the "city of gold." Travelers came from India and the Middle East to admire the city's beautiful architecture and famous Buddhist structures. Given its pervasive hermit kingdom label, it is easy to forget that Korea once basked in the early glow of globalization, using its peninsular position to advantage to create a unique and noteworthy civilization.

In contrast to this earlier golden era, the spatial concepts that dominated Korea in the 20th century are those of colonial occupation or annexation on the one hand and division or fracture on the other. Historically, the occupation of Korea by Japan had its run from 1910 until the surrender of Japan at the close of World War II in 1945. During this time, Japanese policies facilitated introduction of Japanese forms of music (such as the nostalgic popular genre called *enka*), promoted mainly Western and some Japanese-style music in the public school system and took part in documenting and recording of genres of Korean traditional and early popular forms of music.

Although Korean traditional genres were adversely affected by the occupation, they were not suppressed completely. First of all, many long-standing musical institutions were discontinued, altered or severely reduced, as was the case with the renaming of the royal music institution to the much weakened *Aaktae* in 1910. At the same time, a shift in musical activity occurred when female entertainers from the royal court, who were called *kisaeng*, were transferred over to new institutes called *kwŏnbŏn*. These private *kwŏnbŏn* became a very influential locus of Korean expressive activity that thrived in large part because they were considered unthreatening (though appealing) to the Japanese. In fact, many early Korean "stars" were trained in these institutes. By contrast, public expressions of Korean native culture (such as large-scale shamanist festivals) were often prohibited because they wanted to discourage any possible mobilization of large groups of people. Although musical change was bound to accompany Korea's transition to the modern era, the colonial occupation intensified and modulated the tenor of disruption to development of Korean music and culture at this time.

The sense of disruption only continued after Japan was defeated at the end of World War II. In shepherding Korea's transition to modern nationhood, the Americans and Soviets decided to arbitrarily divide the country at the 38th parallel, with the United States in charge of the south and the USSR the north. Soon thereafter, conflicting governments emerged and ideological lines were drawn. In the south, Syngman Rhee (1875–1965) won an election supervised by the United Nations and was declared president of the Republic of Korea in 1948. Meanwhile in the north, Kim Il-sung (1912–1994) led the formation of a communist state called the Democratic People's Republic of Korea. It was not long before the two ideologically opposed states began to clash, and from 1950 to 1953 the peninsula erupted in an international conflict known as the Korean War. It left three million Koreans dead, the division very much intact and much of the country and its cultural artifacts in total devastation.

At the turn of the 21st century, we find Korea in a remarkably different place from where it was a hundred years ago. Although the hermit kingdom metaphor remains somewhat operative in North Korea, visitors to South Korea now encounter a country that has emerged as a rapidly developing "Asian tiger." In light of its increased participation in the global political economy, South Korea has radically reimagined itself vis-à-vis powerful neighbors and experienced unprecedented success in marketing its cultural products abroad. Taking off in the early 2000s in China, Taiwan and Japan and spreading to other parts of Asia with the popularity of Korean acts and television dramas, the transnational embrace of Korean pop culture has come to be known as *hallyu*, or the Korean wave. In a radical departure from previous notions of Korea as a nation that must be protected from outside or divisive forces, the Korean wave is a more external concept whereby culture is seen to emanate outward, crossing borders and language barriers with ease. Given its obvious capitalist transnational influences, many critics have questioned whether the Korean wave is truly representative of Korean culture. Regardless, it is a testament to the power of music as an important medium in reconfiguring global cultural flows within Asia and beyond.

Modernization and Cultural Continuity in North and South Korea
The second theme of this book focuses on Korea's various expressions of cultural continuity in musical practice. Although I will hone in on this theme during various points in its history, this volume does not attempt to be a historical survey of traditional Korean music. Rather, I have chosen to focus on those practices that conform to Barbara Kirshenblatt-Gimblett's notion of "heritage" as a "mode of cultural production in the present that has recourse to the past" (1995: 369). In addition, instead of trying to cover all the forms of music that have been developed over time on the Korean peninsula, I will focus on those that can still be heard and experienced today.

In both the DPRK and the ROK, cultural continuity and modernization are like two sides of the same coin and must be understood each against the backdrop of the other. The forces of modernization began at least 50 or 60 years before the division. However, after the division the vehicles of modernization took decidedly different paths in the two countries. In the late 19th century, Western music was introduced to Korea, including its instruments, art music, hymns, marches and even children's songs. Today, Western music is very much entrenched in both the ROK and the DPRK; in the ROK, its practitioners easily outnumber those who perform traditional music. Modernization also brought various forms of popular music from Japan, Europe, America and beyond. Many of these cultural influences came in the form of transformative music technologies (phonograph, microphone, radio, etc.) and were mostly controlled by transnational companies.

After the Korean War, South Korea became more heavily influenced by American culture while North Korea began to develop a philosophy of socialist realism after the doctrines of Marx, Lenin and Mao. In terms of artistic practice, Kim Il-sung drew on Mao Zedong's "Talks at the Yan'an Forum on Literature and Art" to promote the idea that artists should work toward proper education of the masses, drawing inspiration from ordinary working people in order to better uplift and serve them. In addition to revolutionary songs and military band marches, programmatic music was also favored—all of this similar to what was heard in China and the Soviet Union. Kim's policies were further developed through the *Chŏllima undong*, or "Galloping horse movement," as well as the national policy of *juche* or "self-reliance." This resulted in systematic control of programmatic content, standardization of performance techniques and vocal production, "improvement" of Korean instruments and production of new works that emphasized content over form and control over individualism.

Even with all these changes, both the ROK and the DPRK have made striking efforts to maintain a sense of continuity with older forms of Korean culture, albeit in very different ways. North Korea has drawn actively from traditional folksongs and melodies in reconstructing a strong national repertoire. The South has done much to distinguish Korean aesthetics while working to preserve a plethora of highly localized forms (including the North Korean *sŏdosori*) managed through the Intangible Cultural Asset Preservation system. In addition, South Korean contemporary musicians, from classical to rock to hip-hop, have made consistent efforts to incorporate national Korean elements into their music. As this theme is worked out throughout the volume, careful attention will be paid to how musical practices have evolved through an intertextual process in relation to changing social, cultural and spatial contexts.

Music and Cultural Politics: Articulating the Border Through Song
From the state sacrificial ritual musics of the royal courts to the revival of Korean folk music in the late 20th century and beyond, the third theme of this book explores how music is meaningfully involved in the cultural politics of a given state, movement or group. An important corollary to this process is that music is often combined with other expressive formats, such as lyrics, dramatic narrative, dance, mass demonstrations, ritual, video and film, to create a comprehensive experience that enhances meaning and heightens the overall performative impact. Although numerous examples will be examined throughout this volume, here I focus on those that articulate or imagine the border between North and South Korea. In most cases, this articulation has to do with a literal "joining" or "reunification" of the two Koreas.

"Our Wish Is Reunification": The Story of Im Su-kyŏng
One of the most famous examples of music and politics coming together to imagine an alternative peninsular reality comes to us in the story of Im Su-kyŏng, a South Korean former activist who changed the course of a song and (in so doing, some may argue) history as well. On June 30, 1989,

she entered North Korea as a student representative to attend the World Festival of Youth and Students, an international forum for "progressive" youth that is held regularly in Pyongyang. The late 1980s in South Korea were a period of intense political involvement among student and civilian activists mainly working toward democratization, although reunification was also a galvanizing issue. Im's visit to North Korea carried a great deal of risk because according to National Security Law it is considered illegal for a South Korean to travel to North Korea without prior approval. With her characteristic blend of youthful idealism and irrepressible spirit, Im sang "Our Wish Is Reunification" (a popular Korean children's song) on a number of occasions during her visit.

After the festival, she joined a peace march with several hundred other international activists, beginning at the famed Paektu Mountain near the northern border with China and proceeding southward to Panmunjŏm, located at the DMZ between North and South Korea. Although they hoped to continue all the way down to Korea's southern island of Chejudo, they were refused entry when they arrived on July 27. In the end, Im Su-kyŏng crossed back over into South Korea at Panmunjŏm on August 15, accompanied by Father Moon Kyuhyŏn, becoming the first South Korean civilian to ever cross the demilitarized border. However, as soon as they stepped over into South Korean territory, they were arrested by the government and detained in prison until they were granted amnesty (in 1993). To this day, Im remains beloved in North Korea as the "flower of reunification." Throughout this series of events, "Our Wish Is Reunification" became an integral part of Im Su-kyŏng's performative plea for change and has been interwoven into her legacy.

Popular Visions of Reunification
If we refocus our attention away from the location-specific political dynamics of the DMZ and toward the wider realm of the popular imagination, we see many examples of songs and other cultural "products" that incorporate the theme of reunification promoted on a larger scale. In North Korea, reunification songs are embraced as part of a larger body of state-sanctioned "pop," or what I would call mass popular songs. Well-known reunification-themed songs for the masses include "Reunification Rainbow," "Let's Meet Again" (CD track 6), and "Glad to Meet You." Many are quite catchy, as exemplified in "Glad to Meet You" ("*Pan'gapsŭmnida*," CD track 1). With its moderately syncopated and upbeat rhythm, this song is one of the few North Korean songs that are easily recognizable by South Koreans and diasporic Koreans abroad.

In contrast, reunification songs are generally not promoted by the state in South Korea. Instead, these songs have tended to spring from subcultural musical movements, most notably the highly political "song movement" (*norae undong*) genre of the 1980s. One good example of such a reunification song is a lively number called "From Seoul to Pyongyang" (*"Seoulesŏ Pyongyangkkaji,"* CD track 8), written and performed by the song movement collective Kkottaji (literally, "first fruit"). With the opening words "From Seoul to Pyongyang, the taxi fare is only 50,000 won [approximately $50], we can go to Russia, and even to the land of the moon, there's no place we couldn't go," Kkottaji effectively imagines a united peninsular landscape that is at once completely normalized and pedestrian while at the same time fantastically without bounds.

ACTIVITY 1.2   *Conduct some research on the role of mass media in places such as the United States, South Korea and North Korea. Determine how the media are controlled in each country, and write a few sentences about how this may have an impact on music making in each country. Prepare for discussion in class.*

In the first decade of the 21st century, gestures toward reunification have become more accepted in mainstream South Korean culture. As recently as 2004, major pop groups such as Sinhwa, along with solo artists Yi Sŭng-ch'ŏl, Kim Kŏn-mo and Yi Hyo-ri, have collaborated to create a reunification-themed song called "When That Day Comes." Composed by Ch'oe Chun-yŏng, this song was marketed through an inspirational video that is strongly reminiscent of the feel-good enthusiasm of the 1985 charity single "We Are the World," written by Michael Jackson and Lionel Richie (and recently reprised to aid Haiti in 2010). Heart-wrenching images of divided families who have been allowed to temporarily reunite are interspersed with glamorous shots of Korean pop stars. The video also capitalizes on other North-South juxtapositions: Paektu and Halla mountains, notable North and South Korean athletes and various North and South Korean heads-of-state shaking hands over the years. With words like "let us forget any doubts that we hold in our hearts, because we are one," the overwhelming message of the music and video is to project an image of Korea as one nation and one people whose deeply felt sorrows and painful memories are finally beginning to "melt away."

ACTIVITY 1.3 *Review all of the reunification songs introduced in this section, listening for song structure, vocal production and genre style (CD tracks 1, 6 and 8, and "When That Day Comes" online).*

- *Of all these songs, can you tell which ones are from North Korea and which are from the South? How so?*
- *Write a list of the genres represented and determine how you would tell them apart, by jotting down some distinguishing characteristics of each one.*
- *View the videos for "When That Day Comes" and "We Are the World" (1985 version) online. Write a couple of sentences comparing the two.*

CHAPTER 2

The Court as Cultural Conduit

COURT MUSIC, CULTURAL POLICY AND THE STATE

By the early 1960s, many of Korea's traditional arts had reached an extremely vulnerable state of decline and extinction. This was due to the repressive effects of Japanese colonialism, the ravages of the Korean War, and the inevitable effects of modernization, Westernization and rapid urbanization. Given that the royal Korean court was disbanded in the early 20th century, court-related traditions were especially vulnerable to the state cultural policies of North and South Korea. Some forms of court music have been rigorously maintained under the preservationist agenda of the South Korean government, but court traditions have suffered a markedly different fate in North Korea. In light of North Korea's socialist view of art as a means to serve and revolutionize the masses and embody the philosophy of *juche*, or "self-reliance," many Korean forms of expressive culture with explicit connections to elite court culture were discontinued while folk-oriented forms were selectively collected and "reformed." In contrast, court traditions are still regarded as politically important to the modern South Korean state, even if they are not necessarily considered a pivotal part of the daily lives of its people. To understand the significance of the Korean court and the legacy of its expressive traditions, I will trace its history and introduce you to some of its music.

THE MOVEMENT OF COURT CULTURE FROM EAST TO WEST

By means of the Silk Road, Korea was linked to an early network of trade routes connecting a vast expanse of Asian territory that brought together nomadic cultures from North and Central Asia, emerging dynastic powers in China and Japan, ancient kingdoms such as the influential Buddhist realm of Gandhara and other parts of South Asia. As early as the Three Kingdoms period (Figure 1.4), the Korean court served as an interface where Korean musicians could process musical and cultural influences from abroad, and in some cases, carry them to others. Instruments offer evidence of this. For example, the kingdom of Koguryŏ imported the West Asian lute (*pip'a*), and the cylindrical double reed (*p'iri*, Figure 2.1) from China, while the Paekche kingdom assimilated a Chinese flute with a raised mouthpiece called the *chi* (Howard 1995: 11, figure 2.2).

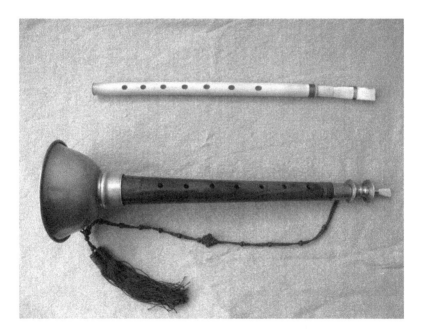

FIGURE 2.1 *Korean double reeds. Top:* p'iri; *bottom:* saenap *or* t'aep'yŏngso. *The* p'iri *has a slim cylindrical shape while the* t'aep'yŏngso *has more of a conical shape that flares out into a detachable metal horn. Both instruments possess distinctive double-reed timbres, but the sound of the* t'aep'yŏngso *is quite piercing and so it is often played outdoors.*   (Photo by the author.)

FIGURE 2.2 Chi *(flute with a raised mouthpiece), an example of an instrument that fits the bamboo category of the* bayin/p'arŭm *system. Here, the* chi *is being played as part of the courtyard ensemble in a performance of* Munmyo Cheryeak *(Confucian ritual music).* (*Photo by the author.*)

In general, Buddhism flowed from China and became recognized in the Three Kingdoms (? B.C.E.–668 C.E.) by the late fourth century C.E (Lee Byong Won 1987: 7). Although it is difficult to tell from the sources what this influence may have sounded like in musical terms, we do know that Korea played a critical role in transferring Buddhist culture from the mainland to Japan. Sharing their music with others from early on, the kingdom of Silla is known to have sent the first envoy of 80 musicians to Japan in the middle of the fifth century.

Korea also created its own stringed and wind instruments, often inspired by instruments found on the mainland. According to the *Samguk Sagi* (History of the Three Kingdoms), King Kashil of the sixth century C.E. Kaya tribal federation (later usurped by Silla) heard a Chinese *zheng* zither and commanded a musician named U Rŭk to create a similar kind of music. U Rŭk then composed music for the Korean 12-string zither called the *kayagŭm*. Just as China sent instruments to Korea, Korea in turn gifted instruments to Japan. In fact, four eighth century *kayagŭm* (listed as *shiragi koto*, or "zithers from Silla") can be found in the Shosoin instrument repository in Nara, Japan (see Wade 2004). In Koguryŏ, the Chinese *guqin*, a delicate-sounding "scholar's instrument" or zither, also seems to have served as a creative impetus (see Lau 2007). The *Samguk Sagi* says that the king of Koguryŏ offered a reward to a musician named Wang Sanak to remodel the *guqin* into what became the Korean six-string *kŏmungo* zither, played with a stick. Despite this remodeling, later dynastic eras continued to make use of an instrument identical to the *guqin*, called the *kŭm*, in Chinese-derived court rituals.

The invention of the large transverse flute or *taegŭm* is recounted in legend (Figure 2.3). According to the *Samguk Yusa*, King Shimun

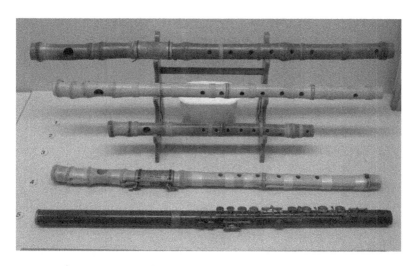

FIGURE 2.3 *From top to bottom:* taegŭm, chunggŭm, sogŭm, sanjo taegŭm, *and* chŏdae. *Unlike the other flutes, the* taegŭm *and the* sanjo taegŭm *(a similar flute that is adapted for the* sanjo *genre) possess a membrane that vibrates when played. In the picture below, the membranes lie just underneath the plate that is fastened onto the flute with two cords. The* chŏdae *is an example of a "reformed" flute with Western-style keywork.* (Photo by the author, courtesy of the National Gugak Center.)

(681–692 C.E.) learned that his deceased father had returned in the form of a dragon. Seeking to help his son, the dragon told the king to cut a special bamboo plant that grew on the peak of a mysterious mountain that was floating in the Eastern Sea. This bamboo grew in such a way that it was split in two during the day but fused during the night. A *taegŭm* flute was created from the fused bamboo; it is said that whenever it was played, "enemies retreated, illnesses were cured, rain came after drought, and the sea remained calm" (Howard 1995: 43). In this way, *taegŭm* came to be called the "flute to calm 100 million waves."

By the Unified Silla period (668–935 C.E.), Korea had developed a form of court music called "three strings, three winds" (*samhyŏn samjuk*). The "three strings" represented a mixture of influences from home and abroad and included the Korean *kayagŭm* and *kŏmungo* and the West Asian *pip'a* or pear-shaped lute. In contrast, the "three winds" referred to indigenous instruments such as the legendary Korean *taegŭm*. From all of this experimentation with various influences, Koreans began to differentiate between the music of native origin and that of Tang China, with whom they had close relations; "native music" was literally called *hyangak*, whereas the music of the Tang was called *tangak*. During this process, both the Koreans and the Chinese were active in transmitting their court music to Japan (see Wade 2004). There, musics from outside were categorized as *tôgaku* for music from China and *komagaku* for music from Korea.

THE DEVELOPMENT OF RITUAL MUSIC OF THE COURT: MUSIC, CULTURAL POLITICS AND THE STATE

Although tensions arose among the dominant religious traditions of dynastic Korea (shamanism, Buddhism and Confucianism), they were generally not seen as mutually exclusive, spreading in an ebb and flow through the courts and to the general populace. The Koryŏ dynasty was a time when all three were practiced in some form, although Buddhism reached its peak during this time. In fact, Koryŏ's first king, T'aejo (reigned 918–943), made it mandatory for his subjects to observe Buddhist rites and festivals during his reign. This practice continued throughout the Koryŏ era (Lee Byong Won 1987: 12). In the temples, simple and more complex melodic chants were adopted from China and gradually Koreanized over time (Lee Byong Won 1987: 11).

In terms of instrumental practice, one of the most significant cultural additions during the Koryŏ period (918–1392) was the introduction of Confucian ritual music, or *aak* from China, reflecting the court's increasing interest in Confucian political philosophy. The term *aak* is derived from the Chinese word *yayue* (meaning "elegant music" in Chinese). Although *yayue* was originally used by Confucius to describe music that was considered good and "proper" for the country, *aak* came to have a more limited meaning in Korea, referring to music that was performed for a set of Chinese-derived state sacrificial rites based on ancient Confucian and Asian cosmological beliefs (Provine 2002a: 861). Comprehensive in nature, these rites included music and dance, elaborate ensemble and performance formats and a diverse array of instruments. When these Confucian sacrificial rituals were introduced during the Koryŏ era, they were performed to pay proper respect and give recognition to various spirits attributed to the heavenly, earthly and human realms (Figure 2.4).

The arrival of *aak* was enabled largely through acceptance of a series of extraordinary gifts sent from King Huizong, the eighth emperor of the Chinese Song court. The first gift, in 1114, consisted of 167 instruments with scores and performance instructions, mainly for use in palace banquets (Howard 1995: 13). However, what the Koreans really yearned for was a set of ritual instruments to use in performing sacrificial rites to Confucius that they believed would improve the peace and prosperity of the state (Figure 2.4). The king generously complied

Category or Realm	Spirits Honored in the Rite
Heavens	Wind, Clouds, Thunder, Rain
Earth	Land and Grain
Human	Royal Ancestors
Human	Agriculture
Human	Sericulture
Human	Elements and Grain
Human	Confucius

FIGURE 2.4   *State Sacrificial Rites during the Chosŏn dynasty.   (Adapted from Provine 2002a: 863.)*

in 1116 by sending more than 400 instruments, as well as notated scores and dance props (Provine 2002a: 862). Under constant threat from attack from neighboring kingdoms, King Huizong may well have sent the unprecedented gifts as a politically motivated gesture to secure an ally in Korea. At the very least, the Song ruler sought to maintain diplomatic relations with Koryŏ by fulfilling Korea's request.

In Korean music history, these gifts and their subsequent legacy are one of the more significant examples of transnational cultural politics at work. Musically and culturally, the gifts added greatly to Korea's instrumentarium and repertoire. Politically, King Huizong's gesture helped advance relations between the Song and Koryŏ courts and also constituted a more powerful and broadly recognizable means to demonstrate the prosperity and glory of the state. This bolstered Korean legitimacy, both among its own people and among its powerful Asian neighbors.

Political instability characterized the 13th century in the region. Despite Song China's efforts to hold on to their power, they were eventually attacked by the Jurchen people and driven beyond the Yangtze River. Without an accessible source of instruction, guidance and instruments, it became more difficult for Korea to maintain the newly imported *aak*. By the mid-13th century, Koryŏ was also a target, greatly weakened by invasions from the Mongols. To make matters worse, the Red Turban brigands (a Chinese rebel faction that formed to resist the Mongols) attacked in 1361 and effectively destroyed almost all of the Chinese instruments that had been gifted to the Korean court (Provine 2002a: 862). Koryŏ soon collapsed, in 1392, and was taken over by the Chosŏn dynasty.

During the early establishment of the Chosŏn dynasty (1392–1910), the court sought to completely reorganize its music. As Buddhism declined from a position of relative importance in the Koryŏ era and Confucianism became more entrenched in the Chosŏn court, King Sejong (1418–1450) – one of Korea's most distinguished and musically inclined kings – was especially determined to restore Confucian *aak*. For a dynasty in transition, Confucianism would have been especially appealing because it promoted the notion of "one ruler" in power under the "mandate of heaven." In this system, everyone is to behave according to a proper code of relationships (e.g., subjects should abide by their king), in order to secure harmony in the world.

Through the assistance of the scholar Pak Yŏn, King Sejong was able to reconstruct *aak* instruments according to the Chinese *bayin* philosophy (literally, "eight sounds"); many were successfully made from Korean materials. According to this philosophy, resonating these materials during a ritual was believed to induce harmony, propriety and peace. In light of this, they worked hard to reestablish and systematize a full set of state sacrificial rites. They also prepared melodies that reflected Korean interpretations of Chinese sources such as Lin Yu's *Dasheng yuepu* ("Collection of Dasheng music"), which they believed corresponded well with the music that was originally received in the 12th century (Provine 2002a: 863). Amazingly, Korea has maintained this music, more or less continuing this tradition long after it disappeared in China.

Chinese-derived *aak* was used for most of the seven sacrificial rites (Figure 2.4) that were restored during the Chosŏn, with the exception of the Sacrifice to the Royal Ancestors. King Sejong argued that Korean music is unlike that of China and that Korea's own royal ancestors should be memorialized with music that sounded "natural" to Koreans. He then composed two large suites of music with vocal texts praising his royal ancestors (Provine 2002b: 869). Given the formal context and political importance of *aak* within the court, this was a significant assertion of Korean identity. In a sense, King Sejong's compositional act was a declaration of the independent spirit of the Korean royal ancestors, and by extension of the Korean people as a whole. King Sejong's musical legacy was continued under the reign of his son, King Sejo, who oversaw further refinement of the original suites into 11 movements each and officially introduced them into the Sacrificial Rite to the Royal Ancestors. Although this music is used for a ritual with Chinese origins, it is now usually classified as *hyangak* or native Korean music because of its native compositional origin.

COURT MUSIC IN PRACTICE TODAY

Of the seven sacrificial rites that were performed during the height of the Chosŏn dynastic court, only two were allowed to continue during the early 20th century under Japanese colonial rule: the Sacrifice to Confucius (with music called *Munmyo Cheryeak*, CD track 9) and the Sacrifice to the Royal Ancestors (with music called *Chongmyo Cheryeak*, CD track 10). By 1945 there were fewer than 30 court musicians remaining in the Court Music Bureau (*Aakpu*). This was down from 772 musicians at the end of the 19th century. Despite this suppression and the disappearance of an active court culture in the 20th century, these two pieces of ritual music are still performed today in South Korea, in ritual and spatial contexts that share at least some continuity with courtly practice.

The continuity of court ritual music is largely due to a cultural preservation system that was initiated by the ROK through the Cultural Properties Protection Law, enacted in 1962. This new legislation was explicitly geared toward developing a stronger sense of Korean cultural and national identity; Article I states that "the purpose of the law is to strive for the cultural progress of the Korean people, as well as to contribute to the development of human culture by preserving cultural properties and their utilization." This people-oriented policy actively promoted inclusion of native folk music genres in selecting cultural properties (as opposed to just elite, aristocratic genres), thereby differentiating Korea's preservation program somewhat from a similar system that was set up in Japan at least a decade earlier.

In the implementation of this new law, four categories were created: Tangible Cultural Properties, Intangible Cultural Properties, Folk Cultural Properties, and Monuments. Under this system, performing arts are considered Intangible Cultural Properties, in which category designated scholars and officials were charged with researching and selecting appropriate genres for preservation and then appointing people to transmit them. Among those appointed to transmit a given genre, the highest position is that of "holder" (*poyuja*), otherwise known under the highly coveted title "human cultural treasure" (*ingan munhwajae*).

In light of Korea's emphasis on people-oriented folk genres, it is ironic that court music was one of the first to benefit from this new cultural preservation policy; in fact, the first musical genre to be appointed for preservation was Royal Ancestral shrine music (*Chongmyo Cheryeak*) as Cultural Property No. 1 in 1964. Today, *Chongmyo Cheryeak* (along with other forms of court music and dance) is transmitted under the well-supported auspices of the National Gugak Center, an organization whose roots can be linked to the royal music institutes of Korea's dynastic past. It is interesting to note that this particular "Koreanized" ritual for the Royal Ancestors (*Chongmyo Cheryeak*) was appointed well before other types of state sacrificial rite. For example, despite its much longer history in Korea, the Sacrifice to Confucius was not designated as a Cultural Property (No. 85) until 1986, under the comprehensive ritual title of *Sŏkchŏn Taeje*. Cultural politics may have played a role here because art forms with a clearer Korean cultural identity were prioritized over others, even those with a longer history of continuous practice (Figure 2.4).

Other types of pieces performed at court have also been preserved as part of the traditional Korean repertoire and continue to be transmitted in university programs and major cultural institutions such as the National Gugak Center. Together, all the music associated with the Korean court has traditionally been organized into three main categories:

1. *Aak.* Ritual court music of Chinese structure and origin. The only surviving works of *aak* are the melodies that are played in *Munmyo Cheryeak.*
2. *Hyangak.* Native court music performed in a variety of contexts, including ceremonies, banquets and processionals. Because of its Korean compositional origin, *Chongmyo Cheryeak* is usually considered *hyangak.*
3. *Tangak.* Ensemble music of Chinese origin performed in a Koreanized style, mainly in a variety of nonritual court contexts.

Of these three categories, *hyangak* is by far the largest in terms of the number of works that remain in the contemporary repertoire. In addition to *Chongmyo Cheryeak*, *hyangak* works include the 80-minute *Yŏmillak* ("Enjoyment of the People"), the widely known "masterpiece" of Korean music called *"Sujech'ŏn"* ("Long Life Everlasting as the Sky," CD track 11), and the military processional suite called *Chwita* ("Blowing and Beating"). The *tangak* category consists of only two pieces today: *Pohŏja* ("Pacing the Void") and *Nagyangch'un* ("Springtime in Luoyang"). Taking into consideration the various invasions and upheavals that have beset the Korean peninsula, these ritual court practices represent a remarkably long and continuous tradition that Korea has worked hard to preserve. The exceptional perseverance of these state ritual traditions is all the more impressive when one considers that the Korean court has become an anachronism in contemporary Korean life.

ACTIVITY 2.1 *South Korea's preservation system was modeled on that of Japan. Compare the two systems by conducting an internet search on the National Gugak Center and the National Theater of Japan. Acquaint yourself with the history and programming of these two organizations, and make note of any similarities or differences in how each country approaches preservation of traditional culture. Prepare in groups and do a short in-class presentation.*

EXPERIENCING STATE SACRIFICIAL MUSIC

Preservation of musical genres has gone hand in hand with preservation of historic sites where the genres are performed. These sites are among the few remaining bastions of tradition in Seoul, a centuries-old city that is now a densely populated and rapidly changing metropolis. The Sacrifice to the Royal Ancestors is held once a year at the Chongmyo Shrine, located near Ch'anggyŏng Palace in the centrally located area of Jongno in Seoul. Preserved in its original form since the 16th century, the shrine is designated as a UNESCO World Heritage site, one of the oldest Confucian royal shrines still in existence today. The Sacrifice to Confucius is performed biannually at the Confucian Shrine (Historic Site No. 143) and is further ensconced within the grounds of Sŏnggyun'gwan University, an educational institution with a long and distinguished royal heritage.

Ritual Format and Cosmology
Both *Chongmyo Cheryeak* and *Munmyo Cheryeak* are performed with two ensembles that play in alternation. One, called the "terrace ensemble," is set up on a formidable stone terrace that leads into the main shrine building. The other, called the "courtyard ensemble," is located at the opposite end of the courtyard. Rows of dancers stand in formation on one side (Figure 2.5). Although the number of instruments and dancers and the spatial positions of the musicians have been adapted to various circumstances over the years, any changes were most certainly made in accordance with ancient Confucian cosmological philosophy. Confucian philosophy extends beyond the geomantic or spatial and is infused into the sonic and melodic realm as well. For example, the instruments that are sounded are all made of materials that correspond with the ancient Chinese *bayin* ("eight sounds") system (*p'arŭm* in Korean). This system classifies instruments according to eight natural materials—bamboo, wood, metal, silk, skin, stone, gourd and clay—that are believed to "resonate" with other elements of the cosmos (Figure 2.6).

Instruments and Music
As artifacts of material culture, the preservation, maintenance and continuation of the instrumental legacy involved in performing state sacrificial music has many advantages for the state. In addition to embodying the cosmological beliefs associated with the *p'arŭm* system, the instrumentation of state sacrificial music creates a unique multitimbral texture that is almost avant-garde in its wide palette of percussion sounds

FIGURE 2.5 *Painted depiction of a ritual court music ceremony. The terrace ensemble is located on the raised platform at the top of the painting. The courtyard ensemble is located toward the bottom center of the painting and is surrounded by rows of dancers in red and blue. (Photo by the author. Courtesy of the National Gugak Center.)*

Type	Instrument Type	Munmyo Cheryeak	Chongmyo Cheryeak
Metal	Bronze bells	P'yŏnjong, t'ŭkchong+	P'yŏnjong, panghyang, ching*
Stone	Stone chimes	P'yŏn'gyŏng, t'ŭkgyŏng+	P'yŏn'gyŏng
Skin	Drums	Chŏlgo+, chingo, nogo*, nodo*,	Chŏlgo+, chingo*, changgo
Gourd	Mouth organs	n/a	n/a
Bamboo	Flutes, panpipes, double-reeds	Chi, yak, chŏk, so	Taegŭm, tang p'iri, saenap*
Wood	Wooden clapper, box drum, and tiger shaped scraper with serrated spine	Pak, ch'uk, ŏ	Pak, ch'uk, ŏ
Silk	Zithers with silk strings	Kŭm+, sŭl+	Ajaeng+, haegŭm*
Clay	Clay bowl, clay ocarina	Pu*, hun*	n/a

Key: + means used only in the terrace ensemble; * means used only in the courtyard ensemble.

FIGURE 2.6 Bayin/p'arŭm *"eight sounds" system in* Munmyo Cheryeak *and* Chongmyo Cheryeak.

(CD tracks 9 and 10). Physically, there is much to admire in the instruments themselves: a unique array of resonant materials, novel shapes and elaborate decorations that are imbued with rich animal imagery and symbolism. Historically, *Munmyo Cheryeak* features instruments that descended directly from China's original instrumental gift of 1116, save for the mouth organ or *saeng*, which fell out of use from deterioration over time. Since the *saeng* belongs to the gourd category in the "eight sounds" system, its absence means the *Munmyo Cheryeak* that we hear today falls just short of completely fulfilling the "eight sounds" philosophy. Lastly, several of these instruments are rarely heard or played in other genres and would have disappeared from the Korean musical soundscape entirely had it not been for the preservationist intervention of the ROK.

Munmyo Cheryeak

Among some of the instruments that would have fallen out of use are the formidable and distinctive metal and stone idiophones, most notably the sets of bronze bells (*p'yŏnjong*, Figure 2.7) and stone chimes (*p'yŏn'gyŏng*, Figure 2.8). The *p'yŏnjong* features 16 elliptical bells that are hung in two rows of eight upon a majestic wooden frame carved with dragons, birds and other mystical animals. The bells are tuned according to a chromatic scale from C to D#. The terrace ensemble also features the *t'ŭkchong* (Figure 2.7), a single tall elliptical bell. Constructed without interior clappers, all of the bells are struck individually by a

FIGURE 2.7 *From left to right:* t'ŭkchong *(single bronze bell),* ch'uk *(wooden box) and* p'yŏnjong *(set of multiple bronze bells). These instruments were set up as part of the terrace ensemble during a performance of* Munmyo Cheryeak *(Confucian ritual music).* *(Photo by the author.)*

FIGURE 2.8   *From left to right: p'yŏn'gyŏng (set of multiple stone chimes) and ch'uk (wooden box). The instruments pictured here are part of the courtyard ensemble used in* Munmyo Cheryeak *(Confucian ritual music).*   (Photo by the author.)

performer wielding a long stick with a special, horn-shaped tip. The *p'yŏn'gyŏng* is made up of 16 L-shaped stone slabs hung onto a similar frame with reddish ropes. These stone chimes are also arranged in two rows of eight and tuned in the same manner as the *p'yŏnjong*. The terrace ensemble also features a stone counterpart to the *t'ŭkchong*, a single stone-slab instrument called a *t'ŭkgyŏng*.

The wood categories are also populated with some noteworthy idiophones that serve to punctuate the beginning and ending of a ritual court piece. Perhaps the most important of these is the *pak*, a clapper made of six hardwood rectangles held together with a cord strung through a hole on one end of each wood slab. In keeping with its importance, the *pak* is played by the director of the ensemble, who signals the beginning of the piece by slapping the pieces of wood together once and the end by playing it three times. Another instrument that can be heard in the opening percussion sequence is the *ch'uk*, a medium-sized wooden

FIGURE 2.9   Front: Ŏ (wooden tiger with serrated spine). The Ŏ is played by running a bundle of split bamboo across the serrated spine. Here, the bundle rests in front of the musician as she waits to perform in the courtyard ensemble of Munmyo Cheryeak (Confucian ritual music).   (Photo by the author.)

box played with a thick stick that is placed in a hole at the center of the top panel (Figure 2.7). With its large open cavity, the *ch'uk* produces an earthy, hollow sound when struck that easily resonates throughout the space. Perhaps one of the most delightful instruments is the *ŏ*, a large wooden tiger with a serrated spine of 27 ridges carved in a representation of the animal's mane (Figure 2.9). The *ŏ* is "played" by striking the head with a bundle of split bamboo and then running it along the spine, creating a wonderfully textured scraping sound.

Another unique idiophone is the *pu*, a large clay vessel that is struck on the rim with a bundle of split bamboo. In *Munmyo Cheryeak*, the *pu* is played in a gradually accelerating pattern and helps fill the considerable empty space between notes (Figure 2.10).

In the "skin" category, there are four membranophones or drums of various sizes. The *chŏlgo* is a barrel drum suspended at a slight angle

FIGURE 2.10   *Front left:* Pu *(large clay vessel struck with a bundle of split bamboo). Back row left:* Hun, *a clay ocarina. Both of these instruments represent the "clay" category of the* bayin/p'arŭm *system. Here, they are being played as part of the courtyard ensemble in a performance of* Munmyo Cheryeak *(Confucian ritual music).   (Photo by the author.)*

FIGURE 2.11   Chingo *(large barrel drum with tacked on heads). (Photo by the author. Courtesy of the National Gugak Center.)*

that is played with the terrace ensemble. The *chingo*, one of the largest drums still in use, plays with the courtyard ensemble within a level frame (Figure 2.11). In addition, there are the *nogo* and the *nodo*, both of which consist of two longer barrel drums mounted at right angles to one another (Figure 2.12). In the case of the larger *nogo*, only one head is played, with a single mallet. In a more novel fashion, the smaller drums of the *nodo* are sounded through rotation of the central pole, which then activates movement of the attached thongs that strike the drumheads.

The bamboo category consists of an array of aerophones that are played only in the Sacrifice to Confucius: three flutes called the *chi, yak* and *chŏk* as well as a panpipe called the *so*. The *chi* is a transverse flute made of dark yellow bamboo and featuring a raised mouthpiece and five finger holes (Figure 2.2). The *yak* and the *chŏk* are simple flutes, played vertically with similarly narrow ranges. In contrast, the *so* is made of 16 notched bamboo pipes arranged in a row by length and held in a wooden frame that is said to resemble unfolded phoenix wings.

FIGURE 2.12 *Front:* nogo *(two small barrel drums attached to a pole). Notice the knotted ropes that are activated by rotation of the central pole. Back:* Nodo *(two large, long barrel drums struck by a mallet). Both are part of the courtyard ensemble of* Munmyo Cheryeak *(Confucian ritual music).* (Photo by the author.)

One final aerophone, called the *hun*, is essentially an ocarina made out of baked clay and therefore part of the clay category (Figure 2.10). Rounding out the "eight sounds" system are the silk instruments called the *kŭm* and the *sŭl*. With strings made of wound silk, these chordophones are basically zithers imported from China that were rarely heard in any other context. As Korea went on to adapt its own native zithers, the *kŭm* and *sŭl* remained in their original form. The *kŭm* is a seven-string zither identical to the Chinese *guqin*. The *sŭl* is a 25-string zither that features a painted soundboard made of paulownia wood.

When listening to *Munmyo Cheryeak* on the recording (CD track 9), imagine yourself seated in the center of a spacious traditional Korean courtyard with the terrace ensemble on a platform in front of you, the courtyard ensemble behind you and several rows of dancers flanking you on each side (Figure 2.5). Despite the array of tones produced by the "eight sound" system, the overall sound is quite stark. The simple unison melodic construction and use of a rising inflection on each note contributes to its unique, unearthly sound. Because of the unusually slow tempo and free-floating melodic quality, the succession of 32 notes resists easy perception as "melody" and therefore transports the listener to a different sense of time and space (Figure 2.14).

Chongmyo Cheryeak
The Sacrifice to the Royal Ancestors (*Chongmyo Cheryeak*, CD track 10) retains some of the Chinese-derived instruments featured in

Section	Ensemble	Dance
Welcoming the Spirits	Courtyard	Civil
Offering of Tribute	Terrace	Civil
Offering of Food	Courtyard	None
First Wine Offering	Terrace	Civil
Second Wine Offering	Courtyard	Martial
Final Wine Offering	Courtyard	Martial
Removing the Vessels	Terrace	none
Ushering Out the Spirits	Courtyard	none

FIGURE 2.13 Munmyo Cheryeak *Ritual Order. (Adapted from Provine 2002a: 862.)*

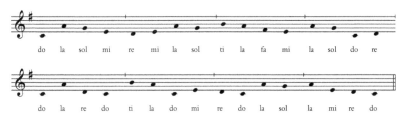

FIGURE 2.14   *Melodic notation for* Munmyo Cheryeak: Hwangjongkung, *CD track 9. Normally, the syllables that indicate the pitches would be written in Chinese characters. For ease of practice, I have replaced them with Western solfège syllables.*

ACTIVITY 2.2   *CD track 9 features the courtyard ensemble playing the first movement or section ("Welcoming the Spirits") of* Munmyo Cheryeak *(Figure 2.13). Although there are eight sections in the ritual, essentially only two melodies are used, each consisting of 32 notes (Figure 2.14). Of these two melodies, the first one is used in various transpositions in all of the sections except for the last, "Ushering out the Spirits," which employs the second melody exclusively.*

In "Welcoming the Spirits," the first note starts on the fundamental pitch of C on the Western scale, which is referred to as the hwangjongkung *in Korean. The melody uses pitches that follow a diatonic scale of C, D, E, F#, G, A, and B. This arrangement of pitches translates into the C Lydian mode in Western practice (on the piano the Lydian mode can be played on the white keys starting on F).*

- *First get a sense of the pulse. After the rhythmic introduction, each note of the melody constitutes one pulse. Think of the pulse duration as one long inhalation and exhalation (about four seconds altogether).*
- *Listen to CD track 9 and follow along with the melody in Figure 2.14. Sing the melody on Solfège syllables (do, la, sol, mi, etc.) along with the recording.*
- *Pay attention to how the rhythm is articulated in the introduction, melodic section and conclusion. In the main melodic*
  (continued)

ACTIVITY 2.2 *(continued)*

section, the clay pu *provides a rhythmic underpinning for each long tone by playing a gently accelerating pattern. Also, two pairs of drum strokes are struck every fourth note, lending some structure to the free-floating succession of pitches.*

- *Now that you have a sense of the pulse, get together with other musicians and play the 32-note melody together in the same tempo as the recording. If possible, try to imitate the ornamental upward slide that punctuates each note. Elect a "percussionist" to lead by playing the gently accelerating pattern of the* pu *part.*
- *The piece is punctuated at the beginning and end with commanding rhythmic patterns played by the wood and skin instruments. Refer to Figure 2.6, and listen to their distinct timbres, listed in order of entry:* pak, ŏ, ch'uk, chingo, nogo, pak

Munmyo Cheryeak (CD track 9) but also incorporates several other instruments, many of them indigenous. Referring to Figure 2.6, one can see that *Chongmyo Cheryeak* retains many of the most distinctive instruments used in *Munmyo Cheryeak*: the stone and metal *p'yŏnjong* and *p'yŏn'gyŏng*, the skin *chŏlgo* and *chingo*, as well as the wood *pak*, *ch'uk* and *ŏ*. This gives sonic continuity with the Confucian ritual tradition while allowing room for a more indigenous instrumental aesthetic.

In the metal category, we see the addition of the Korean *ching*, a large metal gong that produces a low, sustained ring when struck in the center by a soft mallet. Another instrument is the addition of the Chinese-derived *panghyang*, a set of 16 iron-slab chimes that were originally an integral part of ritual court music until the end of the 18th century. Curiously, now it is played only in *Chongmyo Cheryeak*. In keeping with its ubiquitous role in Korean music, the hourglass-shaped two-sided *changgo* drum is the one major addition to the wood category (Figure 2.15).

In the bamboo aerophone and silk chordophone categories, Korean instruments have mostly replaced the more direct Chinese imports that are featured in *Munmyo Cheryeak*, contributing greatly to a shift in the sonority to a more characteristically sustained sound. Much of this has

FIGURE 2.15 *From left to right:* changgo *(hourglass drum) and* puk *(barrel drum). Both of these instruments are used in a variety of genres. The* puk *pictured here, however, is used in* p'ungmul *and has drumheads that are held in place with tied ropes. Other types of puk employ tacked on heads, such as those used in* p'ansori. *(Photo by the author.)*

to do with the addition of the double-reeded *tang p'iri* and the *saenap* (Figure 2.1). As suggested in the name, the *tang p'iri* (literally "Chinese oboe") was imported from China as part of the early 12th-century instrumental gifts from King Huizong. Although the *tang p'iri* is clearly Chinese derived, Korea has definitely embraced this *p'iri*-type double-reed instrument as central to many Korean genres, both inside and outside the court. The *saenap* (also called the *t'aep'yŏngso*) is a conical double reed played in the courtyard ensemble. Rounding out the bamboo section is a large transverse flute called the *taegŭm* (figure 2.3). One of its unique features is an oval hole overlaid with a tissue membrane that can be exposed or hidden with a cover. When exposed, the membrane vibrates with a characteristic buzzing and slightly nasal timbre. This capability lends to the *taegŭm* an extraordinary timbral depth and variety that can sound both natural and calm, plaintive and haunting—making it one of the most difficult Korean instruments to master.

Also contributing to the more sustained sound of *Chongmyo Cheryeak* are the bowed *ajaeng* and *haegŭm* (instead of the plucked Chinese zithers featured in *Munmyo Cheryeak*) in the silk chordophone category. The *ajaeng*, a seven-string zither, most likely descends from the Chinese

FIGURE 2.16 Ajaeng *(bowed zither)*. *The court* ajaeng *has seven strings and is bowed with a rosined bow of forsythia wood. The* ajaeng *used in the* sanjo *genre has eight strings and is usually bowed with a horsehair bow as pictured here. This particular* ajaeng *has been adapted for modern use and has 11 strings. (Photo by the author.)*

yazheng (literally, "creaking zither"). Court *ajaeng* players retain the practice of bowing the strings with a rosined stick of forsythia wood, which produces its characteristic scratchy and earthy sound (Figure 2.16). The other bowed instrument is the *haegŭm*, a two-stringed spiked lute with a bright, nasal tone quality that is similar to that of the Chinese *erhu*. The bow is threaded in between the two strings and must be manually tensed in order to make a clear sound. Adding to an already difficult playing technique is the absence of a fretted fingerboard, which requires the fingers to find the pitches by pulling on the strings in midair. Despite the challenge, this feature allows the facile bending of the pitches that has become a distinguishing feature of the *haegŭm's* sound.

Chongmyo Cheryeak is best experienced within the larger context of the Sacrifice to the Royal Ancestors at the Chongmyo Shrine in Seoul. Once a year in May, visitors enter a grand, palatial courtyard that is set up with the familiar terrace and courtyard ensembles. The music consists of two suites: *Pot'aep'yŏng* ("Preserving the Peace") and *Chŏngdaeyŏp* ("Achieving Great Works"). Consisting of 11 movements each, *Pot'aep'yŏng* addresses civil (or nonmilitary) achievements while *Chŏngdaeyŏp* extols the military exploits of past kings. The terrace ensemble plays the first movement of *Pot'aep'yŏng* (called *"Hŭimun,"* CD track 10) during the rites of "Welcoming of the Ancestral Spirits," the "Greeting of the Spirits" and the "First Offering of Wine." Meanwhile, a large group of dancers perform a civil dance, and vocalists laud the civil achievements of the royal ancestors. In the second and third offerings of wine, the courtyard ensemble takes over and plays the second *Chŏngdaeyŏp* suite, while the dancers and singers perform in praise of the military achievements of former kings.

Given that *Chongmyo Cheryeak* uses many of the same instruments as *Munmyo Cheryeak* in the metal, stone, skin and wood instrument categories (Figure 2.6), there is a discernible sonic continuity between the two forms, especially in the percussive realm. However, when King Sejo sanctioned use of the *hyangak* suites composed by his father, King Sejong, for the Sacrifice to the Royal Ancestors, several major musical changes were set in motion. The double reed sonorities of the *tang p'iri* and the *saenap* (Figure 2.1) in the bamboo category produce a thicker, more strident sound that is tempered only somewhat by the earthy timbres of the *taegŭm* flute (figure 2.3). This dominant sustained sound is bolstered by the bowed strings of the *ajaeng* (Figure 2.16) in the terrace ensemble and the *haegŭm* in the courtyard ensemble.

ACTIVITY 2.3 *Listen to* Chongmyo Cheryeak *on CD track 10. The music of* Chongmyo Cheryeak *is more intricate than what is found in* Munmyo Cheryeak. *How can you tell? First, listen to CD Track 10 (*Pot'aep'yŏng *suite, "Hŭimun" movement). Right away, you should hear the more irregular rhythmic groupings of the pulse.*

- *Compare the instrumental texture and melodic line to that of the* Munmyo Cheryeak *"Hwangjongkung" in CD track 9. On the basis of your observations, what are some of the differences?*

(continued)

ACTIVITY 2.3   *(continued)*
You should be able to hear that Chongmyo Cheryeak *is made up of tones of unequal duration and more variety in ornamentation and inflections of the instruments. In addition, the vocalists take more liberties with the melody, sometimes articulating the text with more stylized ornaments and heavy vibrato. Sometimes the voices rise one tone higher than the main melody, providing intermittent moments of melodic tension with the other instruments. In addition, the stone and metal chimes repeat pitches when other instruments are sustaining, which adds sparks of contrast to the overall texture.*

- *What are some of the similarities in terms of how the pieces begin and end?*

To get a sense of the larger four-part structure, listen for the sharp sound of the pak *(wooden clapper), and write down the timing of every occurrence.*

Chŏlgo/Changgo	Ch'uk	Pak
		X
	/	
	/	
	/	
O		
	/	
	/	
	/	
O		
	/	
	/	
	/	
O		
		X

(continued)

ACTIVITY 2.3 *(continued)*
With the exception of the opening rhythmic sequence, the pak *artic-ulates the end of a section and is usually preceded by three pairs of drum strokes played on the* chŏlgo *and the* changgo.
Now turn your attention to the opening drum pattern. Korean notation is often read from right to left and from the top down. Look at the following approximation of Korean notation for the opening drum part. All the columns should be read simultaneously from the top down. Once you are able to follow the pattern while listening to CD track 10, get together with two others to tap the rhythm, with one person to a part. Or make up vocables (drum syllables) for each drum stroke and say them as you tap them.

TENSION AND RELEASE IN *"SUJECH'ŎN"*

In addition to the ritual *aak* and *hyangak* examples discussed in depth in this chapter, there are several other *hyangak* and *tangak* pieces that were played at court in a variety of contexts. Of the court music pieces that are still performed today, the most well known is the *hyangak* piece called *"Sujech'ŏn"* ("Long Life Everlasting as the Sky," CD track 11). Originally performed for royal banquet ceremonies and processions, this majes-tic 15-minute piece is performed on a "wind" ensemble called *taepung-nyu* ("bamboo *pungnyu"*) and features the powerful sound of the native double-reed oboes called *p'iri* that play the lead melody, as well as the *taegŭm* and *sogŭm* flutes (Figure 2.3), the bowed *ajaeng* zither (Figure 2.16) and *haegŭm* fiddle as well as the *changgo* hourglass drum (Figure 2.15) and a barrel drum called the *chwago*. Within the context of this particu-lar ensemble, the *ajaeng* and *haegŭm* are considered "winds" (instead of strings) because of their ability to sustain a tone, unlike plucked string instruments such as the *kayagŭm.*

"Sujech'ŏn" consists of four continuous sections. The first three are made up of six rhythmic patterns called *changdan* (lit., "long-short"), and the fourth contains only two *changdan*. In this context, a *changdan* refers to a fixed rhythmic pattern of beats; but it also can refer more loosely to a rhythmic grouping or cycle.

ACTIVITY 2.4 *The first step to listening to "Sujech'ŏn" on CD track 11 is to get a sense of the fluid breathing pulse. It is very slow and can be felt as being imbued with the flexible regularity of human breathing.*

- By following along with the notation in Figure 2.18, try to feel how the pulse is articulated throughout this piece. In most cases, it is through the drum strokes of the changdan, but the melodic instruments also play a role in sustaining the pulse.
- Then follow along with the changdan by reading the drum part for the two-headed hourglass changgo, written on the bottom line of the score in Figure 2.18. Refer to Figure 2.17 to learn the two changdans employed in this first section.
- Now play the changdan by tapping your hands on your lap while listening to the first section of "Sujech'ŏn." Altogether you will play six changdan patterns.

1	/	O	/		O	Ø . . .
	Tak	*Kung*	*Tak*		*Kung*	*Tŏng tŏrŏrŏ*
2	/	O	Ø . . .			
	Tak	*Kung*	*Tŏng tŏrŏrŏ*			

Key: Changgo drumstroke vocables

In the first section of "*Sujech'ŏn,*" *changdan* 1 is played twice, followed by *changdan* 2 once. Then *changdan* 1 is repeated three more times.

Vocable	Symbol	Description
Tak	/	*A sharp drum stroke on the right drumhead with a thin stick. Use your right hand on your lap to approximate the drumstroke.*
Kung	O	*A lower-pitched drumstroke on the left drum head with the left hand. Use your left hand on your lap to approximate the drumstroke.*
Tŏng tŏrŏrŏ	Ø. . .	*A gently accelerating roll, using both drumheads.*

FIGURE 2.17 Changdan *for* Sujech'ŏn

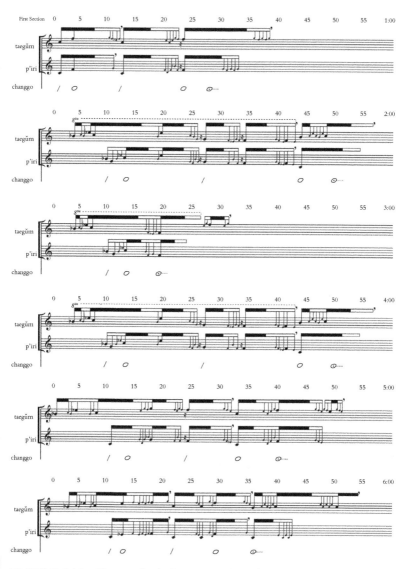

FIGURE 2.18 *Notation for the first section of* Sujech'ŏn, *CD track 11.* *(Adapted from Cho Chae-sŏn 1992: 69).*

In this way, *changdan* can be thought of as a "series of accented and unaccented strokes or beats" (Hesselink 1996: 152), where the pattern of emphasis often reinforces a feeling of tension and release. In *"Sujech'ŏn,"* tension is built up in the strongly accented strokes that begin each *changdan* and is released in the gradually accelerating drum roll that concludes each *changdan* (see Figure 2.17).

Tension and release is also expressed in the melodic expression of *"Sujech'ŏn,"* more specifically through connecting figures called *yŏnŭm* and the subtle inflection of single tones called *nong*. The practice of *yŏnŭm* is most readily discernible in the play of the melodic instruments (see Figure 2.18). For example, you can readily see how some of the melodic parts extend beyond the last stroke of each *changdan*. While the *p'iri* leads the main melody, the *taegŭm* (supported by the *sogŭm, haegŭm* and *ajaeng*) extends the melodic flow either before or after the *p'iri's* main melodic line. The relationship between the two melodic groups creates audible tension through a texture called heterophony, where one melody is played by multiple instruments but with varying inflections and ornaments. Cho Chae-sŏn argues that the practice of inflection and ornamentation is absolutely vital to expressing tension and release in the piece. Even within a given sustained long tone, various types of

ACTIVITY 2.5   *This time, as you listen to "Sujech'ŏn" on CD track 11, refer to Figure 2.18 and listen more carefully to how the instruments build and release tension in the melody.*

- *First, identify the leading instrument sound of the* p'iri *double reed. Note the timing of when you first hear the* p'iri.
- *Then identify the main* yŏnŭm *("connecting figure") instrument, the* taegŭm *flute. How do the* p'iri *and* taegŭm *interact with one another? Do you feel a sense of tension between the two parts? Note their timings.*
- *Now hone in on how the long tones are inflected or ornamented. Try to identify places where the tone is being "pushed" or "pulled back," and note the timing. Also try to tell the difference between "calm in motion" and "motion in motion."*
- *Now try "pushing" or "pulling back" on a long tone by singing or playing a sustained instrument.*

inflections (dynamic shading, vibrato, microtonal slides) called *nong* are used to either "push the sound" or "pull back on the sound." According to Cho, these long tones contrast with bursts of ornamental activity, creating two opposing melodic states that he calls "calm in motion" and "motion in motion" (Cho 1992: 123, 132). These two dynamic states interact powerfully to build and release tension throughout the piece.

In the three pieces presented in this chapter, we can trace the progression of choices: importing influences from abroad in *Munmyo Cheryeak*, to gradual indigenization in *Chongmyo Cheryeak*, to native aesthetic development in *"Sujech'ŏn."* Much of this process of indigenization is reflected in the instrumental and musical choices made by Korean practitioners, choices motivated by both political and aesthetic concerns. Although the power of the Korean court has faded away in the modern era, much of its expressive legacy is retained, in large part thanks to the cultural preservation efforts of the South Korean government. Some practitioners and scholars question whether cultural preservation policies have inhibited or enlivened a given artistic practice, but one cannot deny that the court music forms introduced in this chapter continue to be a part of a living, breathing tradition.

CHAPTER 3

The Politics of Preservation and Revival in Instrumental Music

INSTRUMENTAL PRESERVATION, ADAPTATION AND REVIVAL

All over the world, musical instruments remain potent symbols of a given culture, representing its sounds, people, identity, artistic accomplishments and technological ingenuity. Given its peninsular location, Korea developed and nurtured its own instruments in close cross-cultural dialogue with other countries. This happened initially with other Asian cultures and more recently with far-flung nations. In particular, Koreans have embraced the instruments and genres of Western concert and popular music, greatly affecting their musical sphere. Despite this, or perhaps in response to it, Koreans have remained actively engaged with older Korean instruments and genres in both "traditional" and creative ways. Although this desire to engage with older Korean forms has manifested itself differently in the North than in the South, the impulse is the same: to maintain some semblance of cultural continuity in rapidly changing times. Depending on the context, cultural continuity can be adapted to the needs of various interest groups, whether it serves to bolster the state in power, promote a national ideology or even embolden an oppositional movement. In this chapter, I continue to pursue the intersection of music, culture and politics with a focus on instrumental genres cultivated outside of the court.

South Korea: The Politics of Preservation and Revival
As discussed in the previous chapter, South Korea's cultural preservation system, initiated through the Cultural Properties Protection Law of 1962, was crucial to the survival of court practices such as Royal Ancestral Shrine music (Cultural Property No. 1) and the Sacrifice to Confucius (Cultural Property No. 85). It also served to support a number of other

instrumental genres that developed outside the court. These include *kayagŭm sanjo* (No. 23, CD track 12), *kŏmungo sanjo* (No. 16, CD track 13), *taegŭm sanjo* (No. 45, CD track 14), *nongak* (lit. "farmer's music," No. 11, CD track 15), as well as a number of comprehensive shamanic rituals. Some of these genres have a history of incorporating a great deal of individual improvisation, although others have become more fixed over time.

Although cultural preservation began as a government-sponsored endeavor, some of the folk genres that the government designated as Cultural Properties (such as *nongak*) were later pivotal in fueling a college- and community-based cultural revival that worked in tandem with the *minjung undong*, or "people's movement." In addition to advocating for the democratization of South Korea after a series of repressive military regimes led by Park Chung-hee (1961–1979) and Chun Doo-hwan (1980–1988), the people's movement was instrumental in developing progressive voices in many areas of South Korean society. Here in the beginning of the 21st century, the political impetus of cultural revival has shifted and subsided, giving way to other forces such as cultural tourism, creative experimentation and popularization. Nevertheless, even as South Korean instrumental practices become more diversified, the playing of Korean instruments continues to be an indelible marker of Korean cultural identity.

North Korea: Music and the Masses

Since the division, Korean instrumental musics have been shaped by a radically different ideology in the North, and as a result any comparison with the more preservationist South remains stark and dramatic. Because of this, the two countries stand as an intriguing case study of how political ideology can radically affect the musical practices of a people. In his *Talks with Writers and Artists* from 1951, Prime Minister Kim Il-sung drew from the communist notion articulated by Mao Zedong (1893–1976) that music and art should reflect and serve the masses in their revolutionary development (Howard 2002: 960). Although policies toward music evolved over the next several decades, this tenet positioned art as a "powerful weapon," thereby making bedfellows of music and politics and altering the course of music making in North Korea up to the present day.

Drawing from precedents already set in motion in Stalinist Russia and Maoist China, the early music of the emerging socialist state was dramatically reshaped for mass reception. For the most part, revolutionary songs and military marches with accessible, diatonic melodies and regular duple meters were widely promulgated in the early 1950s and swiftly became a compulsory fixture of the North Korean soundscape. This quickly displaced nonsanctioned forms of Korean music, such as ritual court musics, genres associated with the elite as well as other art forms considered distasteful or corrupt. Governmental policies on music and culture took a slight turn with the development of the *Chŏllima Undong* or "Galloping horse movement" in the late 1950s. Similar to Mao's "Great Leap Forward," this movement placed emphasis on rapid economic development. The *Chŏllima undong* also encouraged musicologists to collect folksongs from the countryside. Once collected, this material was then standardized; lyrics were adapted to suit the state's purposes and melodies and ornaments were shaped into a more homogeneous repertoire. This occurred at the expense of maintaining regional distinctiveness and variety in terms of lyrics, ornamentation and vocal production, all of which stands in striking contrast with the South, where regional distinctiveness is so highly valued.

Korean instruments were also reintroduced in the late 1950s, but with a *Chŏllima* twist. In keeping with the forward momentum of the *Chŏllima* agenda, the Committee for the Improvement of People's Instruments was created to "reform" these instruments. As this work progressed over the next several decades, the design and integration of the "improved instruments" was inevitably influenced by the developing philosophy of *juche* ("self-reliance"). In his influential 1982 essay "On the *Juche* Idea," Kim Jong-il consolidated the principles of *juche*, writing that "we must build culture which is *national in form and revolutionary and socialistic in content* . . . it is also necessary to make strenuous efforts to *develop science and technology* in order to *raise the cultural and technological standards of the masses*" (Kim Jong-il 1982; italics mine). The goal was to "improve" Korean instruments in such a way as to be competitive with Western or Chinese instruments. This enabled practitioners to flexibly integrate Korean instruments with Western instruments while also retaining a sense of Korean national culture and heritage.

Although many types of ensembles mix and match instruments, one of the more significant is the North Korean orchestra, which blends European strings, winds and brass with a selection of these "improved" Korean instruments (Figure 3.1). This hybrid can be heard in the instrumental arrangement of the well-known Korean folksong *"Arirang,"* performed by the Pyongyang Conservatory Orchestra (CD track 2). As heard in the string section, the *haegŭm*, a two-stringed bowed lute, has been reconstituted in various sizes to coincide with the four orchestral string roles of the violin, viola, cello and double bass. All four "reformed" *haegŭms* possess four metal strings instead of the original two and have a fingerboard for more precise tuning. These and other changes produce a bigger sound, expanded ranges and broader spectrum of string timbres

FIGURE 3.1 *Pyongyang Conservatory Orchestra, North Korea.* *(Photo courtesy of Elisa Gahng.)*

to fill out the string section of a North Korean orchestra (Figure 3.2). However, several key instruments were not updated. For example, those with strong associations to elite aristocratic or court cultures have been intentionally neglected, as with the *kŏmungo* and *ajaeng*. In addition, elaborate instruments used exclusively in court ritual forms, such as the stone *p'yŏn'gyŏng* chimes, have not been maintained in contemporary practice.

The wind section contains flutes modeled on the *taegŭm* and the *tanso*, both constructed in three sizes to cover various ranges. Other changes include hardwood construction instead of traditional bamboo and the addition of Western-style keywork that enables more precise tuning and facile chromatic capacity. The Korean double-reed *p'iri* has also been converted into three sizes: the *so p'iri* is much like the native *p'iri* but with a hardwood body, while the *chung p'iri* and *chŏ p'iri* have been altered in the format of the bassoon and contrabassoon. In addition, the traditional conical double-reed *saenap* (or *t'aep'yŏngso*) was modified with Western-style keywork (Figure 3.3), enabling an expanded range with fuller diatonic and chromatic capability (as opposed to the previous model, which was better suited to certain pentatonic scales).

FIGURE 3.2   *The string section of the Pyongyang Conservatory Orchestra. Notice the mixture of cellos and circular "reformed" haegŭms.*   *(Photo courtesy of Elisa Gahng.)*

ACTIVITY 3.1   *Listen to this performance of the Pyongyang Conservatory Orchestra playing "Arirang" in CD track 2 and view the photos of the modified Korean instruments in Figures 3.1, 3.2 and 3.3.*

* *Focusing on the string, wind and percussion sections, compare the sound of this ensemble to the same sections in a Western orchestra. Do you hear any major differences in instrumental timbre, range or expressivity?*
* *Then compare this North Korean orchestral excerpt to a traditional Korean court ensemble, as represented in "Sujech'ŏn" on track 10, and try to articulate some of the differences and similarities.*

FIGURE 3.3 *Modified saenap (North Korean conical double reed modified with metal keys).* *(Photo courtesy of Elisa Gahng.)*

FIGURE 3.4   *North Korean modified* kayagŭm *with 21 strings.*   *(Photo courtesy of Elisa Gahng.)*

Another popular "improved" instrument is the North Korean *kayagŭm*. Having 21 nylon strings (instead of the 12 silk strings of the traditional *kayagŭm*), the North Korean version uses metal pins instead of coiled cords to hold tension (CD track 16, Figure 3.4). Although the new version may lack some of the earthiness of its silk-stringed cousins, the North Korean *kayagŭm* gains by exploiting a louder, brighter and livelier sound and is versatile enough to accommodate diatonic scales and functional harmony.

ACTIVITY 3.2   *Listen to the North Korean 21-string* kayagŭm *on CD track 16, and then compare this to the 12-string South Korean* kayagŭm *in CD track 12. They are both examples of the* sanjo *instrumental form.*

- *Take note of the differences in timbre and playing technique, and see if you can tell the difference between the two instruments.*

(continued)

ACTIVITY 3.2 *(continued)*
- *Both tracks have the presence of the* changgo *drum playing the underlying* changdan. *Tap the pulse on CD track 16, and try to determine the meter (regular grouping of strong and weak pulses). You should be able to count a fast 4/4 that is similar to the* hwimori changdan *in* sanjo *(see Activity 3.4).*

Although some instruments have been discontinued, overall it is safe to say that North Korea has devoted considerable effort to maintaining its own version of instrumental continuity—albeit shaped by North Korean ideologies and clearly without the same eye toward preservation and authenticity so prevalent in the South. It is important to note that South Koreans have also engaged in similar efforts to "improve" the range or dynamic capability of their traditional instruments and create orchestras with Korean instruments. The difference is that the South Korean government did not mandate these changes and was more concerned with pursuing a preservationist agenda. Despite their differences, both North and South Korea maintain instrumental continuity through cultivation of solo and ensemble repertoires. I devote the remainder of this chapter to introducing some of the more distinctive of these forms.

THE FEATURING OF SOLO INSTRUMENTS IN *SANJO*

South Koreans use the umbrella term *kugak* (literally, "national music") to refer generally to Korean music performed on Korean instruments. Music that is newly composed for Korean instruments is further defined as *ch'angjak kugak*. Whereas individual solo pieces are common in *ch'angjak kugak,* such as Hwang Byung-ki's "Spring Snow" ("*Ch'unsŏl*") for the *kayagŭm* (CD track 30), they are less common in the older repertoires of the court and aristocratic salon. Perhaps the most familiar genre that features a solo instrument comes to us from the folk music world and is called *sanjo* (literally, "scattered melody"). Today, *sanjo* is more widely practiced in South Korea, although several well-known *sanjo* practitioners are known to have settled in North Korea.

Originally developed for the *kayagŭm* zither in the 19th century, *sanjo* (Figure 3.5) has easily become one of the most important *kugak* genres to

FIGURE 3.5 *South Korean* kayagǔm *with 12 strings. As seen in the picture, the woman in the traditional Korean costume is teaching the young girl to pluck the strings with the right hand and manipulate the pitches with the left.* *(Photo by the author.)*

feature a solo instrument (CD tracks 12, 13, 14, 16 and 17). Its continued success is due in large part to earlier preservation and revival efforts in South Korea. This may explain why the image of a musician playing *kayagŭm sanjo* and dressed in a vibrant, multicolored Korean traditional costume is one of the more appealing symbols of Korean music and culture. These "scattered melodies" feature a solo instrument that plays intricately ornamented melodic lines. Although the sophisticated artistry of the melody is the focus for most listeners, *sanjo* could not exist without the necessary rhythmic underpinning, dialogue and support provided by the accompanying *changgo* player (Figure 2.15).

Structurally speaking, *sanjo* comprises several connected movements, where each is defined by and named after the underlying rhythmic cycle or *changdan* (with the exception of the optional nonmetrical prelude). The movements usually flow from one to another without a break and can be very difficult to distinguish on first listening. These movements are generally arranged in a sequence of gradually increasing tempo, where the initial movement is said to establish the "emotional core" of the music, giving way to progressively lively movements that build melodic and rhythmic density over the course of a performance (Howard, Lee and Casswell 2008: 5). The length of a *sanjo* performance is extremely flexible and can be condensed to five minutes or expanded to an hour or more. Most performances find a medium ground and last somewhere between 15 and 30 minutes.

Given that East Asia is not necessarily known for its wealth of improvisatory genres, newcomers to Korean music are often surprised to learn that improvisation once played a pivotal role in the development of *sanjo*. Although the melodic content has become somewhat fixed into master-led schools of playing, the rhythmic accompaniment is still by and large improvised by the *changgo* player within the framework of a given *changdan* and in dialogue with the soloist. Spontaneous shouts of encouragement, called *ch'uimsae*, are considered crucial to a live performance and are routinely interjected by the accompanist (or audience members) at key points in the music.

The Development of Sanjo and Its Spread to Other Instruments

Although it may be difficult to pinpoint *sanjo's* exact origins, there is consensus that it evolved in dialogue with other genres that were based, at least in part, in the southwestern Chŏlla provinces of South Korea. These include local forms of shamanist music used to accompany a shaman's ritual movements, chants or dance, called *sinawi*, along with the well-regarded narrative vocal tradition called *p'ansori*. *Sanjo* practitioners most often credit the Chŏlla province aristocrat Kim Ch'ang-jo (1865–1919) as the creator and grandfather of the genre. Later scholars have complicated this story by asserting that *sanjo* developed from a continuum of instrumental music forms that include other chamber music forms, among them *sinawi* and *chul p'ungryu* (Howard, Lee and Casswell 2008: 9). In the early 20th century, the second generation of *kayagŭm sanjo* players contributed to formalizing *sanjo* in a number of ways. In the 1920s and 1930s, second-generation players were among the earliest to make recordings. This supported the notion of *sanjo* as a "fixed object" (as opposed to an ephemeral improvisation) and thereby contributed to gradually fixing the repertory. In addition, recordings made it possible for more people to listen to various styles of playing and better attribute these styles to individual players. Soon, the characteristic styles of key individual players became known as *ryu*, a concept loosely borrowed from Japan that refers to a style or school that is often based on an intensive master-student relationship.

As political conflict began to divide the Korean peninsula, leading up to the Korean War, so did it cause gaps within the *sanjo* world; in the 1940s, two key second-generation *sanjo* performers—An Ki-ok (1894–1974) and his disciple Ch'ŏng Nam-hŭi (1910–1984)—moved to North Korea. For the next four decades, their names were expunged from South Korean accounts of *sanjo* even though they were both among the original disciples of Kim Ch'ang-jo. When *kayagŭm sanjo* was designated in South Korea as Important Intangible Cultural Property No. 23 in 1968, select members were appointed as "holders" (*poyuja*), notably Kim Yun-dŏk (1918–1980), Sŏng Kŭm-yŏn (1923–1986), Ham Kŭm-dŏk (1917–1994) and Kim Chuk-p'a (1911–1989). In North Korea, Ch'ŏng Nam-hŭi is known to have been involved in modernizing the *kayagŭm* into its 21-string form, working at the Pyongyang Music and Dance University. There, he continued to play a form of *sanjo* that has been adapted to exploit the possibilities of the 21-string *kayagŭm* (Howard, Lee and Casswell 2008: 11). Interestingly, Ch'ŏng Nam-hŭi's early style of *sanjo* has been preserved in South Korea through one of his disciples, Hwang Byung-ki, who is now among Korea's most distinguished figures in *kugak*.

At the turn of the 20th century, *sanjo* was starting to gain recognition as a form and began its spread to other instruments. Around this time, Paek Nak-ch'un adapted the *sanjo* form for the six-string *kŏmungo* zither, an instrument prized by the literati class (Figure 3.6). Unlike the *kayagŭm*, the *kŏmungo* is played by striking the strings with a pencillike

FIGURE 3.6 Kŏmungo *(six-string zither plucked with a pencil-like stick).* *Although modeled on the Chinese* guqin *zither, the* kŏmungo *is played with a stick, lending it a more percussive timbre.* *(Photo by the author.)*

stick, lending a characteristic lower timbre and percussive sound (CD track 13). By the 1930s, other instrumental players wanted to expand their expressive range and repertoire, and soon *sanjo* was developed by masters of the *haegŭm* (two-string bowed lute), *ajaeng* (bowed zither, CD track 17, Figure 2.16), the *taegŭm* (transverse flute, CD track 14, Figure 2.3), the *tanso* (vertical flute), and the *p'iri* (cylindrical oboe, Figure 2.1). Of these additional forms of *sanjo* for other instruments, two more were designated as Intangible Cultural Properties: *kŏmungo sanjo* (No. 16) and *taegŭm sanjo* (No. 45).

Thanks to its development for myriad Korean instruments, *sanjo* has become one of the more highly recognized and aesthetically valued forms of Korean music today. That *sanjo* was so successfully adopted by a range of Korean instruments speaks to its incredible expressive power and flexibility as a form. Lastly, because *sanjo* encourages the player to exploit the techniques and capabilities of the instrument (melodic, timbral, rhythmic, etc.), its spread has undoubtedly contributed to cultivating the expressivity and artistry of every Korean instrument embracing its contours.

Changdan: *The Rhythmic Underpinning of* Sanjo

Although the "scattered melodies" may be the main feature of *sanjo* that perks up the ear, one could easily be unmoored by its steady stream of notes without an understanding of the underlying rhythmic cycles

ACTIVITY 3.3   *As noted,* sanjo *was originally developed on the* kayagŭm *and then adapted to other melodic instruments. Listen to examples of* sanjo *being played on all of the Korean zither instruments: the* kayagŭm *in CD track 12, the* kŏmungo *in CD track 13, and the* ajaeng *in CD track 17.*

• *Characterize each of the three zithers according to the pitch range, timbre, playing technique and modes of ornamentation. Make a chart of your findings.*
• *Then listen to* sanjo *being played on the* taegŭm *transverse flute on Track 14. Pay attention to timbre and playing technique; how does the* taegŭm *sound similar to or different from the other zither-based expressions of* sanjo?

called *changdan*. With the exception of the optional unmetered prelude (called *tasŭrŭm*), each movement is named after and defined by its underlying *changdan*; in this way, the concept of the *changdan* forms a kind of structural framework for the movements and as such stands as one of the most important organizational principles of *sanjo*. Although the exact sequence of the movements varies according to the performer and the performance context and time allotted, the player normally proceeds from the slower to faster *changdan* in this approximate order (not including the optional prelude): *chinyangjo, chungmori, chungjungmori, kutkŏri, chajinmori,* and *hwimori.*

A given *changdan* in *sanjo* and other folk genres is distinguished mainly by (1) tempo; (2) meter or "rhythmic grouping," as suggested by Bonnie Wade to refer to *changdans* that feel freer and unmetered (Wade 2009: 71); and (3) a rhythmic grouping of accented and unaccented beats or strokes where strict adherence to a specific drum pattern is less important than maintaining the flow of accented and unaccented beats. Given this philosophy, the *changgo* accompanist varies the drum stroke patterns while maintaining an aesthetic feeling of gathering tension and release within the course of a rhythmic cycle. Practitioners and scholars often explain this aesthetic of tension and release by breaking it down into four stages: mounting, suspension, binding and loosening. Students begin by learning the basic patterns through notation; variations are often learned orally through articulation of *changgo* drum stroke syllables or vocables.

ACTIVITY 3.4 *Graphic symbols and oral vocables are often used to teach these* changdan *and are arranged here in a sequence of boxes where each box represents an equal subunit of the pulse. Bolded boxes represent the larger pulse, where three subunits or "boxes" usually make up one pulse.*

- *Please refer to the key and tap the rhythms. Listen to CD track 18 to help you learn each* changdan. *In this track, each* changdan *is (1) pronounced by name, (2) performed on vocables, and (3) performed on the* changgo *drum.*
- *Once you are comfortable with the basic rhythmic pattern, add the spoken drum vocables.*
- *If you are feeling creative, pick one* changdan *and make up your own variation.*

Drum Stroke Key:

Symbol	Vocable	Description
Ø	Tŏng	Left hand hits the left head while the right hand hits the right head with the thin stick
O	Kung	Left hand hits the left head by itself
/	Tak	The right hand hits the right head with the thin stick with a sharp, clear sound
.	Ta or Ki	The right hand hits or taps the right head a little more softly

Chinyangjo: *slow tempo (18/8, six pulses divided into three subunits each)*

Ø												/			/		.
Tŏng												Tak			Tak		Ta

(continued)

ACTIVITY 3.4 *(continued)*

Chungmori: *moderately slow tempo (12/8, 4 pulses divided into three subunits each)*

Ø	/	O	/ .	/ /	O	O	/	O		O
Tŏng	Tak	Kung	Tak ki	Tak tak	Kung	Kung	Tak	Kung		Kung

Chungjungmori: *moderate tempo (12/8, four pulses divided into three subunits each)*

Ø		/	O	/	/	O	O	/	O		O
Tŏng		Tak	Kung	Tak	Tak	Kung	Kung	Tak	Kung		Kung

Kutkŏri: *moderately fast tempo (12/8, four pulses divided into three subunits each)*

Ø		/	O	. .	/	O		/	O	/	. .
Tŏng		Tak	Kung	Ta ta	Tak	Kung		Tak	Kung	Tak	

Chajinmori: *fast tempo (12/8, four pulses divided into three subunits each)*

Ø		O		O		/	O	
Tŏng		Kung		Kung		Tak	Kung	

Hwimori: *fast tempo (4/4, four pulses divided into two subunits each)*

Ø		/	/	O	/	O	
Tŏng		Tak	Tak	Kung	Tak	Kung	

The Interaction of Rhythm, Mode and Melody in Sanjo

Percussive extemporization on the accompanying *changgo* drum would be meaningless without its melodic counterpart. With this in mind, the goal of the accompanist is to anticipate what the soloist is playing and enhance the flow of the music rather than display virtuosic skills. This may include matching or enhancing the accents in the melody or playing connective fills in the breaks left by the soloist. Whether played on the *kayagŭm*, *kŏmungo* or *taegŭm*, the melody is primarily monophonic, although simultaneous playing of two or more pitches may be used occasionally for emphasis. In addition, the music contains no structural repetition, as may be found in folksongs. Instead, the "scattered melodies" are arranged in phrases that tend to correlate with the rhythmic groupings supplied by the *changdan*. Despite the absence of sectional repetition, short units of melodic material called *motives* are repeated and developed throughout a given section, providing coherence and serving to draw the listener deeper into the music.

Organization and expression of individual pitches, short motives or melodic phrases in *sanjo* can also be understood in terms of Korean modal theory. Like modes in other parts of the world, a Korean mode goes beyond the concept of a scale or set of pitches (see Wade 2004). In addition, Korean modes differ from scales in several dramatic ways: (1) the "home" or tonic pitch is situated in the center of the mode (rather than being the initial pitch); (2) pitches are often articulated with characteristic inflections, vibratos, slides or other ornaments that are associated with a given mode; and (3) Korean modes also contain ideas, melodic tendencies and expressions that convey extramusical feelings, emotions or moods.

A good example of these modal features can be heard in *kyemyŏnjo*, a distinctive Korean mode that many regard as central to *sanjo*. There is some disagreement in terms of the exact pitches that constitute *kyemyŏnjo* although the most important are *la, re, mi* and the passing tones of *fa* and perhaps *sol*, where the central tone or "tonic" is *re*. The distinct tonal characteristics of *kyemyŏnjo* include (1) a heavy vibrato on *la*, (2) a flat inflection on the central tone of *re*, and (3) "falling" or "breaking" tones on *fa* or *sol* sliding down to *mi* (Figure 3.7). Depending on the tuning of a given instrument, the exact setting of these pitches is not fixed and may be transposed. These tonal characteristics impart a heavy and plaintive sound that contributes to the "sad" expressive identity of this particular mode.

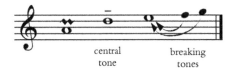

central   breaking
tone   tones

FIGURE 3.7   Kyemyŏnjo *mode. This mode is widely used in several genres discussed in this book, including* sanjo, *southern* minyo, *and* p'ansori. *With its plaintive and sorrowful sound,* kyemyŏnjo *is believed to be characteristic of the southwestern region of Korea.*

ACTIVITY 3.5   *Now that you are familiar with the* sanjo changdan, *you can use this knowledge to help navigate as you listen to the longer* sanjo *excerpts performed on the* kayagŭm *and* kŏmungo. *Follow along and try to tap the* changdan *as you listen.*

"Kayagŭm Sanjo" *(CD track 12)*
* *0:00–0:55* Chungmori changdan *(*kyemyŏnjo *mode starting on F#, melody starts in lower register and moves into the higher registers and builds melodic and rhythmic tension around 0:38, before finally coming back strong on the last phrase; 12 cycles in all. Phrases are through-composed but can be heard in pairs. Also notice the use repeated motives, which bring additional coherence).*
* *00:56–2:11* Kutkŏri changdan *(*kyemyŏnjo *mode; melody explores a transposition of the mode a fourth higher at about 1:40; altogether 21 cycles).*
* *2:12–end* Chajinmori changdan *(*kyemyŏnjo *mode; approximately 15 cycles before fade-out)*

"Kŏmungo Sanjo" *(CD track 13)*
* *0:00–2:41* Chinyangjo *(*kyemyŏnjo; *14 cycles)*
* *2:42–4:53* Chungmori *(14 cycles)*
* *4:54–end Chajinmori (approximately three cycles before fade-out)*

(continued)

ACTIVITY 3.5 *(continued)*

Get together with a friend and test each other to see if you can identify the various changdan *that are represented in the other* sanjo *examples (CD tracks 14, 16, 17). (Hint: CD track 14 features the* taegŭm *playing* Chungjungmori, *track 16 features the North Korean* kayagŭm *playing* hwimori, *and track 17 features the* ajaeng *playing the* chinyangjo *changdan).*

Over the course of a *sanjo* performance, a player may modulate to other starting pitches (usually up a fifth), contributing added dimension to the sound. In addition, the pitches can be arranged, transposed and inflected in ways that suggest other modes, adding interest and richness to the melodic palette of *sanjo*.

Following along with the rhythms in Activity 3.4 and 3.5 and listening to the corresponding *changdan* in CD tracks 12, 13, 14, 16 and 17, you may notice that articulation of a given *changdan* is characterized more by a curious feeling of space and absence than as a clearly delineated presence. The reason is that the performers tend to internalize the *changdan*, rendering its expression more implicit. One might even go so far as to say that mature *sanjo* performers playfully resist, and at times even sublimate, the *changdan*. This poses an added challenge and locus of interest for *sanjo* listeners. Just as dedicated South Indian music audiences internalize the *tala* through the help of hand gestures, avid *sanjo* listeners strive to become attuned with the music by following along with the *changdan* internally, and perhaps even following the drummer's lead by interjecting a shout of *ch'uimsae*.

The interplay of rhythm, melody and mode are tools in the exploration of new musical terrains in *sanjo*. On a micro level, subtle playing techniques that vary according to the solo instrument are a pivotal part of this process. Howard, Lee and Casswell see the pushing of rhythmic and melodic boundaries as characteristic of *sanjo*, noting in their analysis that "the music of *sanjo* constantly extricates itself from absolute organizational principles" (2008: 88). Although this quality may prove challenging for newcomers, over time seasoned listeners learn to find deeper satisfaction in following the performers as they inhabit and resist various melodic and rhythmic territories.

ACTIVITY 3.6   *Listen to the "Kŏmungo" (CD track 13) and "Taegŭm" (CD track 14) examples, paying particular attention to the various playing techniques, ornaments or inflections that are exploited on each instrument. These may include percussive slaps, pitch inflections, upward or downward slides, grace notes, timbral shadings and trills.*

- *Listen to each track, and make a list of some of the playing techniques that you hear. Note their timings within each track.*
- *From your list, which playing techniques seem unique to each instrument, and which seem to occur on both instruments?*

ENSEMBLE FORMS

Collaborative pursuit of performing in a Korean instrumental ensemble has proved especially pivotal in efforts of preservation and revival, especially as South Korea struggles to maintain a sense of cultural identity amidst multiple influences from abroad. Folk music in particular has captured the imagination of certain groups within the general populace, some of whom flock to these forms with genuine revivalist vigor and dedication. Perhaps no other ensemble form enjoys such widespread popularity as *p'ungmul*, a percussion band music and dance form ubiquitous to many rural and village areas on the Korean peninsula. This is the subject of the next section.

Koreans have also embraced various shamanist ritual traditions in the revival era and beyond, especially those individuals who view these traditions as a source and haven of native culture and beliefs. Scholars concur that Korean shamanist traditions serve as a "seedbed" of Korean culture, from which many vocal, instrumental, dance and drama genres derive inspiration and influence. This may also partially explain why there is such a diversity of shamanist and shamanist-derived traditions today. Two representative ritual forms, as well a shamanist musical offshoot called *sinawi*, are the focus of the last section of this chapter.

P'ungmul

P'ungmul is a comprehensive percussion band music, dance and drama form that includes the *changgo* (two-sided hourglass drum), *puk* (two-sided barrel drum), *ching* (the low-pitched large gong) and *soe* (small lead gong, also called the *kkwaenggwari*; Figures 2.15 and 3.8). Although all of the percussionists stand and move while playing, there are some additional roles that are more dance-oriented; these include players of the small hand-held *sogo* drums and character players called *chapsaek*. In addition to performing various acrobatic moves, some *sogo* players are trained to twirl long streamers flowing from specially constructed hats, adding an unmistakably dramatic flare to the *p'ungmul* performance at hand. The *soe* players also manipulate revolving headgear, although the materials are different and more contained. The *chapsaek* are modeled after archetypal village characters who vary from region to region, although common roles include the hunter, monk, aristocrat, grandmother and village maiden (Figure 3.9). Adding melodic liveliness to

FIGURE 3.8   *A* p'ungmul *ensemble from the Honam Chwado P'ilbong region (Important Intangible Cultural Asset No. 11-5) performing on the grounds of the National Theater of Korea in Seoul.*   *(Photo by the author.)*

the mainly percussive texture is the piercing conical double reed called the *t'aep'yŏngso* (Figure 2.1). On some occasions, one may also hear the bracing tones of the long-necked valveless bugle called the *nabal* (literally, "trumpet-bugle"), usually played to herald the beginning of an event or performance or for some other type of signal.

Given its regional ubiquity and diversity of formats, *p'ungmul* (literally, "wind-objects") is actually one of many local and institutional names used to refer to this genre. According to the governmental cultural asset system, this music is referred to as *nongak,* a term derived from pairing the two Sino-Korean characters for "farmer" or "farming" (*nong*) and "music" (*ak*). Interestingly, despite its comprehensive expressive nature, "*nongak*" was among one of the first *musical* categories to be designated as an Important Intangible Cultural Asset (No. 11) in 1966. Since then, scholars and practitioners have argued against usage of *nongak* because it serves to confine the meaning of this genre

FIGURE 3.9 *A close-up of one of the* chapsaek *characters in the Honam Chwado* P'ilbong p'ungmul *ensemble (Important Intangible Cultural Asset No. 11-5). Pictured here is the* taep'osu *or "hunter" character.* *(Photo courtesy of Linda Kwon.)*

to the spheres of "music" and "farming." The subject has even become
a topic of political contestation as some suggest that the semantic creation of *"nongak"* was part of an intentional effort to limit or belit-
tle the genre on the part of authorities during the Japanese colonial
era. Personally, I use *p'ungmul* mainly because it is the term of choice
among my fellow practitioners. I am also in sympathy with Nathan
Hesselink's argument that *p'ungmul's* more open Sino-Korean meaning of "wind-objects" better encompasses the irrepressible spirit and
multiplicity of expressions involved in this outdoor format (Hesselink
2006: 15–16).

Compared to other Korean genres, *p'ungmul* has been adapted to a
wide variety of social and spatial contexts: villages, schoolyards, parks,
city streets, multipurpose rooms, outdoor amphitheaters and the gamut
of stages. In fact, *p'ungmul's* extraordinary adaptability and accessibility makes it a powerful vehicle for exploring Korean cultural identity.
In the process, *p'ungmul* has become one of the more visible markers of
cultural continuity in modern-day Korean life. In exploring *p'ungmul* in
several contemporary contexts—the village, *madang*, street protest and
stage—I hope to give you a sense of its cultural depth, diversity and significance in Korean society.

P'ungmul *in the Village* Madang

Prior to Japanese occupation in the early 20th century, *p'ungmul* was
one of the major forms of expression available to the common people.
Although *p'ungmul* could be heard in marketplaces and small town-
ships, it was nurtured more fully in the villages, where it was played
in contexts of ritual, labor, entertainment and everyday life. In this way,
p'ungmul (and its various local manifestations) was a ubiquitous presence throughout the Korean countryside and could be considered integral to village life. As village life continues to decline in the 21st century,
it is not as common to hear *p'ungmul* within the village context, although
some troupes have revived the practice of performing *p'ungmul*-related
shamanist rituals during special times of the year (called *p'ungmul-kut*).
For example, for many troupes, the first full moon of the Lunar New
Year is considered an ideal time to hold a village *p'ungmul* ritual to stamp
out bad energy, appease the spirits and pray for a year of good fortune
and blessings. On February 23, 2002, I had the fortune of observing a
Lunar New Year ritual performed by the *p'ungmul* troupe from the village of P'ilbong, located in the county of Imsil in Chŏlla province. (This

group is designated as Important Intangible Cultural Asset No. 11-5 and is considered representative of the Honam Chwado region.) The day's events proceeded roughly according to this schedule:

1:30	Flag ceremony; village common *madang*
2:00	Guardian spirit ceremony; guardian spirit tree *madang*
2:30	Village spring ceremony; village water *madangs*
3:00	Household ceremonial visits; individual home *madangs*
6:00	Dinner; village common *madang*
7:00	Full moon *p'an-kut* celebration; mountaintop *madang*
11:00	Bonfire; mountaintop *madang* (see Figure 3.10)

Although these ceremonies all took place within the larger confines of the village, each individual ceremony is associated with a particular type of space called the *madang*. Spatially speaking, the *madang* refers most literally to a traditional courtyard or public common, but it also functions as a figurative frame for a host of other discursive meanings. For example, the *madang* can refer temporally to an occasion, a unit of time or a gathered sequence of things (songs, narrative events, rhythms, rites, etc.). Socially, this term is imbued with evocative connotations of communal gathering and embodied participation. The *madang* derives power from its ability to evoke all of these spatial, temporal and social meanings; as such, it serves as a powerful concept in *p'ungmul* performances. Although villages are not the only place where *madangs* exist, they remain a meaningful place in which to experience folk expressive culture in a uniquely Korean cultural space and contextual format.

To give a sense of what experiencing *p'ungmul* in the *madang* is like, I focus here on the evening Full Moon *pan'kut* celebration, which began just as the new full moon was rising in the sky. *P'an-kut* (literally, "field-ceremony") is a more entertainment-oriented format of *p'ungmul* as opposed to the ritual formats that took place earlier in the day. For example, this *p'an-kut* contained elaborate choreographies, virtuosic solos and opportunities for group singing and dancing. To give a sense of the setting and of the event's meaning for some of the lead performers, I offer an edited excerpt from my fieldnotes.

FIGURE 3.10 *Mountaintop* madang. *This photo shows the* madang *being prepared the day before the festivities. On the left, there is a large conical bundle of pine branches that will be burned in a bonfire during the performance to provide light and warmth. In addition, participants are encouraged to write their wishes for the New Year on a piece of paper and attach it to the pine branches, so that when the bundle is burned, the "wishes will fly up to heaven."* (Photo by the author.)

After dinner, the audience followed the performers up to the mountaintop madang *to participate in the evening* p'an-kut *(entertainment-format* p'ungmul) *and bonfire. Situated on an open plateau high up in the village, surrounded by a ring of hills and freshly laid with sandy earth, this* madang *ranks as one of the most picturesque spots for* p'an-kut *that I have ever seen (Figure 3.10). True to the event's name, a full moon hovered just above the bamboo bonfire set up on the eastern edge of the* madang. *For both Yang Chin-sŏng and Yang Chin-hwan, the image of the moonlit* madang *holds special significance. Yang Chin-sŏng explains:*

> . . . *from when I was young, I was exposed to* p'ungmul *under the natural lighting of the moon. Under this moon just floating by itself, eternal, what I saw was the* madang. *And though the culture of moonlight is not as bright [as artificial light], the kinds of things that happen by the light of the moon*

is what I have come to see as truly beautiful (Yang Chin-sŏng interview, October 8, 2002).

The performers began playing just out of visual range, down one of the paths that led into the mountaintop madang. *As they filed into the playing area with the sound gradually filling the space, the audience began to gather with an excited air of anticipation. Standing around in the cold, bracing night, the audience members were primed to participate in the celebrations. Interestingly, the rhythmic formations seemed to be arranged in such a way that the audience could alternate coming in for one rhythmic formation and then out for the next, and so on.*

I define a "rhythmic formation" as a set of rhythms and movement formations that go together. Generally, p'ungmul *rhythms are not conceived of individually; they are usually grouped into a series of rhythms that flow from one to the next in a particular order. These rhythms commonly proceed in order of tempo, from slow to fast. Each series of rhythms has a corresponding directive in terms of movement, such as to simply circle counterclockwise. This common formation is what I would call an "open" rhythmic formation because it is stable enough to allow people to come into the center of the circle without disrupting the choreography. "Closed" rhythmic formations have more complex choreographies that work better if the performance space is emptied out, or "closed" to the audience. In this way, the rhythmic formations alternated between "open" and "closed" sets, allowing audience members to rest in between bouts of activity.*

In a full p'an-kut, *a performance can last several hours and be divided into a "front ritual"* (ap-kut) *and "back ritual"* (dwi-kut). *In general, the front ritual features more formal choreographies by the performers, while the back ritual features improvisation, audience participation, singing and individual solos. To understand the alternating phenomenon, refer to Figure 3.11.*

The way the audience flowed in and out of the madang *was remarkably smooth. Generally, it is the character players or* chapsaek *who encourage people to come in and participate, but they barely had to lift a welcoming finger to get this particular* madang *filled with people. The space thrummed with bodies moving harmoniously with the music, some with children on their shoulders. During the last double line formation, called* mijigi, *a mass of people gathered around the performers, moving back and forth and waving their arms to the changes in the music. Although some may interpret such a scene as chaos, for those intimately knowledgeable with the form it was an image beautiful in its simplicity.*

Rhythmic Series	Movement Formation Description	Open or Closed
Ch'ae-kut	Counterclockwise circular formation	Open
Hohŏ-kut	1. The group splits into two lines and moves in opposite directions to form curved, wavelike shapes similar to the yin–yang symbol. 2. Eventually they come together to form two parallel curved lines facing in the same direction. 3. Then they proceed in the opposite directions again.	Closed
P'ungryu-kut	Counterclockwise circular formation	Open
Pangŭljin-kut	The group spirals into the center of a circle, then switches directions and unwinds like a corkscrew and proceeds to make another spiral on the other side of the *madang*.	Closed or open
Mijigi	After coming out of the previous formation in a zigzag pattern, the group forms two long lines and moves back and forth in these two lines. The audience is free to mimic their movements on both sides.	Open

FIGURE 3.11 *Order of rhythmic formations in the* ap-kut *(Front ritual)*

The "front ritual" of the *p'an-kut* described here was an integral part of the day's Full Moon Ritual, functioning as a culminating release for all those who participated. Some practitioners see preservation of village-based *p'ungmul* as essential to *p'ungmul's* identity; in other words, to discontinue such a practice would be to lose a crucial avenue of Korean expressive identity in *p'ungmul*. If not for such efforts, the main avenue of experiencing *p'ungmul* would be limited to condensed, hourlong, entertainment-oriented *p'an-kut* performances presented in folkloric venues, festivals, educational institutions and parks.

ACTIVITY 3.7 Norae-kut *or "song-ceremony" occurs in the dwi-kut or "back ritual" and is unique to the P'ilbong regional style of* p'ungmul *(CD track 15). The song proceeds in a simple verse-refrain form that features a call-and-response between the lead singer on the verse and the rest of the musicians on the refrain. Both the verse and chorus are accompanied by a simple dotted rhythm, except for the* p'ungryu *rhythm below, which is used as a transition between verses and chorus. During this transition, the musicians play one line of the* p'ungryu *rhythm below, before launching back into the verse.*

- *Learn the p'ungryu rhythm below, and tap the rhythms as you say the vocables.*
- *Follow along with the verse-refrain structure below. Then try to hum along with the simple melody and tap the* p'ungryu *rhythm in between the verse and the refrain.*

  Opening **P'ungryu** *rhythm 0:00 to 0:05*
  Solo refrain 0:06 to 0:28
  Group refrain 0:29 to 0:50
  First verse 0:51 to 1:24
  Group refrain 1:25 to 1:46
  Second verse 1:47 to 2:18
  Group refrain 2:19 to 2:40
  Third verse 2:41 to end

P'ungryu *(12/8) moderately slow tempo*

Ø	Ø		O	/	O	Ø	.	/	O		/
Tŏng	Tŏng		Kung	Tak	Kung	Tŏng	Ki	Tak	Kung		Tak

P'ungmul *in the Streets: Political Protest Demonstrations*
P'ungmul has also served as a medium of empowerment in the face of physical or political hardship. As such, this demonstrates *p'ungmul's* remarkable flexibility in being adapted to the needs of the times. For example, before the age of industrialized agriculture *p'ungmul* was

once integral to the work of agricultural guilds, where members played *p'ungmul* to enhance the productivity of various farming tasks. More recently, it has become a potent vehicle for political protest. Beginning sometime in the 1970s, *p'ungmul* was adopted as a mode of expression by the *minjung* cultural movement (literally, "people's cultural movement"). In particular, folk genres such as *p'ungmul* (as well as mask dance drama) were seen as especially resonant with the goal of "awakening" the spirit and critical consciousness of the *minjung* or "common people" (Choi Chungmoo 1995: 109). Working primarily toward the goal of democratization, members of the *minjung* cultural movement, who were mostly college students, began to incorporate *p'ungmul* into street demonstrations. By the late 1980s, *p'ungmul* was so intimately associated with public protest that it became one of the primary sonic markers of protest culture in South Korea (Figure 3.12).

Political protest culture emerged in direct response to the increasingly repressive policies of the Park Chung-hee regime (1961–1979). This repression continued after Park's assassination in 1979 as Chun Doo-hwan, another military figure, seized control of the government in a coup d'état. In May 1980, the people of the city of Kwangju rose up against Chun's fledgling dictatorship. In an effort to retain power and restore stability, Chun retaliated by authorizing a repressive attack that left approximately 500 dead and 960 declared missing. Given the extent of the casualties, the Kwangju Uprising became the defining event in the history of the democratization movement. As the 1980s progressed, Koreans grew increasingly frustrated with Chun's policies as well as with what they saw as America's complicity and influence in his regime. Although increased support for the democratization movement succeeded in preventing Chun from running for another term in 1987, it did not stop him from naming another military leader, Roh Tae Woo, as the succeeding candidate of his party and orchestrating his victory despite what appeared to be a democratic election on paper. In the late 1980s, conflict between riot police and protesters intensified and demonstrations grew increasingly violent. The sounds of *p'ungmul* and protest were so intertwined that "South Koreans became accustomed to loud percussion music as students danced to farmers' music [*p'ungmul*], dressed in traditional farmers' white clothes, and battled with riot police" (Choi 1995: 108).

As the goals of the *minjung* movement broadened to include issues of social justice, decolonization and self-determination, *p'ungmul* was used in a more diverse array of causes and spaces. In particular, its "salt-of-the-earth" origins were well suited to supporting members of various

FIGURE 3.12 *An example of* p'ungmul *being used in protest. Here, members of the Korean Peasants League prepare to play* p'ungmul *during a march in protest of the WTO's Sixth Ministerial Conference in Hong Kong in 2005.* (Photo courtesy of Kyung Jin Lee.)

labor and farmers' movements. During a particularly heated time in August 1987, *p'ungmul* was used notably in two well-documented events: (1) a memorial protest for a fallen labor protester, Yi Sŏk-kyu, and (2) the Kochang Tenant Farmers association, who were protesting against Samyang, their landlord company, demanding that the

FIGURE 3.13   *Front row from left to right:* ching, puk, changgo, kkwaenggwari *and* puk. *Back row from left to right:* puk *and* ching, changgo, changgo, kkwaenggwari. *Graduates of the Korean National University of the Arts perform* samulnori *seated on stage at the Kwanghwamun Art Hall.* *(Photo courtesy of Katherine Lee.)*

land be redistributed to the tenants (Katherine Lee 2009: 1; Abelmann 1996: 61–62). Although the power of *p'ungmul* as a medium of protest remains strong into the 21st century, Koreans are more accepting of the cultural value of *p'ungmul*, especially in the realms of education and entertainment.

Adapting P'ungmul *to the Stage:* Samulnori

P'ungmul's acceptance by the general Korean populace is most likely connected to the high-profile success of *samulnori* (literally, "four objects playing"), a staged Korean percussion-based genre that draws from the rhythms, music and performance techniques of *p'ungmul* (Figure 3.13). Around the same time that urban college students were discovering *p'ungmul* as an outlet for political expression, several percussion-based performers with roots mostly in *namsadang* (an itinerant entertainment troupe that integrates six main performing styles, among them *p'ungmul*) were developing a way to translate the exuberance of regional Korean folk rhythms and melodies to a new context: the modern concert stage. Two of the most prominent of these performers are Kim Duk Soo (b. 1952) and Yi Kwang-su (b. 1952), who made their debut in Seoul in 1978 as part of the pivotal group Samul-Nori. This group was so successful that the genre they created also became known as *samulnori* (indicated here with a slightly different spelling to avoid confusion). With their dynamic style, fast tempos, virtuosic rhythmic sequences and grounded sense of togetherness and groove, Samul-Nori was an immediate sensation. Drawing larger audiences than expected for a neotraditional form, they not only toured in Korea but also became somewhat successful as a world music phenomenon in Japan, Europe and the United States. With their fresh and contemporary spin on "tradition," they appealed to the younger generation of Koreans, who began to form groups dedicated to learning and playing repertoire developed by Samul-Nori.

As youths began to clamber to learn how to play *samulnori*, a small "canon" of compositions developed, largely based on repertoire performed and recorded by the original Samul-Nori ensemble in their first decade of existence. Much of the *samulnori* repertoire has currents of continuity with the older cultural form of *p'ungmul*. For example, "Uddhari-Poongmul" (which is based on rhythms from Ch'ungch'ŏng province; CD track 19) incorporates participatory singing, stylistic shouts and of course the basic rhythmic cycles of *p'ungmul*. As the same time, this piece also contains performance practices that exploit more dramatic changes in dynamics and flow, heart-racing tempos as well as sequential arrangements of virtuosic rhythmic variations or patterns that have become more typical of *samulnori*. Building on their spirit of creativity, the *Samul-Nori* group broke boundaries by working on fusion projects with European jazz artists, famous Korean vocalists and even Korean break-dancers. Their success led to creation of other percussion-heavy fusion-oriented groups such as Puri and Gong Myoung, spurring a significant new direction in creative Korean music.

ACTIVITY 3.8 *In the Samul-Nori version of "Uddhari Poongmul" on CD track 19, one can hear incorporation of participatory singing in the introductory 12/8 rhythmic cycle; it is*

(continued)

ACTIVITY 3.8 *(continued)*

strikingly reminiscent of the refrain in the Norae-kut *(CD track 15) excerpt from the P'ilbong* p'ungmul *region. This demonstrates that the influence of* p'ungmul *goes beyond the realm of rhythm. This introduction (0:00–0:08) to the Samul-Nori piece is followed by a transitional series of mixed meter rhythmic cycles (0:09–0:28) that freely intermingle cross rhythms, irregular rhythmic groupings, stylistic shouts and dramatic pauses.*

- *Comparing* p'ungmul *as represented in CD track 15 with* samulnori *in track 19, articulate some similarities and differences that you hear in terms of tempo, ensemble aesthetics and rhythmic complexity.*

Shamanist Ritual Forms

Given its long history, complexity and regional diversity, Korean shamanism can be difficult to grasp, even for native Koreans. In this light, perhaps the simplest route to understanding shamanism in Korea is through the ritual performances or ceremonies called *kut*. Scholars define *kut* as large-scale ritual performances based on indigenous folk religious beliefs and customs. Maria Seo (2002: 3) further categorizes the large-scale *kut* that include music and dance into two main types: (1) *mudang-kut*, or those that are led by trained shamans or ritual specialists called *mudang* (sometimes called otherwise, depending on the region); and (2) *p'ungmul-kut*, led primarily by musicians who play *p'ungmul* percussion instruments during major village celebrations or ceremonies, such as the one described in the "*P'ungmul* in the Village *Madang*" section of this book. Lee Bo-hyung also places emphasis on large-scale rituals but classifies them according to the following functions: household rituals, memorial rituals and village rituals (Lee Bo-hyung 2002: 875). Both Lee and Seo mention that smaller-scale ceremonies can also be called *kut*, such as family offerings made to ancestral spirits or *kosa*, but both acknowledge that these are generally not included in most academic studies on Korean shamanism.

Despite the wide regional variety of customs and rituals and the daunting array of deities, the basic principles of Korean shamanism are fairly simple. In short, Korean shamans strive to create universal harmony by maintaining a balance of the three elements of the universe: heaven, earth and humans. In addition, believers also seek to develop harmonious relationships with other people, nature and the spirits. Although some spirits are considered malevolent or mischievous, most are benevolent. Of the benevolent spirits, the most important are the "three spirits" or *Samsin*: Hwan In (the supreme heavenly god); his son, Hwan Ung; and Tan'gun, the son of Hwan Ung and a bear-woman. Tan'gun is regarded as the mythological founder of the Korean people and is believed to have ruled around 2333 B.C.E. as Korea's first political and religious leader. According to legend, Tan'gun established the Korean nation by opening up the Gate of Heaven and descending into the dramatic mountain landscape of Mt. Paektu (Seo 2002: 32).

Shamans in Korea are typically called on or hired to perform household, memorial or village rituals. During these rituals, they communicate with pertinent spirits in order to maintain balance and harmony and act as a mediator between the human and spirit realms. In Korea, there are two main types of shamans: hereditary and spirit-appointed. Both perform rituals and communicate with spirits and humans; spirit-appointed shamans emphasize spirit possession as the main mode of communicating with the spirit world.

Chindo Ssikkim-kut *(Cleansing Rituals)*

Although *ssikkim-kut* is performed in other parts of Chŏlla province, shamans on Chindo Island have developed an especially rich musical tradition of *ssikkim-kut* that has helped produce many accomplished instrumentalists, vocalists and dancers, notably Pak Pyŏng-ch'ŏn and Kim Tae-rye. Traditionally, Chindo *Ssikkim-kut* (Intangible Cultural Asset No. 72) was performed primarily by hereditary shamans, but as their numbers declined in the era of rural-to-urban migration, *ssikkim-kut* has been performed increasingly by spirit-appointed shamans (Park Mikyung 2003: 355). *Ssikkim-kut* is usually performed in relation to the death of a loved one, often around the time of burial. According to Park Mikyung, the ritual order of a *Chindo ssikkim-kut* typically encompasses four main sections: (1) the beginning ritual (for the house gods), (2) the precleansing rituals (for the gods of smallpox, prosperity and ancestors), (3) cleansing rituals (for the deceased), and (4) the ending ritual (for the three escorts and various other spirits; 258).

The first one open to guests (both human and spirit) is the "invitation ritual," which takes place during the precleansing section (CD track 20). This ceremony is performed outdoors in the main ritual tent (as opposed to the more intimate household quarters for the beginning ritual). The shaman practitioners effectively draw the participants in by performing lyric and epic poetry and dancing over a moderately slow 12/8 rhythm called the *salp'uri changdan*. This excerpt features an extraordinarily husky and expressive vocal delivery of the text by the main female shaman; it stands in contrast to an independent, improvisatory vocal line provided by a second practitioner. Although their individual timbres vary, both voices are exemplary of the more husky, southwestern vocal style. Although shaman rituals are often multidisciplinary in form, Park Mikyung aptly asserts that "music, as a central element, integrates all the other artistic and ritual elements such as dance, drama, divinations, magic, offerings, sacrifices, incantation and possession" (2003: 360). In this light, it is no surprise that these comprehensive rituals are so influential in Korean music, dance and drama forms.

ACTIVITY 3.9 *Shamans are common in many contemporary cultures, and yet they still retain an aura of mystique. Conduct some internet research on shamans. Who are they? What do they do? What role do they fulfill? Write a short paragraph summarizing your findings, and share with the class during discussion.*

Sinawi and Cultivation of Improvisation
Springing from Korea's rich shamanic ritual tradition, dances and instrumental music ("*Sinawi*," CD track 21) have been adapted to the stage. The dance—*salp'uri*—is known for its distinctive use of a long white scarf. The instrumental music—*sinawi*—is used as an accompaniment to *salp'uri* or can be heard on its own. The instrumentation of *sinawi* is flexible, although common instruments include the *changgo* and *ching* percussion instruments; the *ajaeng*, *kayagŭm* and *kŏmungo* zithers; the *haegŭm* bowed lute; and the *p'iri* and *taegŭm* wind instruments.

In a typical performance of contemporary *sinawi* in a dance or instrumental concert setting, *sinawi* proceeds in a manner similar to *sanjo*. Instead of a soloist, a group of professional musicians go through various *changdan*-based sections, beginning with the *salp'uri changdan* (a slow four-beat rhythmic cycle with triple subdivisions, 12/8), and following this with *chajinmori* (a fast four-beat rhythmic cycle with triple subdivisions, 12/8), *onmori* (an irregular four-beat rhythmic cycle with subdivisions of 3 + 2 + 3 + 2, 10/8) and *tongsalp'uri* (a moderate four-beat rhythmic cycle with duple subdivisions, 4/4).

What makes *sinawi* stand out is that it encourages the musicians to engage in simultaneous improvisation. The resulting mix of melodies maintain coherence by adhering more or less to the *yukchabaegi t'ŏri* mode characteristic of the southwestern folk music style (similar to *kyemyŏnjo*), which consists of the pitches *mi, sol, la, do-ti,* and *re,* with *la* as a central cadential tone. Musicians often take advantage of the microtonal slide from *do* to *ti,* which gives this mode a feeling of sorrow and plaintiveness. Although musicians come into a performance with the knowledge of common characteristic phrases that often correspond at the beginning of a section, each instrumentalist then builds on these phrases individually as the section progresses. This leads to an interactive, polyphonic texture that is truly unique in Korean instrumental concert music. These improvisations are anchored by the rhythmic cycle set down by the *changgo* player. However, the *changgo* player promotes rhythmic interest by improvising nuanced variations on the rhythmic cycle while negotiating between the important roles of helping to lead rhythmic transitions and accompanying and responding to the other musicians. In *sinawi,* each musician strives to explore the expressive possibilities of his instrument through use of microtonal slides, multitimbral shadings and effects, dynamics and ornaments; the resulting fabric of sound can be dense, emotional and moody, simmering with a kind of melodic and rhythmic interplay seldom heard in other forms of Korean instrumental music.

ACTIVITY 3.10   *Listen to the "Sinawi" excerpt on CD track 21. This short excerpt stays exclusively in the salp'uri changdan, which is nicely introduced on the changgo in the beginning of the track. Referring to the guide below, see if you can follow along and take notes in the margins as to what is happening melodically during each reiteration of the changdan.*

- *0:00–0:07 Changgo introduction*
- *0:08–0:14 First changdan*
- *0:15–0:20 Second changdan*
- *0:20–0:26 Third changdan*
- *0:26–0:31 Fourth changdan*

(continued)

ACTIVITY 3.10 *(continued)*

- *0:32–0:37 Fifth changdan*
- *0:37–0:42 Sixth changdan*
- *0:43–0:47 Seventh changdan*
- *0:48–0:54 Eighth changdan*
- *Listen again and try to differentiate the individual sounds of the ajaeng, kŏmungo, kayagŭm, p'iri and taegŭm.*
- *Although sinawi is supposed to feature simultaneous improvisation, there are clearly instruments that tend to align with each other. Which instruments seem to be more in sync, and which ones seem to be operating more independently?*
- *Compare this excerpt to the "Chindo Cleansing Ritual" in CD track 20. What are some of the similarities and differences in terms of instrumentation and approaches to improvisation?*

In this chapter, I have explored how solo and ensemble forms of instrumental Korean music have figured prominently in the politics of cultural preservation, development and revival in a time of great change in Korea. Whether one hails from the North or South, city or village, government institution or college campus, the manner in which culture is shaped is highly contested, often bearing social, economic, political and aesthetic implications. In the next chapter, I focus on similar themes as they relate to expressive use of the voice.

CHAPTER 4

The Singing Voice

As emphasized in the opening chapter of this book, the singing voice remains a crucial medium of interpersonal exchange and cultural continuity in both North and South Korea. Although today's singing repertoire is generally more diverse and global in influence, the historic practice of folksongs certainly contributed to the remarkable zeal with which many Koreans incorporate singing into their everyday lives. In North and South Korea, singing most visibly functions as a social lubricant for myriad gatherings and events—formal and informal, public and private. Although much more prevalent in the ROK, karaoke-style singing has become a common and visible outlet. South Koreans prefer to sing in intimate group settings in private rooms called *noraebang* (literally, "song room"). Although karaoke technology exists in North Korea, one may just as often find groups of people singing with the accompaniment of more acoustic options such as the accordion or the guitar. If the aid of music technology, musical instruments or skilled musicians is unavailable, people in both countries sing with no more accompaniment than the clapping of hands. I have found that it is in these moments Koreans seem to truly relish the interpersonal exchange of baring one's voice in front of others. In this sense, singing is a give-and-take whereby Koreans participate in the continuity of culture.

FOLKSONGS

Although folksongs no longer serve to embroider and accompany the everyday activities of most Koreans, they are still viewed as an invaluable repository and resource for Korean expressive folk culture in the DPRK and the ROK (CD tracks 2, 3, 4, 5, 22 and 23). The concept and terminology of the folksong, called *minyo* in Korea, can be traced to the German *Volkslied*, a term that the Japanese adopted and translated (also as *minyo*) and brought to Korea during the early colonial period (Howard

1999: 1). Although *minyo* today can still be considered a living tradition, performance of folksongs now tends to evoke nostalgic connotations of a Korean cultural past that supports a more "traditional" image of national identity. In South Korea in particular, the government perpetuates this rather static conception of traditional folk culture through its agenda of cultural preservation, most notably realized in the Intangible Cultural Asset system.

The notion of folksongs emerging purely from the lips of village-bound farmers appears to be a product of the nationalist imaginary, based on myth just as much as reality. Though the salt-of-the-earth associations of folksongs hold just as much sway in North Korea, there is less concern with preserving distinctions of folk authenticity. In South Korea, folksongs were shaped in different ways when cultural activists involved in the progressive *minjung* movement of the 1970s and 1980s drew on them to promote a self-determined vision of Korean culture as free from foreign influence, and free of Confucian elitism whereby the struggles of the common people represent the ideal. As this trend continued, lyrics were selected, adapted and changed to support nationalist messages (Figure 4.1, "*Chindo Arirang*," last verse, CD track 22). Representing an even more creative approach, some musicians wrote newly composed folksongs or *p'ansori*-style works to better engage with the political struggles of the time.

What these primarily South Korean nationalist agendas tend to miss or obscure is that in Korea folk singing has long blurred the line between the "folk" and the "popular," between amateurs and professionals and between what is considered local and national in character. South Korean scholars grapple with these issues by differentiating between "local" folksongs (*t'osok minyo*) and "widespread" folksongs (*t'ongsok minyo*). Here, local folksongs tend to be known and cultivated by a relatively small number of people limited to a specific geographic area. Widespread folksongs tend to be performed by professional singers and can be said to have more entertainment value, with their complex song structures and intertextual lyrics, colorful timbres and elaborate melodies. As these performers began to record these widespread folksongs, the recording industry further blurred the divide between folk and popular. North Koreans have gone even further in this regard by vigorously integrating folksongs into the mass popular song repertoire.

In part due to the increased exposure and development encouraged by itinerant musicians and recordings, most of the folksongs that Koreans are familiar with (in North and South Korea) fall under the *t'ongsok minyo* or widespread category. Fortunately, many of these

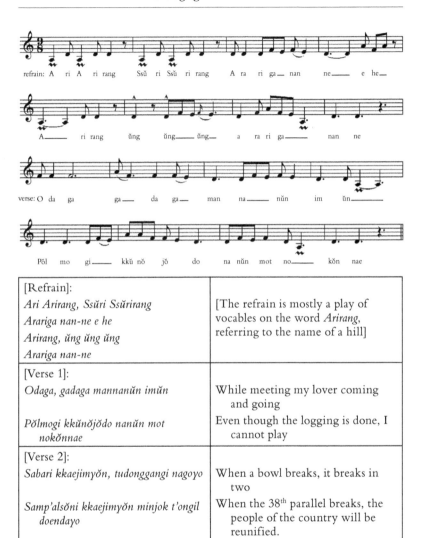

refrain: A ri A ri rang Ssŭ ri Ssŭ ri rang A ra ri ga— nan ne___ e he__

A___ ri rang ŭng ŭng___ ŭng— a ra ri ga___ nan ne

verse: O da ga ga — da ga — man na___ nŭn im ŭn___

Pŏl mo gi___ kkŭ nŏ jŏ do na nŭn mot no___ kŏn nae

[Refrain]:	
Ari Arirang, Ssŭri Ssŭrirang	[The refrain is mostly a play of
Arariga nan-ne e he	vocables on the word *Arirang,*
Arirang, ŭng ŭng ŭng	referring to the name of a hill]
Arariga nan-ne	
[Verse 1]:	
Odaga, gadaga mannanŭn imŭn	While meeting my lover coming and going
Pŏlmogi kkŭnŏjŏdo nanŭn mot nokŏnnae	Even though the logging is done, I cannot play
[Verse 2]:	
Sabari kkaejimyŏn, tudonggangi nagoyo	When a bowl breaks, it breaks in two
Samp'alsŏni kkaejimyŏn minjok t'ongil doendayo	When the 38th parallel breaks, the people of the country will be reunified.

FIGURE 4.1 "Chindo Arirang," *an example of* Namdo minyo *(southern folksong; CD track 22).*

FIGURE 4.2 *Map of Korean folksong regions.*

folksongs have retained their regional distinctiveness and are consequently organized by five regions: central, western, eastern, southern
and the island of Chejudo (Figure 4.2). It is important to mention that
these regional categories were created by South Korean scholars and
consequently have been subject to South Korean musical and political

discourses. In the following sections, I explore these regional distinctions by focusing on two contrasting styles: central and southern.

Central (Kyŏnggi) Minyo

Central minyo is usually called Kyŏnggi minyo, in reference to the main province to which these songs are attributed, although songs from the northern section of Ch'ungch'ŏng province are also included here (Figure 4.2). Centrally located on the peninsula and home to the capital Seoul, Kyŏnggi province has been seen as a center of culture and politics for several centuries. Consequently, many Kyŏnggi minyo are popular as widespread minyo and are beloved throughout the Korean peninsula. Kyŏnggi minyo typically use an anhemitonic pentatonic mode ("anhemitonic" refers to a sequence of pitches without half-steps) of do, re, fa, sol

Refrain: Arirang, Arirang, Arariyo
I am crossing over the Arirang Pass

Verse: After abandoning me, my departing dear one
I cannot even walk ten li without getting sore feet

FIGURE 4.3 "Arirang," an example of Kyŏnggi minyo (central folksong; CD tracks 2 and 3).

and *la* but can cadence on any of these tones. Representative Kyŏnggi *minyo* include *"Arirang"* (CD tracks 2 and 3, Figure 4.3) and *Kunbam T'aryŏng* ("Roast Chestnut Song," CD tracks 4 and 5). Although *Arirang* eclipses the popularity of most folksongs—so much so that it is considered the unofficial folk anthem of both the DPRK and the ROK—both songs continue to be recorded in a variety of settings.

In addition to sharing a modal expression, Kyŏnggi *minyo* can have other characteristics in common, such as (1) a clear, bright and generally higher vocal timbre in men and women; (2) a lively and upbeat mood and tempo; (3) cheerful, highly ornamented melodic lines; and (4) a more lyrical, smoother and gentler melody. Not every song demonstrates all of these qualities; they are usually accompanied by a *changgo* or a small ensemble of Korean instruments.

ACTIVITY 4.1 *Listen to the various versions of "Arirang" (CD tracks 2 and 3) and "Kunbam T'aryŏng" (CD tracks 4 and 5) from the DPRK and the ROK.*

- *As you listen to the tracks, see if you can sing the pentatonic mode of* do, re, fa, sol, la *(in movable* do*).*
- *Looking at the central folksong characteristics, which do you think apply to* "Arirang" *and which best apply to* "Kunbam T'aryŏng"*?*
- *All four of these tracks represent contemporary versions of Korean folksongs. Can you identify some of the "outside" influences that have influenced each track? What are they?*
- *Referring to Figure 4.3, see if you can learn the melody to* "Arirang" *and sing it as a group.*

Southern (Namdo) Minyo

The "southern province" folksong area covers North and South Chŏlla provinces, although part of southern Ch'ungch'ŏng province is also included (Figure 4.2). It is worth noting that South Chŏlla province also includes the island of Chindo, which is well known for producing exceptional singers, musicians and shamans. With its clear ties to other well-recognized genres such as *p'ansori* and *sanjo*, Namdo *minyo* is one of the more distinctive folksong types and therefore one of the easiest to distinguish. One key to the sound of this folksong area has to do with its characteristic *kyemyŏnjo* mode. We encountered this mode earlier in *sanjo*, a genre that is also believed to have taken root in the same region. To reiterate, *kyemyŏnjo* consists of a fourth and a whole step (*la, re, mi*) with the presence of *fa* and *sol* as passing tones; *re* is considered the central tone. Building on what was said previously, this is a good example of a "weighted" scale where the individual tones carry different weights or characteristic ornamental tendencies. In this case, the first tone, *la*, is sung with a wide vibrato or "shaking voice," the central tone *re* is sung flat with relatively little vibrato and the highest tones (*fa* and *sol*) that want to slide down to *mi* are considered the "breaking tones" (see Figure 3.7). These modal qualities are clearly defined in the song "*Chindo Arirang*" (Figure 4.1), and can be heard on CD track 22 and practiced in Activity 4.3. With its wide vibratos and dramatic appoggiaturas, *kyemyŏnjo* conveys a sense of gravity, earthiness and unrestrained emotion, and it is often associated with expression of sorrow or deep loss.

Adding to the emotional quality of *kyemyŏnjo* is the unmistakable aesthetic of unabashed strength and huskiness in the voice. In addition, the melodies often incorporate microtonal inflections and a variety of ornaments that often closely amplify the meaning of the lyrics. Southern folksongs also tend to use regular rhythmic cycles with a compound triplet feel: *chinyangjo* (slow 18/8), *chungmori* (moderately slow 12/8), *semach'i* (moderate 9/8) and *kutkori* (lilting 12/8). Many of these rhythmic cycles can be heard in other styles, such as central and eastern folksong, and genres such as *sanjo* and *p'ansori*. As in many of the other folksong styles, traditional verse-refrain song structures predominate, although one may also hear complex call-and-response song structures as well.

ACTIVITY 4.3   *Listen to* "Chindo Arirang" *on CD track 22.*

- *This is an example of a mode where* re *is considered the central tone or tonic (Figure 3.7). As you listen to the track, see if you can hum the contours of this mode.*

(continued)

ACTIVITY 4.3 *(continued)*

- *Practice the unique inflections of the three main tones (Figure 3.7): (1) the wide, shaking vibrato on* la; *(2) the* re *with little or no vibrato; and (3) the* mi *that starts higher on* fa *and falls down to* mi.

- *The refrain of "Chindo Arirang" demonstrates these characteristic ornaments perfectly. Refer to Figure 4.1, and try to learn the refrain and incorporate the various ornaments and inflections by imitating the singers on CD track 22.*

- *Lastly, compare and contrast the vocal timbres of southern (CD track 22) and western (CD track 23) folksong. Then compare this with the central folksong examples in CD tracks 4 and 5.*

SIJO-CH'ANG: CULTIVATING AN APPRECIATION FOR SUNG POETRY

Korea is also home to a rich and contemplative lyric "art song" tradition that includes three interrelated forms: *sijo-ch'ang, kagok* and *kasa*. Though all three forms are characterized by slow tempos, long sustained tones and a subtle and restrained aesthetic, *sijo-ch'ang* is the most accessible and therefore serves as a wonderful introduction to Korea's beautiful tradition of sung poetry. Both *kagok* and *sijo-ch'ang* are set to Korea's distinctive three-line poetic form, called *sijo*, while *kasa* has a more narrative emphasis. To avoid confusion, the suffix *ch'ang* has been added recently to differentiate the sung genre from the poetic form.

Unlike *kagok* and *kasa*, *sijo-ch'ang* is the most likely to be performed by both amateurs and professionals alike. Like folksongs, *sijo-ch'ang* is usually accompanied by a *changgo* that outlines the *changdan* or rhythmic cycle. Here, the *changgo* player fulfills the role of marking time by coordinating closely with the articulations of the singer. In more formal performance, a *p'iri, taegŭm* and *haegŭm* may be added. With the exception of the prelude and interludes, these melodic instruments follow the vocal line, adding ornaments to create a light heterophonic texture.

Although *kagok* emerged as early as the 15th century, it was not until the reign of King Yongjo (1724–1776) in the 18th century that *sijo-ch'ang* began to surface. Interestingly, that emergence coincided with development of a new middle class in Korea. *Kagok, kasa* and *sijo-ch'ang* were regularly cultivated by the higher class of aristocrats called *yangban*; *sijo-ch'ang's* accessibility made it especially popular with this newly emerging middle class, who consisted of rural scholars, children of aristocrats and concubines of lower status, provincial officials and *chungin* professionals (merchants, craftspersons and technicians). In addition, female courtesans or *kisaeng* (who were of lower status) were also well versed in writing and performing *sijo* for their elite clients. Even though this mixture of scholars, government officials, courtesans and *chungin* were influenced by Confucian ideas about music as a mode of cultivating the mind and conveying restraint, they were also interested in music that spoke more to the present and to the emotions of daily life.

Of the three vocal genres, *sijo-ch'ang* enjoyed the most widespread popularity, in part because it was able to move from the scholar's salon, where *kagok* was likely to be performed, to the meeting rooms of merchants and other middle-class people. Short, simple and yet elegant, *sijo-ch'ang* also embodied the ideals of the times, especially during the reign of Yongjo, who was king during its inception. In particular, he worked hard to discourage overly luxurious living by aristocrats, advocated for more widespread education by promoting the Korean writing system (*han'gŭl*) and supported indigenous artistic traditions. Through his patronage, both *sijo* as poetic verse and *sijo-ch'ang* as song served as a unique bridge between classes. As this music spread to the emerging merchant and middle class, *sijo-ch'ang* was appreciated across regions and developed a healthy dose of regional variation. I have chosen to focus on *sijo-ch'ang* in the next sections not only to elucidate Korean expressive approaches to the integration of poetry and song but also to shed some light on an overlooked but still vital pathway through which Koreans maintain a continuous "voice" in Korean culture.

The Poetic Form of Sijo

The *sijo* poetic form is usually introduced to students at an early age and can be thought of as Korea's equivalent to Japanese *haiku*. Based loosely on a three-line syllabic and rhetorical structure, *sijo* has each line of text made up of four groupings of usually three or four syllables each. Though the syllabic structure is rather flexible, there is a basic form, found in Figure 4.4. The poem exemplified here is a famous one attributed to a legendary *kisaeng* named Hwang Chini (16th century). The slight deviations in the syllabic structure (as indicated by the asterisks in Figure 4.4) are common and point to the inherent flexibility of the form.

This syllabic flexibility suggests that it might be necessary to consider other ways of theorizing the structure of *sijo* lyrics. David McCann writes that *sijo's* syllabic structure must "be analyzed only within another, overriding structural design," which would be its rhetorical form or sense structure (1988: 2). Scholars concur that *sijo's* rhetorical form follows the Chinese quatrain, in which the theme is stated in the first line and developed in the second, and then a twist is introduced in the third and resolved in the fourth line. The first two lines of *sijo* follow the Chinese quatrain, but the third and fourth lines are collapsed into one line, so that the twist must be introduced and resolved in the third and final line. For example, in *"Ch'ŏngsanri Pyŏkkyesuya"* in Figure 4.4 (CD track 24), the first line states the theme of addressing the "jade blue stream" and develops it by pondering the force of its inevitable trajectory out to sea. The third and final line introduces the twist in the form of the "bright moon" that resolves by entreating the stream to "stop and rest." Objects of nature are cleverly personified here, although the mischievous and playful tone of this poem can only be truly understood

No. of syllables	3	4	3–4	4
Line 1 STATEMENT	Ch'ŏngsanri	pyŏkkyesuya	Su-i kamŭl	charang mara
	Jade blue stream, rippling through these green hills, do not boast so			
Line 2 DEVELOPMENT	3 (here only 2) Ilto	4 ch'anghae hamyŏn	3–4 Tora ogi	4 oryŏwora
	Once you reach the wide open sea, you may find it difficult to return			
Line 3 TWIST/ RESOLUTION	3 Myŏngwori	4–8 man'gongsan hani	4 Suyo kandŭl	3 (ottori)
	As the bright moon still floods these bare hills, why not stop and rest on your way?			

FIGURE 4.4 Sijo *syllabic and rhetorical structure* ("Ch'ŏngsanri Pyŏkkyesuya")

knowing that "jade blue stream" and "bright moon" are puns on the names of two lovers. According to legend, "jade blue stream" refers to a man noted for his virtuous actions, while "bright moon" refers to the pen name for Hwang Chini, the well-known *kisaeng* famous for her seductive powers.

ACTIVITY 4.4 *Write your own original* sijo *poem (in English) by adhering to the three-line rhetorical structure. Try to follow the syllabic structure as well (see also Figure 4.4).*

- *First line: Introduce your theme (3 + 4 + 3-4 + 4 syllables)*
- *Second line: Develop your theme (3 + 4 + 3-4 + 4 syllables)*
- *Third line: Provide a twist and resolve your theme (3 + 4-8 + 4 + 3 syllables)*

Text, Rhythm and Melody in Sijo-ch'ang

Musically, *sijo-ch'ang* is made up of three distinct sections that correspond to the three lines of poetic text. The musical setting of the lyrics follows and supports the syllabic groupings of the text but does not stop there; it reinforces the three-line rhetorical structure, almost to the point of exaggeration. If one looks at the poem by itself, the syllabic groupings of text appear more or less equally weighted and evenly distributed. However, this is far from true when overlaying the musical/rhythmic structure of the music. The musical setting serves to draw out and extend the first two lines of the poem (introduction and development), but it contracts significantly in the last and third line (twist and resolution). This musical truncation of the last line accentuates the succinct wit that the last line of *sijo* should convey (Figure 4.5). The principal outcome is that the latter part of the first two lines is given more weight, time and space, making the third line sound abrupt in comparison.

Sijo-ch'ang is based on a limited number of melodic and rhythmic formats to which various three-line *sijo* poems are set. The basic format is called *p'yŏngsijo*. There are two rhythmic patterns or *changdan*

Group	I	II	III	IV	Extension
SECTION 1				Last syllable	delayed
No. of syllables	3	4	3–4	3 +	1
Beats	5	8	8	5	8
STATEMENT	Ch'ŏngsanri	pyŏkkyesuya	Su-i kamŭl	charang ma-	ra
SECTION 2				Last syllable	delayed
No. of				3 +	
syllables	3	4	3 – 4	5	
Beats	5	8	8	oryŏwo-	1
DEVELOPMENT	Ilto	ch'anghae hamyŏn	Tora ogi		8
					ra
SECTION 3			Last syllable	delayed	
No. of syllables					
Beats	3	4–8	3 +	1	
TWIST/	5	8	5	8 (rest 7)	
RESOLUTION	Myŏngwori	man'gongsan hani	Suyo kan-	dŭl	ottori (omitted)

FIGURE 4.5 *Rhythmic and textual patterns in* P'yŏngsijo *(*"Ch'ŏngsanri Pyŏkkyesuya"*)*

in present-day *sijo-ch'ang*, one consisting of five beats and the other of eight. In the basic form of *p'yŏngsijo*, each of the first two sections is made up of a total of thirty-four beats (5 + 8 + 8 + 5 + 8), while the third section is made up of only twenty-six beats (5 + 8 + 5 + 8). The five-and-eight-beat *changdan* is distributed in relation to the poetic text as displayed in Figure 4.5 and can be heard in CD track 24. In performance, the last section is even shorter than suggested in the score because the singer holds the final syllable for only one beat, ending abruptly with no instrumental postlude.

Key:		
Symbol	**Vocable**	**Description**
Ø	Tŏng	Left hand hits the left head while the right hand hits the right head with the thin stick (called the *yeol chae*).
O	Kung	Left hand hits the left head by itself.
/	Tak	Right hand hits the right head with the thin stick with a sharp, clear sound.
.	Ta or Ki	Right hand hits or taps the right head a little more softly.

Five-Beat Pattern: 5/8

Ø		/ . . .	O★	.
Tŏng		Tak ta ta ta	Kung	Ta

Eight-Beat Pattern: 8/8

Ø		/ . . .	O		O	. / /	O
Tŏng		Tak ta ta ta	Kung		Kung	Ki tak tak	Kung

★ Asterisk notes where the rhythmic articulation first becomes audible in performance practice. In other words, the first three beats of the first five-beat pattern are silent.

FIGURE 4.6 Sijo-ch'ang changdan *patterns.*

ACTIVITY 4.5 *Although it is essential to understand how the poetic and musical structure interlocks in* sijo-ch'ang, *it is also important to grasp other characteristics in order to truly appreciate this form: (1) a sense of the pulse, and (2) an awareness of how tension is sustained and released through applying subtle gradations in dynamics, inflections and ornaments. Developing a sense of the pulse is especially challenging because it is slow (between 30 and 35 beats per minute) and occurs somewhat irregularly (every two to four seconds or so). This seeming irregularity is somewhat*

(continued)

ACTIVITY 4.5 *(continued)*

compounded by combination of irregular 5/8 and regular 8/8 meters or changdan *that make up the basic form of* sijo-ch'ang *(Figure 4.6). However, with practice the pulse becomes more predictable and a more organic regularity seems to emerge. The exercises here will help you get a sense of the pulse and follow the* changdan.

- *Listen to CD track 24 and see if you can sense a regular "breathing pulse." Embody the pulse by moving your body in a way that represents this pulse. This could be as simple as moving your hand in a circular motion.*

- *Keeping the tempo of this pulse in mind, tap the rhythms of both the 5/8 and 8/8 patterns in Figure 4.6. Add the drum vocables as you are tapping.*
- *Referring to Figures 4.5 and 4.6, listen to CD track 24, tapping the rhythms along with the piece. Remember that the rhythmic groupings or meters will change frequently, so be careful. Also remember that the first three beats of the first 5/8* changdan *are silent.*

In Korean music, melodic movement in musical space or time often activates tension between opposing states. This movement is then charged with and sustained by a desire to be either resolved or released. Though tension is produced in moving away from a central or starting tone in Korean modes, this pull is not the all-determining force in the music. Rather, each sustained tone, in and of itself, can be subject to the process of tension and release through application of dynamic shading, inflections and ornaments. In particular, the emphasis on the contrast between straight sustained tones and those inflected with vibratos or ornaments is characteristic of Korean art musics and especially audible in the relatively bare vocal setting of *sijo-ch'ang*. In this way, inflection ornaments are not merely aesthetic or "ornamental" in *sijo-ch'ang*; they are the life force of this music.

P'ANSORI: INTERTEXTUALITY AND CULTURAL CONTINUITY

> The intertextual effort: "The complex and variegated play of borrowing, citation, implicit or explicit references . . . and substitutions, which substantiate the relationships between the texts of a given culture (and even between texts of different cultures)." (De Marinis 1993: 4)

Although the voice is central to *p'ansori*, it also incorporates elements of storytelling and dramatic gesture (Figure 4.7). Because of this, *p'ansori* has been touted as Korea's national version of musical theater or opera. But in its original form *p'ansori* can be more simply described as "story singing," as coined by Chan E. Park (2003). More specifically, *p'ansori* is an oral narrative genre in which a single performer employs song, narration, dialogue and gesture to deliver a work of narrative literature. Although there is a *puk* drum player who creates the underlying *changdan* and provides rhythmic and expressive support, it is the responsibility of the main performer to give the narration as well as embody all of the characters in a kind of musical one-person show.

Perhaps more so than any other "traditional" Korean form, *p'ansori* captures the imagination of contemporary audiences through its various musical, dramatic and literary developments. This may be due to its inherent flexibility, comprehensiveness and omnivorous quality, enabling it to both incorporate older forms (such as *minyo* and *sijo-ch'ang*) and be adapted to and retold in other formats (such as novels, film and forms of musical theater). In this way, *p'ansori* is a productive locus of intertextuality, a process through which a new text is created in part by referencing, borrowing or interweaving various "texts." Here, "texts" can be interpreted broadly to include specific words, story lines, themes, folksong lyrics, melodies, characters and other content. Intertextuality often leads to traversing boundaries of time and genre and can bolster a sense of cultural continuity by encouraging substantive links between various Korean texts. Although this occurs more directly in South Korea, it can be argued that *p'ansori* has influenced modern developments in North Korean musical drama more indirectly. In addition, with the abundance of Chinese literary references in *p'ansori*, one can argue that intertextuality engenders transnational creativity as well.

History and Development Through Multiple Formats
Although the etymology of *p'ansori* is made up of two relatively simple words (*p'an* and *sori*), each word carries rich connotations that afford a

FIGURE 4.7   *A* p'ansori *performer holding a fan, performing with* puk *accompanist on the straw mat* p'an *of the* p'ansori *stage.*   *(Photo still from the film* Ch'unhyang, *by Im Kwon-taek.)*

fascinating glimpse into *p'ansori's* origins, meanings and development. Although the *p'an* is most easily understood as a spatial location or place of gathering (such as a courtyard or town square), it also carries a tempo-ral dimension that delineates a moment or occasion in time. According to Chan E. Park's eloquent synthesis, the *p'an* is a "mental and physi-cal space for wholehearted participation" (2003: 1). *Sori* literally means "sound," but it refers more specifically to the act of "singing" within the context of vocal genres. Thus the choice of *sori* ("sound") over more spe-cific musical terms such as *norae* ("song") suggests a more comprehen-sive meaning. Park asserts that *sori* "refers to all sounds whether real, imagined, agreeable or disagreeable. . . [It] goes beyond just 'singing' to become narrative expressiveness, a musical metalanguage, or a 'second language' that is acquired through method and process" (1).

Itinerant folk entertainers, called *kwangdae*, first developed *p'ansori* in the early 18th century, mainly by performing for the lower and middle classes. Back then the *"p'an"* consisted of a straw mat that was laid out in a public place: in a busy marketplace or festive fairground, a village common or a town square. Gradually, *p'ansori* began to attract the attention of the literati, or *yangban* class, and by the mid-18th century the *"p'an"* permeated more private spaces such as a gentleman's salon, the inner courtyard of a *yangban's* mansion or perhaps a teahouse or drinking establishment where *yangban* would gather in town. This transition was not necessarily always smooth; certain neo-Confucianist factions reacted by criticizing *p'ansori* as crude, common and even vulgar. Even so, the practice of elite patronage continued and deepened in the 19th century, and consequently the repertoire was shaped and canonized to suit more scholarly tastes. The early 19th century gave rise to the age of the "eight great singers," who were known to develop their own individual styles, which encouraged the emergence of regional stylistic distinctions and schools. They also contributed to a developing canon of approximately 12 *p'ansori* works, only five of which are performed today: (1) *Ch'unhyang-ga* (*The Song of Ch'unhyang*), (2) *Simch'ŏng-ga* (*The Song of Simch'ŏng*), (3) *Hŭngbo-ga* (*The Song of Hŭngbo*), (4) *Sugung-ga* (*The Song of the Underwater Palace*), and 5) *Chŏkbyŏk-ga* (*The Song of the Red Cliff*).

The paring of the larger canon of works down to five is the result of literati efforts to censor the more "indecent" narrative material while revising it to clearly reflect Confucian values. Suffice it to say that *The Ballad of the Hussy* (*Walcha T'aryŏng*) and other stories involving baudy themes did not make the cut. The five works passed down to the present are the result of considerable refinement by members of the literati class such as Sin Ch'ae-hyo (1812–1884), who is often cited as a pivotal figure in refining the *p'ansori* repertoire. Because of the literati influence, the five remaining works were selected and shaped to reflect the Confucian philosophy of *oryun*, or the "five moral rules governing the five human relations." Loyalty between subject and king is addressed in *The Song of the Underwater Palace*, filial piety between child and parent in *The Song of Simch'ŏng*, fidelity between wife and husband in *The Song of Ch'unhyang*, proper love and respect between siblings in *The Song of Hŭngbo*, and chivalry between friends in *The Song of the Red Cliff.*

Introduction of proscenium stages radically altered the course of *p'ansori* in the 20th century and spurred an era of theatrical adaptation where the simple format of one person standing on a straw mat was replaced by a stage-oriented form called *ch'anggŭk* (literally, "singing theater") that progressively included stage props, lighting, costumes, multiple performers playing individual parts, a chorus, dancers and more elaborate musical accompaniment. Despite a temporary decline caused in part by the rise of women's theater groups, *ch'anggŭk* now enjoys privileged status as a premier form of national musical theater. However, as cultural revivalists and preservationists began to question the authenticity of *ch'anggŭk* in the 60s and 70s, there was a movement to restore and promote *p'ansori* in a manner more coherent with its original format. Along these lines, *p'ansori* was designated Intangible Cultural Asset No. 5 in 1963. Though contemporary *p'ansori* performers have not necessarily given up the concert hall for the open-air *p'ans* of the past, the straw mat remains on stage as a reminder of all that it has meant to participate in *p'ansori* over time.

Performance and Repertoire

In contrast to the spectacular sets of *ch'anggŭk*, *p'ansori* is usually performed today in a concert hall (or perhaps during an outdoor festival) with little adorning the stage except the aforementioned straw mat, and perhaps a painted folding screen that serves as a simple backdrop for the performers. In lieu of theatrical costumes, the performers wear traditional Korean clothing called *hanbok* (Figure 4.7). The drummer plays a specialized medium-sized barrel drum with tacked-on heads called a *sori puk* and sits stage left of the main performer, who clutches a paper fan as a prop. Figure 4.7 gives you a better mental picture, but viewing the opening scene of director Im Kwon-taek's film adaptation *Ch'unhyang* would be ideal.

The indoor concert hall setting is a 20th-century development, but it does preserve some important elements of the *p'an*: (1) the minimal setting places emphasis on the experience of orality, of being told a story with nothing but the voice as a guide; (2) the presence of the "fourth wall" is diminished, encouraging the audience to use their imagination and participate more fully in the performance; and (3) the accompanying drummer is situated prominently on stage and is allowed to dialogue with the performer by interjecting shouts of encouragement, called *ch'uimsae*. In general, the spirit of participation is important as both the drummer and audience are expected to yell out stylized *ch'uimsae* that contribute significantly to the energy and flow of the performance. So that you become more intimately acquainted with the experience of *p'ansori*, I will describe some of the elements of a typical performance.

Warm-up Songs (Tan'ga)

As faithfully depicted in Im Kwon-taek's clever "story-within-a-story" approach to the opening of the feature film *Ch'unhyang*, a *p'ansori* performance typically begins with a warm-up song called a *tan'ga* (literally, "short-song"). This not only allows the singer to warm-up his or her voice and body but is also an opportunity for the singer, accompanist and audience to become more attuned to each other in the *pan*. *Tan'ga* songs generally fall into two categories. The first type consist of songs excerpted or adapted from passages of a major *p'ansori* work, such as *"Sarangga"* ("Love Song") from *The Song of Ch'unhyang* (CD track 7, at 7:28). To see a good example of the first type, view the opening of *Ch'unhyang*. Here, Im aptly chooses the "Love Song" (*Sarangga*) *tan'ga* to introduce the core value of the story to his viewers, that of the love between a husband and wife. The second type consists of songs composed exclusively as *tan'ga*, independently from a *p'ansori* narrative, such as *Sach'ŏlga* ("Song of Four Seasons," CD track 25).

Descriptions of nature and Chinese literary references abound in the second type of *tan'ga*. In this instance, the focus is more topical with the overall format tilted toward singing rather than narrative storytelling. The melodies and rhythms in *tan'ga* are simpler and more straightforward than can be found in *p'ansori*. *Tan'ga* are also relatively shorter in

ACTIVITY 4.6 *Not only is* tan'ga *a warm-up for the singer, but it can be a warm-up for the listener as well, especially for those new to* p'ansori.

- *Review the* chungmori changdan *from Activity 3.4 (in the previous chapter) on* sanjo. *Although the drum used in* p'ansori *is a* puk *instead of the* changgo, *the rhythms are played similarly.*

- *Once you are able to tap the* chungmori changdan, *listen to "Song of Four Seasons" (*"Sach'ŏlga"*) on CD track 25 and tap along with the track. Note that the first beat of the* changdan *begins firmly at 0:07 seconds. Note too that the* puk *player is playing quite minimally here, so you will have to be dutiful in tapping out the full rhythm, even if the drummer is not playing every stroke.*

- *Do the same with the* chungjungmori *rhythm on* "Ch'unhyang-ga Sarangga" *("Love Song" from* The Song of Ch'unhyang*) on CD track 7, at 7:28. Keep in mind that the first beat of the* changdan *starts on 7:34 in the track.*

length, averaging from four to eight minutes. Although a typical scene in *p'ansori* usually involves shifts in rhythm (i.e., from metered to unmetered, or from one rhythmic cycle or *changdan* to another) and vocal style (ranging from spoken narration to singing to recitative), *tan'ga* are usually more consistent from beginning to end and employ a single *changdan* throughout (usually *chungmori*). Thus *tan'ga* tend to be accessible to general audiences.

Narrative Performance: The Song of Ch'unhyang
After a *p'ansori* singer warms up with a *tan'ga*, the singer will then perform his or her version of a full *p'ansori* narrative. A single performance of *p'ansori* can last anywhere between two and eight hours. Today, a performer generally tailors her performance to fit within the standard concert length of two hours. It is also common to see singers perform excerpts or more condensed versions of a *p'ansori* narrative. In this way, a *p'ansori* performance can be seen as a dynamically evolving flow that allows the performer a great deal of flexibility to respond to the particular needs of a given audience or event. In *The Song of Ch'unhyang*, the "traditional" notion of love between a husband and wife is challenged through focusing on an unorthodox relationship between a courtesan's daughter and a young nobleman whose secret marriage is put to the test by a covetous local magistrate.

I now present a synopsis and an excerpt from this, one of the most beloved *p'ansori* stories of all time. *The Song of Ch'unhyang* is a quintessential Korean love story told in about six major scenes. In the first scene, a dashing young son of the local magistrate, Yi Mong-ryŏng, is prompted by the beautiful spring weather to take a trip to Kwanghallu Pavilion with his spirited servant, Bangja. There, he is mesmerized by the sight of an enchanting young woman swaying back and forth on a swing. In the second scene, a smitten Yi Mong-ryŏng courts Ch'unhyang at her home, where he becomes increasingly intrigued by her wit and intelligence (see Figure 4.8 for the text of this scene, CD track 7). He immediately requests her hand, and the two are unofficially married by Ch'unhyang's mother, Wŏlmae, a retired courtesan. They enjoy a brief period of bliss before receiving the news in the third scene that Yi Mong-ryŏng must leave to follow his father, who is being summoned to the capital. Due to Ch'unhyang's tenuous status as the daughter of a former courtesan and Yi Mong-ryŏng's inability to take a concubine with him before passing the national civil examination,

Yi has no choice but to leave Ch'unhyang behind. The scene concludes with sad farewells.

The fourth scene opens with the arrival of the new magistrate, Pyŏn Hak-to. Having heard of Ch'unhyang's legendary beauty, Pyŏn demands that Ch'unhyang succumb to him as his concubine. Boldly declaring her status as a married woman, Ch'unhyang refuses and is tortured, put into prison and threatened with execution. In the fifth scene, Yi Mong-ryŏng returns to Namwŏn, in the guise of a destitute scholar in tattered clothes. In truth, he has just passed the highest civil examination in Seoul and is returning as the royal secret inspector. In the sixth and final scene, Yi Mong-ryŏng announces himself during a birthday banquet for the new magistrate. Exposing the corruption of the officials, the royal inspector punishes the evil magistrate and even has Ch'unhyang come forward to ask her whether she will serve him instead. Unaware of his true identity, she refuses until he reveals the jade ring that she had given him as a symbol of her abiding love. Having endured much hardship, the two are reunited, with hearts bursting with joy.

Expressive Elements of P'ansori

A *p'ansori* performer brings a *p'ansori* story to life through masterful deployment of three main elements: song (*sori*), dialogue or spoken narration (*aniri*), and movement or gesture (*pallim*). *Sori* or "song" usually follows a rhythmic cycle or *changdan* and consists of melodies set to various Korean modes such as *kyemyŏnjo* (also encountered in *sanjo* and southern folksongs). Mastering *sori* requires development of a strong, supple voice that is capable of projecting many timbres, from a robust and unobstructed sound to a husky deep rumble, from a mournful wail to a ghostly whisper. Perhaps it is no mistake that this vocal diversity and richness stands in stark contrast to *p'ansori's* economy of gesture and minimalist aesthetics, making the voice that much more central to the *p'ansori* experience. *Aniri* or narration often takes center stage during the opening of a scene, with additional dialogue or narration interspersed throughout. It may take the form of plain speech (as in dialogue) or occupy some continuum between speech and song (as in recitative). Either way, it must be delivered with an actor's sense of conviction, comic timing, drama and spontaneity—the execution of which can make or break a *p'ansori* performance. Gesture or *pallim* is used to enhance what is happening in a scene. Although *pallim* can be performed with the entire body—some performers fall dramatically to the floor in certain

[Aniri] (0:00 to 0:21)

*Kuttaeyŏ Ch'unhyanggwa toryŏnnimi
haruga kago it'ŭli kago
oryuk-iri nŏmŏgani.*

*Na ŏrin saramdŭri bukkŭrŏmŭn hwolssin
mŏlli kago.*

*Chŏngman tambukdŭlŏ harunŭn sŏro
saranggaro noninnandŭi.*

*With Ch'unhyang and the young master,
As one day, two days, and
several days pass.*

*The young lover's shyness dissipates considerably
And they grow fondly intimate of each other
As they enjoy the "Love Song"*

[Jinyangjo] (0:22 to 7:16)

*Manch'ŏpch'ŏngsan nŭlgŭn bŏmi
salchin amk'aerŭl mullŏda nohko inŭn ta
tŏpssuk ppajyŏ mŏkdŭn mot-hŏgo.
Ŭ-rŭrŭrŭrŭ.*

*Ohŏng nŏmnonan tŭt tansan ponghwangi
chukshirŭl mulgo
odong sok'ŭl nŏmnonan tŭt;
bukhae hŭkyongi yŏ-ŭijurŭl mulgo ch'ae-
un kanŭl nŏmnonan tŭt;
kugok ch'ŏnghaki nanch'orŭl mulgo
songbaekkanŭi nŭmnonan tŭt;*

Nae sarang nae alttŭl nae kanganijiya!

*Oho-ŏ tung tung niga nae sarangiji.
Mokrakmubyŏnsuyŏchŏnŭi ch'anghae
kat'i kipŭn sarang; samosinjŏng tal
palgŭndŭi musan ch'ŏnbong.Wanwŏl
sarang saengjeon sarangi irŏhani sahu
kiyaki ŏpsŭlsonya?*

*Nŏnŭn chugŏ kkoch'i toedoe,
pyŏkdohŭng samch'onhwaga toego.
Nado chugŏ pŏmnabi toe-ŏ.*

*Deeply enfolded by green mountains, like an
old tiger that has grabbed a dog in its mouth but
cannot bite it because its teeth have fallen out.
Ŭ-rŭrŭrŭrŭ.*

*Like the phoenix of Dan-shan Mountain
carrying a bamboo fruit in its beak and
playing among the paulownia trees;
like the black dragon from the north sea
holding its magic stone in its mouth playing
in the clouds; like a blue crane of the nine
marches carrying an orchid in its beak and
playing among the ancient pines.*

My love, my lovely one, my love!

*Oho-ŏ tung tung you're my love.
Love boundless as the sky over the sea and
deep as the ocean; love like the full moon
shining on a thousand peaks. If we love like
this in life, how can our wedding end in
death?*

*If you die, you'll be a
heavenly peach blossom.
If I die, I'll be a butterfly.*

FIGURE 4.8 *Excerpt from the* "Song of Ch'unhyang": *"Love Song"* *("Sarangga"; CD track 7).*

Ch'unsamwŏl hosijŏrae ni kkotsong-
irŭl naega tŏmssuk ango nŏ-ul nŏ-ul
ch'umch'ugo tŭmyŏn niga narinjul
arŭryŏmuna.

When the spring breeze blows gently, I will
dance a swaying dance nibbling your antlers
and you'll know that it's me.

Hwarohŏmyŏn chŏpbul laera nabi
ch'ajaganjŭk kkot doeginŭn
naega silso.

If the flower withers, butterflies won't come
again. Although butterflies and birds come
in, I don't want to be a flower.

Kŭrŏmyŏn chugŏsŏ doel kŏt itta nŏnŭn
chugŏ. Chongno ingyŏngi toego.
Nado chugŏ ingyŏng mach'iga toe-ŏ.
Pamimyŏn isippalsu naji toemyŏn
samsipsamch'ŏn kujŏ taeng ch'igŏdŭn.

All right then, I'll tell you what
you'll be when you die. When
you die, you'll be the bell in Chongno.
When I die, I shall be the wood bell-hammer
of the bell. Counting the twenty-eight
constellations at night and thirty-three
heavens in the daylight.

Niga narinjul arŭryŏmuna.
Ingyŏng toegido naesa silso.
Kŭrŏmyŏn chugŏ toel kŏt itta. Nŏnŭn
chugŏ kŭlchaga toedoe, ttang kon kŭnŭl
ŭm anae ch'ŏ: kyejip yŏja kŭlchaga toego.

You'll know it's me.
I don't like the bell either.
Then, when you die, I'll tell you what you'll
be. When you die, you'll be a Chinese
character, the character for earth, for shadow, for
wife, and for female: the element of woman.

Nado chugŏ kŭlchaga toedoe, hanŭl
ch'ŏn hanŭl kon nal il pyŏl yang chiabi
pu kitŭk ki sana-i nam: adŭl cha cha
kŭlchaga toe-ŏ.

When I die, I shall be a character for the
sky, for the sun, for husband, for man: the
element of a son.

Kyejip yŏ pyŏnaega ttokkkach'i putyŏ
sŏsŏ chohŭl ho charoman norarŭl poja.

Put that by the element of woman and we
have the character for "good" so let's play.

[Aniri] (7:17 to 7:27)
Toryŏnnimŭn ŏtchi iroke chŭlgŏ-un nal
sahu malssŭmŭl hana-ikka kŭrŏmyŏn
nŏwa ŏpkodo norabogo chŏngdamdo
hanbŏn hayŏboja.

The young master exclaims that after such
a joyous day, "why don't we ride on each
other's backs and whisper sweet nothings into
each other's ears."

FIGURE 4.8 *(continued)*

[Jungjungmori] (7:28 to 9:35)
Iri onŏra ŏpko nolcha.
Iri onŏra ŏpko nolcha.
Sarang sarang sarang nae sarangiya.
Sarang sarang sarang nae sarangiya.
Hi-i-i nae sarang-iroda amado nae
sarang-a.
Niga muŏsŭl mŏgŭryanŭnya?
Niga muŏsŭl mŏgŭryanŭnya?
Tunggŭltunggŭl subak utbangji ttettŭrigo?
Kangnŭng baekch'ŏng'ŭl ttarŭrŭrŭrŭ-
puwŏ? Shillang palla pŏrigo pulgŭn
chŏm-uppŏk ttŏ pangan chinsurŏ
mŏguryanŭnya.
Ani kŭgeŏtto nanŭn silko.
Kŭrŏmyŏn muŏsŭl mŏgŭryanŭnya?
Niga muŏsŭl mŏgŭryanŭnya?
Tangdongjiji ruji hŏni woe kaji
tangch'amoe mŏgŭryanŭnya?
Ani kŭgeŏtto nanŭn silso.
Kŭrŏmyŏn muŏsŭl mŏgŭryanŭnya?
Niga muŏsŭl mŏgŭryanŭnya?
P'odorŭl churya aengdorŭl churya?
Kyulbyŏng satangŭi hyehwadang'ŭl churya?
Amado nae saranga.
Shigŭm t'ŏlt'ŏl kaesalgu
chagŭn idoryŏng sŏnŭn dŭi
mŏgŭryanŭnya?
Chŏri kagŏra twi t'aerŭl boja.

Iri onŏra apt'aerŭl boja.

Ajang ajang kŏrŏra kŏnnŭn t'aerŭl boja.
Ppanggŭt ussŏra ip sogŭl boja.

Amado nae saranga.

Come here, ride on my back and let's play.
Come here, ride on my back and let's play.
Love, love, love, my love.
Love, its like this, my loved one
Hee, hee, hee, you are my love.

What would you like to eat?
What would you like to eat?
What about a poked round watermelon?
Poured with white sweet honey?
Take the seeds out and taste a juicy red piece,
savor it all in one big bite.

No, I don't want any.
Then what would you like to eat?
What would you like to eat?
A short, thick and oval
sweet cucumber, eggplant or melon?
No, I don't want any.
Then what would you like to eat?
What do you want to eat?
Would you like cherries or grapes,
A taffy or tangerine candy my dear?
Whatever you what, my loved one.
Are you craving tart, wild apricots,
Because of the little Idoryong that you are
bearing?
Go over there, so we can take a look at your
backside.
Come back here, so we can look at your
front.
Saunter around, let's see you how you walk.
Smile sweetly, so we can see the gaps in your
teeth.
Whatever you want, my loved one.

FIGURE 4.8 *(continued)*

scenes—many actions can be articulated with the humble assistance of a fan (sometimes a handkerchief) as a prop. Demonstrating great economy of expression, the fan can signal an entrance or exit, demarcate various types of scene changes and symbolically morph into an array of objects. Although all of these expressive elements are crucial, it is the element of *sori* that takes the most effort, time and detailed attention to learn and transmit.

ACTIVITY 4.7   *Listen to CD track 7 and follow along with the text in Figure 4.8.*

- *Although you cannot view the gestures (*pallim*) from the sound recording, you can still differentiate between the narration (*aniri*) and the singing (*sori*). In Figure 4.8 the* aniri *sections are marked as such, but the* sori *sections are marked by the rhythmic* changdan. *Take note of what is being conveyed dramatically in each mode, and write a short paragraph reflecting on how the chosen mode or* changdan *enhances the action, meaning or sentiment being expressed.*
- *Focusing on the* Chungjungmori *section that begins at 7:28, listen to the voice and see if you can find any examples of the vocals mimicking the general gestures or emotions of what is being said. To do so, listen line by line and compare the vocals with the translation. Take note of the timings of any examples you find.*

P'ansori *Aesthetics*
Heavy reliance on oral transmission is common in Korean folk forms. And though it may be time-consuming and painstaking at times, oral transmission does help to preserve certain aesthetics or values that are essential to *p'ansori*: (1) close, almost mimetic attention to vocal shadings, inflections and ornaments; (2) appreciation for both repertoire and artistry that is highly individual as opposed to standardized; and (3) adherence to a highly dependent master-student relationship in which the master possesses a great deal of authority over the pace of learning, not to mention input into subsequent performance and teaching activities. It is important to note that although close attention to learning the

individual style of one's teacher is stressed in the beginning, a mature singer is expected to draw upon his or her own personality, experience and creativity to develop a genuine style and interpretation. This aesthetic expectation is coherent with oral transmission; there is little sense that the artistic "work" resides in a particular written score. Rather, the intangibility of oral transmission encourages a more flexible approach where the "work" resides in the individual who tailors expression to the *p'an* in a particular space and moment in time.

P'ansori aesthetics are also quite specific in terms of what kinds of sounds or expressive capabilities are valued in a *p'ansori* singer. Although *p'ansori* is best known for its husky vocal quality, the ideal voice is actually more of a combination of what is considered a "clear, springy or gifted voice" (*ch'ŏngusŏng*) plus other sounds such as "husky voice" (*surisŏng*), "sorrowful voice" (*aewŏnsŏng*), "tubular projection" (*tongsŏng*) or "metallic voice" (*ch'ŏlsŏng*). A voice that is just purely husky might be considered too "dry," "crackled," "starchy" and "tasteless." Other vocal tone qualities that are avoided include "nasal," "quivering" or otherwise lacking in abdominal support or the necessary tension required to project properly. In addition to developing a strong base, a good singer should be able to exploit various timbres to express the various moods and personalities of the characters. For example, a high falsetto that alternates with glottal stops may be used to convey playfulness or humor, while a wailing falsetto might be used to invoke otherworldly spirits, weeping ghosts or even the cries of animals or birds (Park, Chan 2003: 192–201).

Whatever particular combination of tonal qualities or other performance skills a given singer possesses, practitioners often mention that the ultimate goal is to express *imyŏn*, or the emotional interiority and deeper meaning of the text. Some even go so far as to assert that to truly convey the emotions of a *p'ansori* story, one has to have lived them. In particular, a sentiment considered prominent in *p'ansori* (and in Korean music and culture generally) is called *han*. An elusive trope in Korean society, *han* encompasses feelings of sorrow, suffering, regret and longing; taken to its extreme, *han* can move toward an outpouring of emotion or catharsis. Spurred by the *minjung* cultural movement from the 1970s forward, some argue that the concept of *han* was reappropriated to express a national sense of suffering, especially in the context of the Japanese colonial experience and the Korean War. Even so, no one can argue that the sound of *han* is meaningful for many contemporary Koreans. For new listeners especially, *han* is a striking and easily distinguishable aesthetic characteristic of *p'ansori*, not to mention many other Korean cultural forms.

CONTEMPORARY DEVELOPMENTS IN KOREAN MUSICAL THEATER AND FILM

Just as *p'ansori* exploited the power of the voice and crafted it into a distinctive story-singing art, other forms drew upon Korean vocal arts and adapted them in new directions, thereby maintaining valuable threads of aesthetic continuity into the 20th century and beyond. In this section, I examine how *p'ansori* served as an artistic base, point of reference or locus of creativity in new hybrid forms, namely North Korean opera and film. This creative activity produces work that can be seen as simultaneously intertextual, transnational, culturally continuous and even political at times, intersecting with all the themes pursued in this book.

North Korean Revolutionary Opera

In the aftermath of the Korean War and into the 1960s, *p'ansori*-derived musical theater or *ch'angguk* lived on in North Korea as *minjok kaguk* or "national opera." However, the music changed significantly as the more elaborate melodies and diverse timbres of *p'ansori* were replaced with simplified folk melodies and standardized vocals. Although folksongs were seen as important sources for composing "music in a Korean style ... in accord with the feelings of our people," they were not considered revolutionary in and of themselves. In the early 1970s, *minjok kaguk* was not deemed adequately revolutionary, according to the philosophy of *juche* ("self-reliance"), and a new set of operatic productions were composed to fill this gap. According to comments attributed to Kim Jong-il, "revolutionary opera requires not only revolutionary content but also a revolutionary change in its form" (1995: 265). Along these lines, the first revolutionary opera, entitled the *Sea of Blood* (*P'ibada*), was composed in 1971. It featured combined orchestras of Western and reformed Korean instruments, dancers, singer/actors, elaborate stage sets as well as formal changes that included lyrics arranged in stanzas and the addition of *pangch'ang*. Considered an important revolutionary innovation, *pangch'ang* are popular operatic songs meant to draw the audience deeper into the drama; they are sung off-stage so that the actor can focus on conveying the emotions of the character without distraction. In terms of content, *Sea of Blood* dramatizes the story of a resistance fighter who struggles against the Japanese forces brutally cracking down on a mining village that is suspected of providing refuge.

Following the success of the *Sea of Blood*, other revolutionary operas were created, notably *True Daughter of the Party* (1971), *Flower Girl* (1972),

Oh Tell, Forest (1972), and *Song of Mount Kŭmgang* (1973). These were most likely influenced by the "model works" (*yangbanxi*) that were promoted in China during the Cultural Revolution (1966–1976; see Lau 2007). Despite its diverse influences, revolutionary opera cannot fully escape the directive of being "Korean" or "national" and cannot help but be interwoven with traditional Korean motifs, costumes and dance sequences.

P'ansori *and Film: Director Im Kwon-taek*

In South Korea, director Im Kwon-taek (b. 1936) is a figure who many believe brought *p'ansori* into contemporary mainstream consciousness. Some even credit him for legitimizing *p'ansori* and spurring renewed interest in Korean traditional performing arts in general. As a film director, Im is extremely prolific, and his films have made breakthroughs both domestically and abroad. Many of his films explore themes of Korean traditional culture and identity, often in dialogue or tension with the forces of Japanese colonialism, modernity and U.S. imperialism. Bridging the gap between one storytelling medium and another, Im Kwon-taek devoted two of his films to the subject of *p'ansori*: *Sŏp'yŏnje* in 1993 and *Ch'unhyang* in 2000. *Sŏp'yŏnje* is an original story that details the lives of a struggling family of *p'ansori* musicians as they experience the transition from the late colonial period (1930s, 1940s) to the industrial era (1960s, 1970s); *Ch'unhyang* is a more direct filmic adaptation of the *p'ansori* narrative based on the same character. Though *Sŏp'yŏnje* is more indirect and disjointed in its reference to *p'ansori* texts, both of these films stand as creative contributions to the intertextual endeavor, securing *p'ansori's* indelible position in contemporary popular culture in South Korea.

ACTIVITY 4.8 *Research the life and work of the Korean film director Im Kwon-taek (b. 1936), and present your findings in class. Try to ascertain how his films have redefined traditional Korean culture, gender roles, art, and music for contemporary Koreans.*

Sŏp'yŏnje

When *Sŏp'yŏnje* was first released in 1993, few could predict that it would become such a huge cultural phenomenon. At a time when Hollywood movies dominated the Korean box-office market, *Sŏp'yŏnje* struck a national chord and became a huge sleeper hit, going on to become one of the most popular domestic movies in South Korean history. With its masterful weaving of diagetic clips of *p'ansori* and popular southern folksongs such as *"Chindo Arirang"* (CD track 22, Figure 4.1), *Sŏp'yŏnje* reawakened a mainstream yearning and interest in Korean culture. At the same time, the plot provides numerous intertextual twists on the Confucian themes of love and filial piety (in direct reference to *The Song of Ch'unhyang* and *The Song of Simch'ŏng*), making *Sŏp'yŏnje* one of the most widely discussed movies of Im's oeuvre. In particular, the extent to which some of the characters go in the name of *han* (suffering) is disturbing and incomprehensible for some, but sublimely cathartic for others.

In short, *Sŏp'yŏnje* follows the lives of a wandering *p'ansori* musician named Yu-bong; his adopted daughter, Song-hwa; and his stepson, Dong-ho (Figure 4.9). Although the film attributes *p'ansori's* decline to the rising popularity of competing modern entertainments, Yu-bong's difficult position is exacerbated by his estrangement from his teacher and his refusal to compromise by moving to Seoul. The story is told in flashbacks as Dong-ho, now in his 30s, goes searching for his stepsister, Song-hwa, whom he has not seen since running away from his

FIGURE 4.9   *From left to right: Dongho, Songhwa and Yubong singing* Chindo Arirang *in the film* Sŏp'yŏnje *by Im Kwon-taek. (Photo still from the film.)*

family in his youth. From childhood, Yu-bong trained Song-hwa in *sori* and Dong-ho in *puk*. However, unable to fathom the value of continuing *p'ansori* during inhospitable times, Dong-ho ran away, leaving a despondent Song-hwa in his wake. In response to her state, Yu-bong gave Song-hwa some "medicine" that he procures to induce her blindness. He did this believing that the *han* (suffering) she would then experience will somehow make her a better *p'ansori* singer (or at least keep her from running away, like Dong-ho). The story culminates in the reunion of Song-hwa and her stepbrother, who spend the evening sublimating their longing for each other by performing *p'ansori*, only to go their separate ways the next day.

None of the musical/lyrical selections are made at random in *Sŏp'yŏnje*; they intersect both sonically and narratively with what is happening in the film. Here are some of the key intertextual references to watch for:

- *Kalkka Puda* ("I Want to Go") frames Dong-ho's search for his long-lost sister. This is from a scene in which Ch'unhyang longs for her departed lover in *The Song of Ch'unhyang* (Chapter 1, *Sŏp'yŏnje* DVD).
- *Sarangga* ("Love Song") frames the contrast between the innocent love of Song-hwa and Dong-ho and her growing sexual desirability as a female *p'ansori* entertainer. This is from *The Song of Ch'unhyang* (Chapter 5, *Sŏp'yŏnje* DVD, CD track 7).
- *Chindo Arirang*, a southern folksong with adaptable lyrics that speak to the twists and turns of the road of life, frames the early stages of their itinerant lifestyle (Chapter 7, *Sŏp'yŏnje* DVD, CD track 22).
- *Okchungga* ("Prison Song") underscores the feeling of entrapment and helplessness that Dong-ho and Song-hwa begin to experience under such harsh conditions. This is from the imprisonment of Ch'unhyang in *The Song of Ch'unhyang* (*Sŏp'yŏnje* DVD, Chapter 8).
- The *tan'ga* entitled *Sach'ŏlga* and also called *Isan Chŏsan* ("Four Seasons" or "This Mountain, That Mountain") is a *tan'ga* that marks the passing of the seasons and frames Songhwa's maturation as a *p'ansori* singer, as well as submission to her father and her dependent blind state (*Sŏp'yŏnje* DVD, Chapter 12, CD track 25).

However one chooses to read the many threads that run through *Sŏp'yŏnje*, it will surely remain as a powerful tour-de-force that articulates many important aesthetic discourses about *p'ansori*, *han* and its relevance to the historical hardships of the Korean people. Through the numerous intertextual critical readings emerging since it was made, *Sŏp'yŏnje* has become one of the most significant Korean cultural texts of its time.

ACTIVITY 4.9 *If time permits, view the film* Sŏp'yŏnje, *by Im Kwon-taek, taking note of the intertextual references listed above. Answer these questions:*

- *What does the film say about* han *and its connection to* p'ansori *training? How does* han *play out in each character's life?*
- *What modern 20th-century forces "threaten" the livelihood of* p'ansori *performers in this film? How are these forces connected to the ways in which* han *is played out symbolically on a societal, cultural or national level?*

Ch'unhyang
Created seven years after *Sŏp'yŏnje*, Im Kwon-taek approached the depiction of *p'ansori* with a much lighter hand in *Ch'unhyang* (2000, Figure 4.10). Unlike *Sŏp'yŏnje*, *Ch'unhyang* is a more straightforward retelling of *The Song of Ch'unhyang* story, packaged as a fresh period piece for a 21st-century audience. This time, Im preserves the sound of *sori* and the narration and uses them nondiagetically (where the sound source is not present or implied on screen). This is a radical departure from traditional conventions of musical theater and film (*Sŏp'yŏnje* included), in which the characters act as well as sing on stage. Instead, the film *Ch'unhyang* opens by fading into a contemporary "live" concert-hall

FIGURE 4.10 *From left to right: Ch'unhyang, her mother Wŏlmae and her lover Yi Mongryŏng. In this picture, Yi Mongryŏng is sealing his love privately by writing on her dress before he has to leave for his official duties. Because Ch'unhyang is the daughter of a courtesan (kisaeng) and an aristocrat (yangban), her status is somewhat ambiguous and an official marriage with the aristocrat Yi Mongryŏng would be somewhat difficult and require special approval.* (Photo still from Ch'unhyang by Im Kwon-taek.)

performance of *p'ansori*, where we encounter a male performer standing on a straw mat, accompanied by a lone *puk* player, singing *Sarangga* as a *tan'ga* from *The Song of Ch'unhyang*. As we continue to hear the singer, the film segues into the introduction of the story. We are visually transported to Namwon, the home of Ch'unhyang and Yi Mong-ryong. In this way, the movie is a kind of story-within-a-story, and as implausible as it may seem Im Kwon-taek manages to seamlessly link back to the live performance at various points throughout the film. The result is quite liberating; it frees the director from having to use real *p'ansori* singers as actors and enables the actors to focus on the dialogue and acting.

ACTIVITY 4.10   *If time permits, view the film* Ch'unhyang, *by Im Kwon-taek, and answer these questions.*

- *Who is Ch'unhyang? What is her social status? How does she push the boundaries of her status as a woman in the film?*
- *How does Im incorporate intertextuality in* Ch'unhyang? *How is it different from his approach in* Sŏp'yŏnje?

In this chapter, I have examined how the voice served as a powerful vehicle for the cultivation and continuation of culture in Korea. In *p'ansori* in particular, intertextuality proves to be a strategic and effective tool in this process. In the next chapter, intertextuality remains relevant as I explore how Koreans rearticulated their culture as they began to grapple with Japanese and Western influences during the first half of the 20th century.

CHAPTER 5

Colonial Legacies in Korea

Although Korea's history as a colony of Japan (1910–1945) has long since passed, this period had a lasting impact on Korea's musical practices. In addition to the heavy influence of Japan, this was an era of greater international contact with such Western powers as Great Britain, Germany, Russia and the United States. Japan played a pivotal role in prodding Korea's emergence from self-imposed seclusion when it initiated the first official treaty of commerce and trade (also known as the Kanghwa treaty) in 1876. Fortified by 400 troops on the island of Kanghwa and as many as 4,000 soldiers offshore, Japan literally forced the "opening" of Korea "at the point of a gun" (Cumings 1997: 95–101). This maneuver opened the door to other treaties with foreign powers, most notably with the United States in 1882. Soon thereafter, American protestant missionaries were able to reside in Korea for the first time, among them the pioneer medical missionary Horace N. Allen in 1884, followed by Henry Appenzeller, Mary Scranton and Horace Underwood in 1885 (Choi Jai-Keun 2007: 8). Since Chosŏn law forbade them to proselytize directly, these missionaries turned their attention to setting up schools and medical clinics, contributing greatly to the reform of education and health care in Korea.

Meanwhile, domestic peasant discontent had been brewing since the 1850s with the development of the *Tonghak* ("Eastern Learning") movement. Korea's opening in the 1870s only exacerbated peasant conditions as the increased foreign demand for rice and other goods contributed to a steep hike in inflation. As Japanese fishing boats appeared more frequently in Korean waters, competing with local fisherman for the same resources, domestic sentiment became increasingly antiforeign. Owing to the combined conditions of a weakened royal court, ruling class corruption and worsening domestic unrest, Korea had become especially vulnerable; all the Japanese needed to do was wait for the right time to strike. Opportunity beckoned when the Tonghak rebellion broke out in 1894. Fearing that Korean troops would not be able to sustain the rebels,

King Kojong called for the help of China, while also notifying Japan of the situation. Although the official call for help was to China, Japan seized on it as an excuse to send warships as well. By the time China and Japan arrived, the rebellion had been suppressed, but it was too late to turn back. On July 23, Japan took over the palace, seized King Kojong and installed the regent Taewŏngun in his stead. A few days later, Japan stunned China by attacking its ships off the Korean coast, thereby instigating the first Sino-Japanese war.

Continuing in this vein, the Japanese annexation of Korea in 1910 resulted from a tangled web of colonial period intrigues. Exercising its newly acquired military might, Japan swiftly defeated China in 1895 and demanded that China yield the island of Taiwan, its centuries-old tributary relationship with Korea as well as its rights to the Liaodong peninsula (Figure 1.1). Taiwan became Japan's first colony. As for the Liaodong peninsula, the handover attracted the attention of Japan's new rival, Russia, who then brought France and Germany into a Tripartite Intervention, forcing Japan to repatriate the peninsula back to China. Without China as Korea's protector, Japan began to assert control over Korea by sending a series of Japanese ministers to oversee reforms. Meanwhile, they worked to dissolve the power of the royal court by exploiting internal power struggles between the regent Taewŏngun and King Kojong's consort, Queen Min. As she grew more vocal in her opposition to the Japanese, she was assassinated by a combination of Japanese and Korean soldiers in 1895. This prompted King Kojong and his son, the Crown Prince Sunjong, to flee to the Russian legation in 1896. Under Russian protection, King Kojong was able to return to the palace in 1897, and he promptly declared the founding of the Korean Empire.

Korea was able to temporarily fend off Japan's colonial ambitions by appealing to the Russians. But just seven years later, Japan attacked Russia, resulting in the Russo-Japanese war. Ending in 1905, Russia agreed to cede its interests in Korea to Japan. Although King Kojong made a last-ditch appeal to the United States, little did he know that it would be to no avail because the United States had already agreed not to challenge Japan's protectorate of Korea, in exchange for Japan's promise to respect American control of the Philippines in the Taft-Katsura agreement. Although many Koreans protested Japan's actions, which culminated in the dramatic assassination of the prominent Japanese general Ito Hirobumi in 1909, they could not prevent the Japanese-leaning Prime Minister Yi Wan-young from signing the

Treaty of Annexation in 1910. With King Kojong dethroned, there was nothing that his supporters or his son, Sunjong (who was mentally weak), could do but yield. So, with what barely qualifies as a last gasp, Japan finally wore down every possible barrier Korea could put up, ending a long history of relative autonomy that Korea had worked for centuries to preserve.

As evident in this brief history, Japan's annexation of Korea did not take place in a vacuum. It was a process that facilitated closer or more intense relationships with a range of foreign governments, including China, the United States, Great Britain and Russia. In more ways than one, Korea's colonial relationship with Japan must be understood in tandem with myriad influences from the United States and Europe. Furthermore, Japan's prior engagement with Europe and the United States during the Meiji period (1868–1912) meant that many of the forms and technologies it introduced to Korea were already quite hybrid and "Western" in nature (Wade 2004). With Japan controlling the reforms that were needed to bring Korea to the modern era, the first half of the 20th century placed greater emphasis on assimilating transnational influences from abroad than maintaining cultural continuity. Consequently, this chapter first highlights forms that were introduced during the colonial period and ends with a discussion of Korea's substantial engagement with Western concert music.

THE LEGACY OF THE JAPANESE COLONIAL OCCUPATION (1910–1945)

As discussed in the first chapter, Korean culture was strongly suppressed or curtailed during the colonial era, although the degree to which this occurred was somewhat inconsistent depending on the stage of the occupation. In the first decade, they established cultural control by banning use of the Korean language in magazines and newspapers as well as in government or educational institutions. They also suppressed the teaching of Korean subject matter in the classroom. In this restrictive environment, new Western-style school songs and *ch'angga* were among the few musical forms to gain a foothold.

With the advent of the recording industry in Korea, cultural production began to shift toward commercialization, popular consumption and specialized adaptation to the recording format of the times.

Ch'angga-type songs were among the first to be recorded; they "marked the birth of Korean popular song (*taejung kayo*)" (Lee Young Mee 2006: 3). These early *ch'angga* were usually based on previously composed melodies from Japan (children's songs), America (hymns, folk or popular songs) or Europe (anthems, folk or popular songs). However, by the late 1920s, Koreans began to compose both the words and the music, often preferring Korean-inspired triple meters over the duple time signatures prevalent in most popular music (2006: 4).

The Enduring Popularity of Trot

In the early 1930s, a new genre of popular song arrived on the scene that developed in close dialogue with the Japanese popular genre *enka*, eventually coming to be known formally as *trot* (pronounced "*t'ŭrot'ŭ*") in Korean. Most Koreans, however, know it more colloquially as *ppongtchak*, a term that some people see as a derogatory riff on its characteristically simple 4/4 rhythm, which could be represented onomatopoetically as "*ppong tchak-tchak, ppong tchak.*" Despite various critiques leveled at its lack of sophistication or tastefulness, *trot* remained prominent in the Korean popular song scene for several decades and helped to define the musical and expressive contours of the colonial period for many older-generation Koreans. Given that most scholars agree *trot* was heavily influenced by Japanese *enka*, it is one of the few Korean popular genres with distinct Japanese musical characteristics: (1) the Japanese pentatonic *yonanuki* minor (*la-ti-do-mi-fa*) and major (*do-re-mi-sol-la*), although the minor mode is more prevalent; (2) the jaunty, off-beat emphasis of the *enka* rhythm; (3) a penchant for emotional subject matter having to do with nostalgia, longing, love and feelings of loss; and (4) a dramatic vocal style filled with affective ornaments and inflections, such as use of wide vibratos, dramatic slides and various timbral inflections.

You can hear all of these characteristics in the popular *trot* song "Tear-Drenched Tuman River" ("*Nunmul chŏjŭn Tuman-gang*," CD track 26). Written at the height of the colonial era and a year into the Second Sino-Japanese War in 1938, this song is such a potent expression of the sentiments of longing and separation that it is known to bring tears to Koreans at home and abroad. It is important to note that the Tuman River lies at the border between North Korea and what was then Manchuria (Figure 1.1). In the early 20th century, Koreans migrated over the river to Manchuria, seeking political and economic independence and freedom, but were nevertheless caught up in competing Chinese and Japanese interests (Park Hyun Ok 2005: xi–xvi). Although this song possesses all of the *enka*-like traits listed above, some elements of the song, such as the lyrics, demonstrate how a popular transnational genre can become localized to a new cultural context:

Verse 1:	*On the blue waters of the Tuman River, a boatman is rowing.*
	In the old times that have flowed past, my lover is embarking
	Where did that departed ship go?
Refrain:	*Calling the lover that I long for, the lover that I long for.*
	When will my lover ever come back?
Verse 2:	*By the river water on a moonlit night, cries rack my body.*
	Having lost my lover, I breathe a deep sigh.
	My memories are choked with heartbreak and sorrow.

Most obviously, the lyrics localize the song geographically through its reference to the Tuman river, a landmark that doubles as a border and therefore carries associations of separation, made even more poignant for South Koreans since they have lost direct access to the Tuman's waters. In addition, the lyrics detailing "cries" that "rack [the] body" and "memories" that are "choked with heartbreak and sorrow," coupled with vocal inflections of anguish, resonate with the Korean expressive aesthetic of *han* or suffering. Despite these localizations, or what some scholars have aptly termed "glocalizations" (the localization of a global genre or phenomenon; Mitchell 2001: 11), many Korean critics have difficulty accepting *trot* as a legitimate Korean genre because of its strong Japanese associations. Although Christine Yano's research on *enka* suggests that there may have been some key interactions between Koreans and Japanese that contributed to the development of both *enka* and *trot* (1995: 66), this narrative of hybridity is usually dismissed by Korean scholars. Nevertheless, thanks to its unmistakably Japanese colonial associations, *trot* has been the target of much debate and controversy over the years. In this way, the choice to even listen to *trot* (or not) becomes a political one, challenging Koreans to come to terms with the complexities of their colonial past.

The Emergence of Sin Minyo

Directly influenced by older Korean folksongs, *sin minyo* ("new folk-songs") emerged in the early 1930s and served as a more indigenous counterpoint to *trot.* Together, they defined the Korean popular song market during the remainder of the colonial period. Given that the Japanese sought to suppress Korean cultural identity, it is somewhat surprising that *sin minyo* was even allowed to develop. Although the loosening of Japanese colonial policy during the 1920s and early 1930s was certainly a contributing factor, I would argue that Korean forms of music that were commercially appealing and therefore profitable were more likely than others to avoid suppression. In addition, the hybrid nature of *sin minyo* further helped its cause because integration of "foreign" elements into Korean culture very much fit with the modernizing agenda of the colonial period.

One of the first *sin minyo* pieces to be recorded was the song entitled "Paulownia Tree" ("*Odong namu*"), recorded by the singer Kang Sŏ-gyŏn in 1931. As illustrated in this song, many *sin minyo* make reference to seasonal landscapes, natural objects and landmarks as well as to aspects of traditional culture and rural hometown life. These characteristics can be heard in the song "*Kkolmangtae Arirang*," recorded in 1939 (CD track 27). The tendency to refer to rural life is evident in the central subject of a cowherd, as well as in the titular word "*kkolmangtae*," which is a rustic wooden tool used to feed fodder to farm animals. In the chorus, the lyrics describe the act of herding the cows, which needs to be done in haste before sunset. The "haste before sunset" image chafes against the idyllic manner in which pastoral life is normally portrayed and could be a subtle metaphor of the darkness, disruption and hectic pace of life during the colonial period.

The lyrics are based on the experiences of everyday Korean rural life, but the music betrays more of a mixture of Korean and Western elements. The form of the song is a simple verse-refrain, a song form found in both Western and Korean culture. Even though the vocalist is adept at ornaments and inflections typically found in Korean folksongs, there is some influence from Western vocal music practices audible in the lighter tone and the smoother vibratos heard in the higher sustained notes. The clarinet adds a jazzy feeling to the introduction and fills in with countermelodies in a manner reminiscent of early urban blues or jazz. The end of the chorus adds some novelty and humor when the vocalist breaks from song to speech and embodies the main character telling the cows to "Hurry up before the sun sets, let's go!" which is followed by a mooing cow sound. This sound effect is somewhat reminiscent of the menagerie of animal sounds that can be heard in "Livery Stable Blues" (1917), by the Original Dixieland Jazz Band, often mentioned as one of the earliest examples of recorded jazz. Although one may never know if there was any direct influence here, this novelty effect is certainly a delightful example of early Korean transnationalism and experimentation in recorded music.

Despite the charming inventiveness of *sin minyo*, its appeal was relatively short-lived. *Trot*, on the other hand, outlasted *sin minyo* by decades and continues to be enjoyed by the older generation today. Although scholars remain perplexed as to why it was *trot* and not *sin minyo* that managed to outlast the colonial period, Lee Young Mee offers that *sin minyo* "looked to the Korea of the past, lacking the edge to face the challenges of the modernizing world," whereas *trot* was more effective in reflecting the real hopes, frustrations and feelings of longing of the colonized youth (2006: 8). I would add that *trot* developed a more lasting formula for commercial

ACTIVITY 5.1 *Listen to "Kkolmangtae Arirang" (1939) on CD track 27 and try to get a sense of its verse-refrain structure.*

- *How does the song define the verse from the refrain in terms of instrumentation? Identify the Western or Korean instruments that are used in each section.*

- *Melodically, "Kkolmangtae Arirang" exhibits clear Korean folksong features. Compare this piece with "Chindo Arirang" (CD track 22), and take note of any similarities or differences in vocal timbre, ornamentation or phrasing.*
- *Rhythmically, the piece is literally split between two metric feels, one Western and one Korean; the first is a marchlike 4/4 in the verse and the second is a Korean triple rhythm called* semach'i *in the refrain. Try to tap the beat in each section, and take note of the timings in the track when the meter changes.*

pop success than *sin minyo*. In terms of rhythm, the 4/4 off-beat rhythm of *trot* is much more compatible with Western popular songs than the rhythms of *sin minyo*. Despite *sin minyo's* decline, it remains an important genre in Korea's colonial and popular music history as the first example of hybrid indigenous pop (Finchum-Sung 2006: 11).

ENGAGING WITH WESTERN CONCERT MUSIC

Koreans have become avid listeners, performers and composers of Western art music in a relatively short time. In the late 19th and early 20th centuries, tonal harmony was introduced through Christian hymns, military band music and children's songs. During this early period, Western music was embraced as part of the modernization process, while Korean music was clouded in paradox. Some Koreans viewed traditional music as a nostalgic marker of Korean identity; others simply saw it as backward.

The first original art song (also known as *kagok*) composed in the Western style was "Balsam Flower" *Pongsunga* by Hong Nan-p'a (b. Hong Yŏng-hu, 1897–1941), written in 1919. Despite its "foreign" sound, "Balsam Flower" became a hit by touching on the sentiments of the Korean people during the colonial period. In general, song-based repertoires were quickly embraced in part because the song texts served to ground this otherwise foreign-sounding music in the Korean culture and language. In fact, Korean composers did not venture beyond the song format until the late 1930s. Eventually, however, musicians developed facility in solo and chamber music, as well as choral and symphonic repertoires.

Today, Koreans who study Western music far outnumber those who study Korean music (*kugak*). Many of the best students of Western music often choose to pursue studies in Germany, France, Japan, Italy and the United States, among whom some of the best known are siblings Kyung-Wha Chung (violin), Myung-Wha Chung (cello), and Myung-Whun Chung (piano and conducting), as well as the coloratura vocalist Sumi Jo. Koreans who emigrated to the United States and elsewhere often instilled a love of classical music in their children, nurturing talents such as Sarah Chang and the Ahn Trio. As was evident in the unprecedented New York Philharmonic exchange with the DPRK in February 2008, North Koreans have also devoted considerable time to Western music, although general exposure to Western art music is somewhat more limited and indirect. Many of these forms of engagement are significant, so I focus the next two sections on exploring creative developments in composition in both South and North Korea.

ACTIVITY 5.2   *Pick one of two short research topics below:*

- *Research one Korean classical musician (perhaps one of those mentioned above) and prepare to introduce the person's life and work to the class.*
- *Research the New York Philharmonic's historic visit to the DPRK (2008), and prepare to present to the class.*

South Korea: Tradition, Innovation, Synthesis and Popularization
The concept of musical composition as an individual work of art crept into Korean consciousness with the introduction of Western music in the late 19th and early 20th centuries. In the realm of Korean traditional music, pieces may have been attributed to an individual (usually a sovereign or high-status individual) but were more likely seen as developing through the contributions of many people over time. Performers could improvise and make small changes in a "received" piece of music as they saw fit. Within such a practice, there was no strong differentiation between composer and performer. Although the phenomenon of the performer/composer resurfaced in recent decades with the success of figures such as Hwang Byung-ki (b. 1936) and Wŏn Il (b. 1967), introduction of Western art music did encourage several generations of Korean musicians to focus mostly on composition.

These composers are often organized into three generations. The first closely modeled their work on traditional formats (both Western and Korean) and include the aforementioned Hong Nan-p'a and Ahn Eak-Tai (1906–1965), who wrote in the Western format, and Kim Ki-su (1917–1986), who based his work on Korean models. These two approaches resulted in a division between composers who wrote mostly *yang-ak* (literally, "western music") and *ch'angjak kugak* (literally, "creative national music"). Although there is some overlap between the two, *yang-ak* can be defined primarily as music composed for Western instruments in a

Western style, while *ch'angjak kugak* refers mainly to newly composed music written for Korean instruments using Korean idioms. The second generation of composers incorporated Korean concepts into a more cerebral, modern sound that strove to innovate in ways that broke with earlier musical practices. The most recent generation has broken down walls by working toward a synthesis of Korean and Western sounds, or making their music more accessible through popularization and global fusion. In what follows, I introduce you to some of the key figures who were pivotal in the second and third generations.

The most prominent second-generation composer is also perhaps Korea's best-known international composer, Isang Yun (1917–1995). He was a true pioneer who led an extraordinary life crossing boundaries, both physical and musical. Not only was he the first to engage with 20th-century post-Romantic compositional techniques, he was also extremely innovative in translating Asian cosmological and religious philosophies as well as more specific Korean musical concepts into a Western musical aesthetic. Moving far beyond simple quotation of Korean melodies or rhythms, Yun developed a technique he called "main-tone" or "main-sound" by drawing inspiration from the long tones that are so central to the sound of Korean court music pieces such as *"Sujech'ŏn"* (CD track 11) and even literati-based vocal genres such as *sijo-ch'ang* (CD track 24). As discussed in Chapters 2 and 3, the key to the vitality of Korean melodies made up of long tones lies in how tension is built up and released through microtonal shading, inflection and ornamentation of the long tones that make up the melody.

A sophisticated example of Yun's synthesis of Korean and Western elements can be heard in his landmark work of 1971 entitled *"Gagok for Voice, Guitar and Percussion"* (CD track 28). In terms of its instrumentation, structure and text, *kagok* correlates strongly with the Korean vocal genre of the same name. For example, Yun imaginatively translates the texture of a traditional *kagok* ensemble (voice, *kŏmungo, haegŭm, p'iri, taegŭm* and *changgo*; sound is approximated on CD track 28) into a

ACTIVITY 5.3   *Research the life and work of composer Isang Yun, focusing on how he crossed (and could not cross) boundaries in his lifetime. Also look into his relationship with North Korea and how this relationship had an impact on his life.*

minimal Western format by keeping the voice and employing a guitar to fulfill the *kŏmungo* zither role as well as 10 assorted percussion instruments to provide additional rhythmic and melodic material. Unlike in traditional *kagok*, however, Yun's choice of primarily nonsustaining instruments contrasts with the voice and leaves it quite exposed, making it easy to hear the main-tone technique in the vocal line. In terms of structure, there are 13 subsections: a prelude followed by a combination of seven vocal sections and five interludes (Figure 5.1). Not including the prelude, the remainder can be organized into five sections that correspond roughly to the five sections of *kagok*. Rhythmically speaking, Yun's use of 5/4 meter is reminiscent of the irregular meters of Korean *kagok* (16/4 and 10/4) and *sijo-ch'ang* (5/4 and 8/4). Although Yun's text is made up of vocables, its structure also correlates with the way in which the three-line *sijo* poetic form is stretched and dispersed across the five sections in *kagok*. Crossing genre lines, Yun also playfully requires the instrumentalists to perform *ch'uimsae*, the stylized shouts that so

Part	Subsection	Section	Time
Introduction	1	*Tae-yo-ŭm* (Prelude)	0:00 to 0:22
Part 1	2	Voice 1	0:23 to 0:55
	3	Interlude 1	0:56 to 1:10
	4	Voice 2	1:11 to 2:05
	5	Interlude 2	2:06 to 2:20
Part 2	6	Voice 3	2:21 to 2:58
	7	Interlude 3	2:59 to 3:11
	8	Voice 4	3:12 to 3:53
	9	Interlude 4	3:54 to 4:10
Part 3	10	Voice 5	4:11 to 5:07
	11	Interlude 5 *Chung-yo-ŭm*	5:08 to 5:52
Part 4	12	Voice 6	5:53 to 6:50
Part 5	13	Voice 7	6:51 to 9:28

FIGURE 5.1 *Sectional structure of* gagok, *by Isang Yun (CD track 28).*

enliven the performance of folk genres such as p'ansori and sanjo (Kim Jee-Hyun 2008).

On a more conceptual level, Yun integrates his main-tone technique into the vocal and guitar lines, soliciting various microtonal shadings, inflections and ornaments that help to build and release tension. Yun also conveys the yin-yang principle in the way he balances contrasting elements of the piece and explores the continuum between speech and song, pitched and nonpitched sound and low-to-high slides in pitch (and vice versa). In this way, Yun subtly inserts an earthy, natural aesthetic and timbral sensibility that is preferred in many Korean folk genres.

Although several composers followed in the footsteps of Isang Yun, few pursued integration of Korean elements into a Western instrumental

ACTIVITY 5.4   *The following excerpt is from Part 2 of "Gagok" (subsections 6–9), by Isang Yun (CD track 28).*

* *Listen to the relationship among the voice, guitar and percussion. Take notes on the melody, rhythm and musical texture for each subsection enumerated in Figure 5.1.*
* *Describe the interaction among the vocalist, guitarist and percussionist in each subsection. Does any one instrument or voice predominate, or is there more of a dialogue? Do they seem to be supporting each other or operating independently? Would you describe the texture as monophonic, heterophonic or polyphonic?*
* *Yun uses several Asian or Korean-derived concepts, including his "main-tone" technique, ch'uimsae (shouts of encouragement) and the concept of yin-yang. Find examples of each one, and note their timings in the excerpt.*

framework with as much intentionality and consistency. Instead, yang-ak composers sought other ways to define themselves while staying true to their Korean heritage and identity; notable examples are Kang Sŏkhŭi (b. 1934), Paek Pyŏng-dong (b. 1936), Pagh-Paan Younghi (b. 1945) and Unsuk Chin (b. 1961). Like Isang Yun, many of these composers came to prominence through what I would call the "German interface," studying with Yun in Berlin and other composers in Germany. Although Kang Sŏkhŭi and Paek Pyŏng-dong returned to work in Korea, Pagh-Paan Younghi and Unsuk Chin (both women) remain based in Germany (and are consequently better known internationally as Younghi Pagh-Paan and Unsuk Chin).

Of these composers, Unsuk Chin, in particular, is enjoying growing international recognition (Figure 5.2). She serves as resident composer at the Deutsches Symphonie-Orchester Berlin and the Seoul Philharmonic, receives commissions all over the world and has been invited to festivals in Manchester, Turin and Milan and Strasbourg. Unlike the other Korean composers trained in Germany, Chin has

ACTIVITY 5.5 *Listen to "Double Concerto" for piano, percussion, and ensemble, by Unsuk Chin, CD track 29.*

- *Although the piano has a pretty strong entrance in the beginning of the excerpt, the density of the work makes it challenging to identify other instruments. Name at least a few instruments that you hear from the brass, string, wind and percussion families.*

- *Chin's facile use of keyed percussion ostinatos (repeated patterns) that interlock with other melodic cells is reminiscent of Balinese gamelan music (Griffiths 2003). If you have not heard Balinese gamelan, listen to or view a clip (online, or see Gold 2004,* Music in Bali, *in this series). Then decide whether you hear this influence in this piece, and if so, note the timing.*

- *Chin's placement of the ascending string glissandos (slides) in the strings toward the end of the excerpt serves as a brilliant moment of respite from the preceding whirl of activity. Find this spot and note the timing. Does this gesture sound like a nod in the Korean or the European direction? Although there are no explicit references to Korean music per se, are there any places that remind you of the Korean musical practices you have heard thus far?*

FIGURE 5.2 *The composer Unsuk Chin, winner of the 2004 Grawemeyer Award for her Violin Concerto as well as the 2005 Arnold Schoenberg Prize.* *(Photo courtesy of Eric Richmond ArenaPAL.)*

chosen not to distinguish herself by integrating Korean concepts, but instead defines her compositional identity by working primarily within a contemporary Western musical language. Although not opposed to using non-European instruments or sounds, she admits to being "wary of mixing things together which have completely different heritage lines" (Allenby 2009). Paul Griffiths even wrote that "her music makes no parade of national flavor: her preferences for the sounds of plucked or struck strings, for slowly drifting glissandos and for arrays of bells and gongs all carry no specific cultural overtones, and that indeed is one of her strengths" (Griffiths 2003). In *"Double Concerto"* (for piano, percussion, and ensemble), Chin displays a remarkable ability to weave dense, glittering soundscapes in which the various elements vibrate with astonishing clarity and kineticism (CD track 29). She is able to achieve this through her imaginative mastery of timbre and her ability to combine and contrast instrumental clusters of sound.

In the 1980s, a "third generation" of *yang-ak* composers in South Korea searched for ways to express an alternative modernity that resulted in another set of priorities. In response to South Korea's surging democratization people's movement (*minjung undong*), composers such as Lee Geon-yong (Yi Kŏn -yong; b. 1947) sought to create a "musical democracy," where musical elements could be equally combined to create a national music more accessible to the majority of the Korean people, be judged on its own terms and be free of the burden of fitting into a foreign aesthetic framework. These third-generation composers also rejected the modernist notion of pure, absolute music to favor music with programmatic cultural themes and roots in folk expressive culture (Howard 2006a: 167–68).

As composers began to more actively engage with Korean music, the gap between *yang-ak* (Western-style music) and *ch'angjak kugak* (newly composed Korean-style music) began to narrow as the project of creating a contemporary, indigenous and accessible sound resonated with composers on both sides of the divide. In the *kugak* world, one of the most prominent figures in this regard is Hwang Byung-ki (b. 1936, Figure 5.3). Trained from masters in *kayagŭm* in both the folk (*sanjo*) and court styles, Hwang is perhaps best known as a pioneer in writing modern music for the *kayagŭm*; he created a significant body of work that exploits the rich, idiomatic capabilities of the instrument, contributing greatly to the modern *kayagŭm* canon. Injecting his music with subtle inventiveness and a playful but restrained programmatic spirit, Hwang's music is generally seen as a valuable model for how to further develop Korean music in

FIGURE 5.3   *The virtuoso* kayagŭm *performer and composer Hwang Byung-ki.*
(Photo courtesy of Hwang Byung-ki).

a manner that creatively takes flight from prior repertoires while also
maintaining a strong sense of continuity with tradition.

A good example of Hwang's distinctive sound can be heard in
"*Ch'unsŏl*," or "Spring Snow" (CD track 30), a five-movement work
adapted in 1991 for the 17-string *kayagŭm* and *changgo* from an earlier
composition for *kayagŭm* and orchestra called "*Saebom*." Demonstrating
Hwang's adventurous spirit, "*Ch'unsŏl*" takes advantage of the newly
modeled *kayagŭm*. With an increased number of strings (from 12 to 17)
that are made of nylon instead of silk, this new instrument is capable

of more consistent string resonance across a three-octave range. With its adaptability to a range of traditional and modern repertoires, the 17-string *kayagŭm* is a common fixture in *kugak* orchestras. As in many of Hwang's other pieces, "*Ch'unsŏl*" is based on a programmatic theme, drawing inspiration from the subtly shifting soundscapes of snow falling on an early spring day in a country village. Hwang deftly exploits

ACTIVITY 5.6   *Listen to "Spring Snow: 3 Mysteriously," by Hwang Byung-ki (CD track 30)*

- *The expanded range of the 17-string* kayagŭm *is used effectively to depict the changing tempo of free-floating snowflakes as the* kayagŭm *shifts from the slow, midrange introduction to the higher and quickly pulsing motion of the following section. Note the timing of when this happens.*
- *Although Hwang retains the familiar sound of the accompanying* changgo *used in* sanjo *accompaniment, he departs from the triplet-based pulse of most Korean* changdan *and is otherwise quite inventive in evoking mystery through use of subtle tempo changes and multiple meter. Starting from the faster section, can you determine what some of the metric groupings are and when they change?*

- *Compare this excerpt to* kayagŭm *sanjo in CD track 12. What similar playing techniques or ornaments do you hear? Also pay attention to how Hwang stretches the melodic and timbral capabilities of the instrument by employing novel techniques such as repeated notes, chords, ostinatos, varied timbral articulations and addition of countermelodies enabled by both hands plucking the strings. Identify when these occur and note their timings.*
- *This piece is programmatic in nature. Can you hear a "story" develop in this piece? If so, describe the story. Does the story develop in sections? Alternatively, do you hear a sense of "mystery" in this piece? If so, how does he capture this mood musically?*

the larger range of the instrument to capture the moods suggested in the evocatively titled movements "Calm morning," "Peacefully," "Mysteriously," "Humorously" and "Excitedly."

As composers continue to blur the lines between *yang-ak* and *ch'angjak kugak*, several have ventured outside the academy and into the popular/ social realms by writing music for film, television, radio, political or community events and even sports events. Here, boundary crossing is the norm; not only are composers drawn by a more diverse array of cultural influences but they also freely traverse genre lines, experimenting with new age sounds, world music, religious music and of course various types of popular musics. Further, as was the case with Hwang Byung-ki, the line between composer and performer is increasingly blurred as a result of this trend. Although all of this has become commonplace in the last decade, it is worth noting that some of this experimentation was presaged in the spectacular collaboration of composers and producers in the 1988 Seoul Olympics, so nicely discussed in the work of Margaret Dilling (2001).

Today, the *ch'angjak kugak* field is broad enough to include ensembles (such as the *kayagŭm* quartet Sagye) and artists (such as Jang Goon) that are marketed to the mainstream consumer. Here, the tendency toward a free-form and sometimes unexpected mixing of genres has led some to call this music "*kugak* fusion." A fearless pioneer in this arena is Wŏn Il (b. 1967), a composer/performer and professor (of composition) at Korean National University of the Arts (Figure 5.4). Wŏn was an important member of the ground-breaking group Seulgidoong in the mid-1990s. He formed the percussion-based group Puri in 1995, released a solo record and has written many ensemble compositions. As can be heard on "Moonlight Dance" (CD track 31) from his solo album *Asura*, Wŏn experiments with a variety of fusions, incorporating pop, rock, hip-hop and free jazz; minimalist textures, uilleann pipes and a variety of Korean and world percussion instruments. Wherever his musical journeys take him, Wŏn Il always remains grounded in Korean music and believes that its unique musical characteristics and sensibility should not get lost in the process of fusion. For him, the key to maintaining continuity is to remain faithful to the Korean *changdan* or "rhythmic cycle." In describing his compositional philosophy to me in 2007, he explained:

> For me, the most important aspect of Korean music is the Korean *chang-dan or rhythm. This is my basic guide. And though my philosophy changes according to the context, my goal is to express the ways in which the human*

FIGURE 5.4 *From left to right: composer/performer Wŏn Il and the author.* *(Photo courtesy of the author.)*

spirit as well as musical forms flow, build tension and are ultimately released, from an Asian viewpoint. I also don't want the average person to be chased away by music they cannot understand. I essentially want people to be able to find meaning in my music. In terms of my own musical experience and process, I am trying to put into musical form my own maum *or "heart, mind and soul," which is essentially like a quest for water, or finding my own flow.*

In part thanks to creative pioneers such as Wŏn Il and all of the South Korean composers mentioned in this section, more young people today have the freedom and the opportunity to "find their own flow" within an increasingly global musical marketplace that not only nurtures

ACTIVITY 5.7 *Listen to "Moonlight Dance," by Wŏn Il (0:00 to 2:00 minutes) on CD track 31.*

- *This piece combines many elements from various genres and cultures. Make a list of musical elements that serve as markers of Korean culture. Do the same for any non-Korean elements. As you are doing this, try to identify as many instruments as you can.*
- *Try to follow the various rhythms used in this example. Does Wŏn Il remain faithful to the concept of the Korean* chang-dan, *or does he use other methods of rhythmic organization? See Wade's* Thinking Musically *volume to help you determine your answer. Use this guide:*

  - *0:00–0:28 15/8 meter (or five pulses subdivided by three)*
  - *0:29–0:50 9/8 (3+2+2+2) changgo and pipes*
  - *0:51–1:20 9/8 (3+2+2+2) changgo and string sounds, later piano*
  - *1:21–1:27 9/8 (3+2+2+2) Korean percussion interlude*
  - *1:28–2:00 9/8 (3+2+2+2) strings and piano*

preservation of Korean music and culture but has also come to support creativity in exploring alternative pathways.

North Korea: Music, Synthesis and Politics

Engagement with Western concert music has taken a markedly different course in North Korea. For one, new composition has come to be less an outlet of individual expression and experimentation and more about working toward the ideal of revolutionary change and "collective creation." As stated in previous chapters, music and politics go hand in hand. The current DPRK leader, Kim Jong-il (b. 1941), asserted that "music must serve politics" and says that "music without politics is like a flower without a scent" (Yi Hyŏn-ju 2006: 167). Certain elements of Western music have been adopted to become symbolic markers for not only modernity but, more important, revolutionary change. For example, leading up to the Korean War and beyond, diatonic choral harmony, military marchlike rhythms and structured, anthemlike melodies signaled revolution and progress; they helped to "awaken a new political consciousness." The importance placed on political content also explains why much compositional creativity is focused on vocal or choral music with lyrics.

Similar to the "people's music," or *minzu yinyue*, of the People's Republic of China (see Lau 2007, *Music in China*, in this series), North Korean "people's music," or *minjok ŭmak*, evolved according to the governing ideology of the time. From early on, Korean folksongs and newly composed folksongs were pivotal in the creation of *minjok ŭmak* and continue to be important until the present day. After the Korean War, the "galloping horse movement" and the ideology of self-reliance (*juche*) gave rise to reform of Korean instruments so that they could be played together in large, hybridized, Western-style orchestral ensembles (see Chapter 3). Although folksong formed the basis of newly composed light music and opera, much of this material was developed according to Kim Il-sung, who dictated that the lyrics should be modified according to socialist ideology and that the sound should be refined to suit the sensibilities of the younger generation of North Koreans. Believing that the husky, earthy and noisy timbres favored in Southwestern folk genres were "crude" and "defective," Kim argued to eliminate these sounds from both voices and instruments. Instead, the high, bright and more nasal sound of the northwestern style of folksong was considered the new standard of creation. This was mixed with smoother Western vocal production to create a new female vocal ideal that emulated the "pure, beautiful voice of a young girl" (Yi Hyŏn-ju 2006: 142–43). In both vocal and instrumental production, "people's music" developed into a synthesis of Korean and Western aesthetics, formats and ideals.

The priority remained with production and performance of "people's music," but from the 1960s onward Kim Il-sung also encouraged learning the Western musical repertoire. From the 1970s, artists were encouraged to develop new compositions for Western instruments, as long as they focused on *minjok ŭmak* first. As self-reliance became the dominant ideology, this period marked the development of more explicit political repertoire, such as the revolutionary operas discussed in the Chapter 4. Because self-reliance favored collective creation, these large-scale works were often created by collectives of artists. In this way, the socialist approach to artistic creativity privileges the power and expression of the masses and downplays the common notion of the individual artist as innovative or original.

In addition to large-scale works, such as operas, chorales and orchestral arrangements, many famous *minjok ŭmak* pieces have been arranged for a range of chamber ensembles. You can hear an example in "Song of Nostalgia" (CD track 32), arranged for Western instruments, here for marimba and piano. This arrangement is based on a song said to have been favored and sung by Kim Il-sung when he thought longingly of his homeland while fighting with the anti-Japanese guerrilla groups in Northeast China in the 1930s. This piece, an arrangement as a single movement violin concerto, serves as an effective showpiece of North Korea's symphonic mastery; it is often performed when the State Symphony Orchestra of the DPRK is invited abroad. "Song of Nostalgia" may sound predominantly Western, but its multiple narrative associations and implied lyrical content fit with the directive of putting "people's music first" while simultaneously working toward development of Western concert music styles and formats. As such, this piece stands as a good encapsulation of North Korea's approach to integrating influences from the Western concert tradition.

Even when performed instrumentally, most contemporary North Korean audiences could easily recall the lyrics of "Song of Nostalgia" immediately on hearing its hymnlike melody (Figure 5.5). A typical North Korean would also be able to recall the background story of the song, which gives voice to the struggles of the guerrilla movement, and by extension the so-called humanity and heroism of its main figure, Kim Il-sung. What makes this song even more powerful is that the "nostalgia" can be interpreted in many ways. For example, the song not only speaks of the nostalgia for one's homeland or mother but also reinforces nostalgic sentiments for the late "Great Leader," Kim Il-sung. Since the DPRK has suffered many crises since his death—floods, drought, famine

[Verse 1]
A Nae kohyang-ŭl, ttŏ naolttae   When I left my hometown
Naŭi ŏmŏni, mun apesŏ   My mother stood at the front door
Nunmul hŭllimyŏ   With tears in her eyes saying
Chal tanyŏ-ora hasidŏn malssŭm   "Come back safely"
A—kwi-ae jaengjaenghae   Ah, ah her words linger in my ear

[Verse 2]
A Taedonggangmul arŭmdaun   The beautiful waters of the Daedong
Mangyŏngdae-ŭi pom   river
Kkumgyŏledo ijŭlsu ŏpne   of Mangyŏngdae in spring
Kŭriun sanch'ŏn   Are like a dream that I cannot forget
Kwangbokŭi kŭnal   To those precious mountains and
                                          streams

A—tora karira   On the day of independence
                                          Ah, ah I will return

FIGURE 5.5   *The music and lyrics for "The Song of Nostalgia"* ("Sahyangga";
CD track 32).

and energy shortages—many North Koreans may also be wistful for the better times when its development actually surpassed that of the South.

ACTIVITY 5.8   *In "Song of Nostalgia" ("Sahyangga") you will hear the piano and marimba play through two verses of this piece on CD track 32. Listen while referring to Figure 5.5, and imagine the words being sung.*

- *In your opinion, does the melody fit the meaning of the words? Does the melody conjure up feelings of "nostalgia" for you?*
- *How does the arrangement help to convey emotion in the two verses excerpted here?*

WESTERN MUSIC AND MODERN NATIONHOOD: THE MAKING OF KOREA'S NATIONAL ANTHEMS

Toward the end of the 19th century, as Korea was moving into the modern era, the first attempt to create a national anthem began by setting a nationalist Korean text to a well-known preexisting anthem (which happened to be "God Save the Queen"). The tune was then swapped in 1896 to the Scottish folksong "Auld Lang Syne" during a ceremony commemorating the laying of the foundation stone of the Independence Gate in Seoul. This combination of text (beginning with the words *Tonghae Mulga*, or literally, "East Sea Waters") and tune did not change until the time of division, after which the new ROK and DPRK were compelled to negotiate their separate identities by crafting different anthems.

The story of the South Korean national anthem begins a little earlier than for the North, with the composer Ahn Eak-tai (1906–1965). Like many others of his generation, Ahn's life was entangled in part in the conflicting forces of colonialism, nationalism, Westernization, capitalism and World War II politics. Growing up as a young man in Pyongyang during the early colonial period, he was an active participant in the March First Independence movement that began in 1919.

These activities led to his expulsion from school, after which one of the few avenues remaining to him was to leave Korea and attend the Tokyo National School of Music (studying cello). In this way, Ahn's nationalist spirit had a way of propelling him further away from his homeland. After realizing that his return to Korea from Japan was accompanied by intense Japanese surveillance, he resolved never to return until the country was liberated.

Despite his nationalist fervor for Korea, Ahn was also drawn to things Western, especially its music. This led him to the United States, where he eventually studied at the University of Cincinnati College-Conservatory of Music. Within a matter of years he became the first Asian member of the Cincinnati Orchestra, as the first chair in cello. During this time, he began thinking about composing an original national anthem for Korea, but he soon left to study composition in Europe, where he completed the anthem that would become known as *"Aegukga"* ("Patriotic Song") in 1936. He also used the *"Aegukga"* melody in the rousing choral finale of *Symphonic Fantasia Korea*, which he debuted with the Ireland National Symphony in 1938. Ten years later, on August 15, 1948, *"Aegukga"* was performed at a ceremony celebrating the founding of the Republic of Korea and was soon accepted as its official anthem by a presidential decree from the new South Korean leader, Syngman Rhee.

Meanwhile, in North Korea, it became clear soon after the division of the peninsula that they would also need a new anthem to embody their developing revolutionary ideals. South Korea retained some continuity with the original text (*Tonghae Mulga*), which is believed to have originated in the late 19th century; North Korea chose to break from tradition and used a text written by the poet Pak Se-yŏng, who traversed into North Korea in 1946. Although both sets of lyrics call for the longevity of the nation and claim a love for landmarks such as Mt. Paektu, Pak's lyrics reflect a more socialist philosophy by emphasizing the nation as a "nest for the spirit of labor" and a "country established by the will of the people." Around the same time, the farmer turned composer Kim Wŏn Gyun began experimenting with writing music in a format designed to serve the goal of social revolution. Along these lines, he wrote the "Song of General Kim Il-sung" (1946) as well as music for the new anthem, also called *"Aegukga"* ("Patriotic Song"), which was adopted as North Korea's anthem in 1947 (Howard 2002: 961). For these accomplishments alone, Kim Wŏn Gyun is highly regarded as one of North Korea's most influential proletarian composers.

Kim's *"Aegukga"* remains the DPRK's official national anthem, but it is not considered as important domestically as the "Song of General Kim Il-sung." Although elevation of the "Song of General Kim Il-sung" is said to have been by directive from Kim Jong-il after his being named successor, I would argue that *"Aegukga's"* diminished role is also a direct reflection of the DPRK's limited emphasis on international engagement. During the New York Philharmonic's historic visit to North Korea in February 2008, it was noted that North Koreans did not display the gestures of reverence that normally accompany the playing of a national anthem. This is likely due to the North Korean *"Aegukga"* not being widely performed and usually reserved for the international contexts of visits with foreign dignitaries or large-scale competitive games such as the FIFA World Cup. This contrasts dramatically with South Korea, where its version of *"Aegukga"* is highly regarded and widely used in both domestic and international contexts. However, in comparing the cases of North and South Korea, it becomes apparent that the anthem also acts as a musical representation or negotiation of its relationship with the rest of the world.

In many ways, these anthemic stories resonate with the main themes of this volume, most notably the role of music in articulating Korea's transnational influences and activities and the powerful ways in which music becomes embroiled in politics. Interestingly, the North and South Korean anthems have become so politically charged that they cannot even be played in the "other" country (much less together in one context) without inciting major attention. Although musically the anthems possess many of the features typical of European anthems, over time Koreans have invested them with strong feelings of national identity and pride, albeit in the North a little less so. North and South Korea have carved out very different national identities since the division, yet their anthems are remarkably similar; indeed, they even share the same title. That two such similar-sounding anthems could stir such divergent emotions is a testament to the human ability to transform music. As such, they both stand as examples of how a Western musical format such as the anthem manages to transcend cultural boundaries in profound ways. In the final chapter, I continue exploring the impact of other transnational forms on Korean culture, particularly in the realm of popular culture.

ACTIVITY 5.9 *1. Find online versions of both anthems, and listen to them in the same sitting. If you read musical notation, you may also want to download the sheet music for both anthems.*

2. Musically, the two anthems share a form and chord progression that consists of an eight-bar verse that is followed by an eight-bar refrain. What other similarities do you hear in terms of the chord progression, melody, melodic contour, rhythm and tempo?

CHAPTER 6

Negotiating Transnational Flows of Culture

SHIFTS IN THE GLOBAL MEDIASCAPE

It is widely recognized that modern advancements in technology have spurred the unpredictable movements of culture. Korea is a fascinating case study in this regard because the DPRK and the ROK have responded to these cultural global flows in such contrasting ways. It should be no surprise that North Korea exerts almost total control over the kinds of outside cultural influences that enter the country, a policy that is directly linked to its adherence to the philosophy of self-reliance (*juche*). It may not be as widely known that the South Korean government also played an active hand in censoring and even banning certain cultural products from the United States and Japan. In fact, South Korea only recently lifted its ban on Japanese imports as part of a four-stage Open Door policy that was initiated in 1998 and completed in 2004 (Jung 2007: 180).

Despite these efforts to control the flows of cultural traffic, South Korea has had much more exposure than the North to outside musical influences, not only from the United States and Japan but also from a host of other less likely places such as Ireland, India, Puerto Rico, Argentina and Spain. As the global cultural landscape grows more complex, the "center-periphery" model is becoming less relevant because culture no longer simply flows from the more powerful, developed centers to the less-developed peripheries. For example, even though South Korea is not seen as a global powerhouse, it is successful in exporting cultural products overseas, a phenomenon that was dubbed initially in China as the "Korean wave." The Korean wave signals a significant global shift in which smaller countries such as South Korea increasingly disrupt past

patterns of transnational cultural traffic to compete with more powerful nations such as China and the United States (Cho Hae-Joang 2005:
178–79).

The Korean Wave

Beginning in China, Taiwan and Hong Kong and spreading quickly
to Japan and Southeast Asia (and later to South Asia, Central Asia, the
Middle East and even parts of Africa, Russia and Eastern Europe), interest in Korean culture began to rise in the late 1990s but gained notice as
a full-fledged "wave" or trend at the turn of the 21st century. This wave
continued to ebb and flow throughout the first decade, with noticeable
resurgences in 2003 and 2004 and later with the popularity of Rain,
the Wonder Girls, Se7en and Super Junior. Although Korean television
and music have not yet significantly penetrated the American, Western
European or Latin American markets, the Korean wave is certainly cap-
turing the attention of diasporic Koreans, and those interested in Asian
culture, helping to raise the international profile of Korean performers,
music and film. Korean popular music and its stars are a significant
component of the wave, but narrative visual media forms for television
and film have been an especially vital driving force. Serial TV melodramas (with their trademark ability to elicit addictive viewing behavior)
have become one of the most profitable exports of the Korean wave,
bringing in as much as $70 million dollars in a given year. This trend
also yields additional profits as Korean culture influences the realms of
fashion, cosmetics, hairstyles, gaming and mobile phone technology in
other countries.

Even though transnational networks of fans are crucial to the success
of the Korean wave, it would be nothing without its stars. In Taiwan,
the first Korean group to gain recognition was the male pop music
and dance duo CLON, who debuted in 1999 (Sung 2006: 170). Their
success opened doors for other groups such as H.O.T. ("High-Five Of
Teenagers"), NRG ("New Radiancy Group"), Baby V.O.X. ("Baby Voices
of Xpression"), S.E.S. ("Sea, Eugene, Shoo") and Shinhwa, among others.
The appeal of these bands also spread to China and Hong Kong, which
has led to successful music tours by Korean artists in these countries.
Although the Korean language proves a barrier for these artists, many
fans are drawn to Korean popular music for its high energy, dance-oriented fast tempos and the high production values of its music videos
(Sung 2006: 171–72). In Japan, the first Korean star to be groomed for
the lucrative Japanese market was BoA. However, since BoA's musical
releases there were so tailored for Japanese consumption, her Korean

identity was not initially known until she was touted as a Korean wave artist (Jung 2007: 205). Because of this, the Korean wave did not register in Japan until 2003 and 2004, with repeated broadcasts of the hit drama series "Winter Sonata."

One popular explanation for the Korean wave's regional success has to do with its promoting familiar Asian faces and more traditional themes, constituting a change from some American imports that audiences may find too edgy or alienating. In this way, Korea's geographic location and historical role as a cultural conduit (as opposed to an aggressive power) positions South Korea in a unique way to reach out to various Asian populations. This may explain the wide appeal of the Chosŏn period court drama "The Jewel in the Palace," about a talented, bright and determined female palace chef who overcomes numerous societal obstacles to become a court physician. Although the Confucian court setting is certainly accessible to any Asian country with a similar history of governance, it is the story of how the main character, Chang Kŭm, pursues a path of filial piety, excellence and justice (even if it means disrupting the established Confucian social order) that many find so compelling. For countries whose citizens struggle to reconcile the conflict between deeply entrenched cultural values and the global forces of modernity, I can see how "A Jewel in the Palace" could be read as an allegory for this common condition.

On the other end of the spectrum, as a number of Asian countries modernize and incorporate popular music elements from the United States, a pan-Asian pop music middle ground has developed. Although language remains one of the most recognizable markers distinguishing one Asian popular music style from another, incorporation of snippets of English (typically sprinkled in the choruses or intros) is swiftly becoming part of a Pan-Asian vernacular. Some Korean wave artists are capitalizing on this trend in order to begin breaking into the U.S. market, among them BoA, Rain, Super Junior and the Wonder Girls. Rain (or *Bi* in Korean) was the first to gain recognition in 2006 with his inclusion in *Time* magazine's "100 Most Influential People Who Shape Our World." Since then, he has been invited to perform in a DDR (Dance Dance Revolution) "dance-off" with Stephen Colbert in 2008, starred in the film *Speed Racer* (2008) and played the lead role in *Ninja Assassin* (2009). Because of problem-ridden music tours and a lackluster response to his U.S.-targeted 2008 singles "Rainism" and "Love Story," Rain's American musical career has not exactly lived up to the hype. Fortunately, this has not discouraged other acts from trying to make it in the United States. For example, the dynamic and youthful group

Super Junior managed to captivate some U.S. fans as one of the largest boy bands ever, debuting with as many as 12 members. In a recent surprise, the Korean female group the Wonder Girls was invited to perform in the 2009 Jonas Brothers tour, which coincided with the release of the English version of their hit song, "Nobody."

Over the course of the first decade of the 21st century, the Korean wave has attracted a lot of press, even if its international impact is somewhat small compared to similar "waves" from historically more powerful countries such as China, the United States or Japan. Those concerned with promoting Korean entertainment industries are happy to keep pushing the trend, despite any negative backlash. Critics argue that the overcommercialized nature of most of the content carries very little distinctive Korean cultural value. Some might even go so far as to say that through a combination of physical, artistic and linguistic training (not to mention cosmetic surgery) Korean wave stars are being shaped into mimics of their Western counterparts; such critics conclude that this is potentially detrimental to the Asian psyche. However, the Korean wave is more varied and unpredictable than these statements suggest, often with wide-ranging results. Many have declared the Korean wave dead several times over, but I think that it still has a few surprises in store for us.

ACTIVITY 6.1   *Select one of these Korean wave topics for a potential five-minute class presentation.*

- *Pick a solo artist such as Rain or BoA, and introduce his or her music and bio to the class.*
- *Pick one of the boy bands mentioned and analyze their music and style, paying particular attention to how they contribute to the definition of masculinity.*
- *Pick one of the girl bands mentioned and analyze their music and style, paying particular attention to how they contribute to the definition of femininity.*

K-Pop and the Influence of Seo Taiji and the Boys

In terms of music, the Korean wave could not exist without the K-pop industry. Although Koreans often refer to their own popular music by the more generic term *kayo* (literally, "song") or *taejung kayo* ("popular song"), since the early 1990s it has increasingly been called K-pop, especially abroad. It is known for dance-oriented music that is often inflected with rapping, techno or hip-hop beats as well as R&B and pop vocals. Although the K-pop industry suffered when growing piracy and copying resulted in the switch from CD to MP3 and other online technologies in the late 1990s, it also benefited from K-pop artists securing greater online access to their work from abroad. The related rise in global interest in K-pop that manifested in the Korean wave was a surprising boost; the Korean popular music industry took advantage of it as they sought to make up lost domestic profits in the expanding global market.

Although much of what constitutes K-pop today may seem relatively apolitical in nature—dealing more with relationships, love and hanging out with friends—many of today's K-pop artists owe a great deal to the overtly political star Seo Taiji, who was active in the 1990s. Although he became famous as part of the group Seo Taiji and the Boys, Seo was the main creative force while the other two members were more active as performing entertainers. With his many talents as a rock musician and guitarist, songwriter, rapper, singer, dancer/entertainer and producer, he is widely regarded as a revolutionary figure in Korean popular music. Musically, he changed the landscape of Korean pop most notably by introducing rap and hip-hop rhythms when debuting his group in 1992 with the hit *"Nan Arayo"* ("I Know"). He was also extremely creative in freely mixing samples and styles from heavy metal, techno and even Korean folk music. Though melodic ballads remain a mainstay in Korean music, Seo Taiji opened the door to a more diverse and dance-oriented K-pop landscape, stimulating the formation of a number of groups who tried to replicate his success.

Seo Taiji's impact on music was considerable, although his status as a Korean cultural icon has more to do with the way he helped to define a newly emerging youth voice associated with a vocal and confrontational younger generation coming of age in the early 1990s. Seo was able to appeal to this new generation through his style, attitude and rap-based lyrics. Although many of his influences were derived from American pop culture, he mixed and matched them to the Korean context, thereby creating a new hybrid marker of Korean youth identity. For example, in terms of style Seo Taiji and the Boys was one of the first groups to borrow directly from American hip-hop culture, donning colorful, baggy clothes and statement-making accessories. To this, they added spiky Asian hairdos, heavy metal sounds and postures and a dance-oriented performance style that portrayed a more forward and bodycentric image than the Korean public was used to seeing at the time. Lyrically, Seo Taiji and the Boys stirred controversy by delivering critical messages in several key songs, taking aim, for instance, at the oppressiveness of the Korean education system in "Classroom Idea" (*"Kyoshil idea"*) and the corruption of the government in "Regret of the Times" (*"Sidaeyugam"*). However, what set Seo Taiji apart from the previous generation of socially conscious songwriters was his embrace of high entertainment values combined with a more confrontational and in-your-face attitude. In this way, Seo Taiji was able to achieve a fusion of commerce and politics that was perfectly in sync with the new generation.

Although few groups or artists have been able to tap into the sociopolitical zeitgeist of the times as well as Seo Taiji, there is no doubt that his continuing influence is felt in K-pop. Most obviously, boy bands such as DJ DOC ("DJ Dream of Children"), H.O.T. (High-five Of Teenagers") and G.O.D ("Groove Over Dose"). followed in a similar vein by combining rap with R&B-style choruses and placing added emphasis on their dance routines in performance. In addition, the other two members of Seo Taiji and the Boys continued to be active in the music industry. In particular, Yang Hyŏn-sŏk created the music production company YG Entertainment and produced a number of successful artists and groups (including Se7en and Big Bang) who sometimes collaborate on projects under the umbrella term of YG Family. Women have also gotten into the act and formed groups such as S.E.S. ("Sea, Eugene, Shoo"), Fin.K.L ("Fine Killing Liberty"), Baby V.O.X. ("Baby Voices of Xpression"), and the Wonder Girls. Not to be excluded, solo artists such as the aforementioned BoA and Rain also capitalized on the dance-oriented K-pop formula. Although many of these artists have not taken on political topics in their songs, they do adopt the body-conscious attitudes of Seo Taiji and the Boys and take them into more sexually provocative and physically demanding directions than was considered acceptable before. In this way, the long-lasting influence of Seo Taiji on K-pop may have more to do with instigating change in the performative Korean body than in lyrical content, at least in the commercial mainstream.

MUSIC AND POWER

Although Seo Taiji's connection to the emergence of a more youthfully defiant generation in South Korea is well recognized and documented, other examples of music's entanglement with power have had just as much of an impact on Korean society. Seo Taiji's efforts reflect a confluence of supercultural (the entertainment industry) and subcultural (the new youth generation) interests; some of the other examples I introduce in this section more clearly align with one or the other. In the first example, I explore the presence of a foreign superculture in Korea during a pivotal time—namely, the American Forces in South Korea during and after the Korean War—and their role in introducing American music that was popular during the time. In the next example, I look at a dramatically different superculture at work in North Korea, by examining state-sanctioned pop songs. The last example considers songs that arose out of the subculture of the democratization movement in South Korea in the 1970s and 1980s.

> **ACTIVITY 6.2** *Write out a statement of what you consider to constitute the "subculture" and the "superculture" in the United States.*
>
> *In the context of North and South Korea, identify the musical traditions discussed in the chapter that are considered "subcultural" versus "supercultural." How does this differ from your experience with these terms?*

The Presence of American Armed Forces and the Dawn of a New Era in South Korean Pop

Although Koreans were exposed to some aspects of American popular culture in the early 20th century—either directly through foreign missionaries or filtered through the Japanese—it was the increased American military presence in the South during and after the Korean War that opened the floodgates to a new era of American influence in Korean pop. In particular, the advent of AFKN (American Forces Korea Network) radio in 1951 opened the Korean airwaves to American music consistently throughout the day. Although AFKN was targeted at American soldiers, college-age Koreans gradually began to tune in after the Korean War (1950–1953). By the late 1950s, American music was so popular that other Korean stations began to follow suit, offering their own programs featuring American pop (Maliangkay 2006: 23). It is also important to mention the powerful role that film and television played in exposing Korean audiences to American popular culture.

Through this process, South Koreans gained much more consistent access to a variety of popular genres: swing jazz, dance music (foxtrot, waltz, tango, cha cha, mambo), light vocal-based pop, blues, rhythm and blues and early rock 'n' roll. Much of the diversity encountered in this music was soon incorporated into existing Korean pop genres. For instance, *trot* benefited from the addition of exotic dance rhythms, bluesy motifs and jazzy instrumental arrangements. However, creating a completely new branch of Korean pop music based on all of these new genres would prove to take some time. In the interim, many young Koreans participated more fully by incorporating dance and other body movements into the experience of enjoying popular music. Couple-style dances such as waltz, foxtrot, mambo, cha cha and swing rose in popularity among young Koreans despite being discouraged by the government. This did not stop some Koreans from attending the clandestine dance clubs that began to appear in Seoul, opening up spaces for Koreans to embody the music through dance. The opportunity to actually perform this music came when the U.S. military began to recruit Koreans to perform in the military USO (United Service Organizations) shows for soldiers who were stationed in South Korea. Although these shows were created for American soldiers, they became well known to Koreans as the *mip'algun sho* (literally, "American Eighth Army shows"), named after the U.S. troop commanding formation that still exists today.

Although famous American entertainers made their rounds on the USO tours in Korea, there was still a great need for locals who could perform regularly at the South Korean military camps. It is important to keep in mind that the mass devastation of the Korean War had a leveling effect; there were very few Koreans, if any, who were not affected by poverty, hunger and loss. Given that Americans were spending between $80,000 and $120,000 per month on Korean entertainers, the opportunity to perform in the USO show circuit was both culturally and economically compelling (Sŏn Sŏng-wŏn 1993: 25). Consequently, the American military was able to exert its power to open up a new entertainment sphere that had not existed before.

Furthermore, the American military was able to dictate and shape the shows according to the specific needs of the male soldiers. Some talented Korean individual musicians successfully auditioned to perform for the USO shows, but many of the acts that were approved were all-female sister acts, similar in sound and format to the Andrews Sisters. It was much easier for attractive women to succeed because they could employ their looks as well as their talent to appeal to military audiences. Of the many sister acts, the best known were the Kim Sisters, the Lee Sisters, the Arirang Sisters and the Pearl Sisters. All-male groups also began to appear in the 1960s, among them the Arirang Brothers, the Key Boys, the Johnny Brothers, and the Kimchis. However, in contrast to the sister acts the all-male groups gained an edge by defining themselves more in terms of performing rock 'n' roll than light pop (Maliangkay 2006: 26). Some solo stars, notably Patty Kim and Hyŏn Mi, also got their start in USO shows. Kim, who exhibited a confident performing style and a rich and rounded vocal tone, was influential in defining a more diatonic style of pop that contrasted with the highly ornamented and nasal vocal quality of *trot*, which was still very popular at the time.

Most of these acts learned American hit songs as a matter of course; many of them maintained their Korean identity by including arrangements of Korean folksongs or other popular songs in the Korean language. For Americans, this lent a sense of Asian novelty that was not so out of place in the late 50s and early 60s. For Koreans, performing Korean material not only was more familiar but opened a pathway to "crossover" to Korean audiences as well. By the 1960s, the USO shows were a major jumping board for Korean artists to break into the domestic Korean market. In fact, the format of the USO show was used as a model for Korean television programs such as *"Sho, Sho, Sho"* ("Show, Show, Show") on KBS (Korean Broadcasting Station; Lee Young Mee 2006: 171).

The American military played a major role in shaping Korean popular music and culture after the Korean War. The USO shows and related military entertainment clubs created a market that supported Korean performers who could adapt to this foreign and very male-oriented environment. This set in motion a whole new era in Korean popular music and entertainment, one that followed American models much more closely than ever before and encouraged women, in particular, to enter the spotlight. New strains of popular music developed (such as rock 'n' roll and a light pop that Lee Young Mee refers to as "easy listening"), both of which contrasted with the more modal melodies of *trot* and *sin minyo* (Lee Young Mee 2006: 167). Successful artists were those who could flexibly adapt to both American military and Korean domestic audiences. One group was so successful that they were able to parlay their popularity into the mainland American market. This was none other than the Kim Sisters, who went on to become regulars on the Ed Sullivan and Dean Martin shows. Although the USO shows may seem like a "forgotten era" in Korean popular music, the sister and brother groups should at least be remembered as important forerunners to the immensely popular boy and girl groups of K-pop today.

ACTIVITY 6.3   *Find online videos of the Kim Sisters and the Andrews Sisters, and view a couple of each. As you are watching, take note of any similarities or differences in terms of:*

- *Dress and appearance*
- *Vocal style*
- *Performance style (just singing? or also dance and playing of instruments?)*
- *Repertoire*

After you have done this, summarize your findings and determine in what way the Kim Sisters were modeled after the Andrews Sisters and how they fashioned their own identity.

State-Sanctioned Popular Music in North Korea

For those accustomed to choosing what music they want to listen to in a free-market economy, the very notion of "state-sanctioned popular music" may seem like a contradiction in terms. In the North Korean context, however, state-sanctioned music can be seen as popular simply because it is everywhere; it is blared in public spaces, taught in the schools and piped into private living rooms. Even so, it is important to further qualify what I mean by popular music here. On the one hand, most music in North Korea is popular in the sense that it is created with the express purpose of mass consumption. Because of this, much of the North Korean music repertoire is composed in an accessible song format. On the other hand, North Korean music resists Western notions of the popular because it is not distributed in a way that is governed by commercialism or the logic of free market capitalism. Most North Korean popular music is not made primarily to generate profit, but to support and convey the ideology of the state. This conundrum suggests that there is no universal definition of popular music that works across all cultures.

In the context of North Korea, I would like to propose a more music-based definition. The popular music that I refer to may not be produced as popular music is in the West, but at least it *sounds* like it. For example, there are some obvious commonalities in instrumentation, with use of the electronic keyboards, guitar, saxophone, prominent vocals and drum set. More important, North Korean pop also draws on the rhythms, harmonic chord progressions and song structures commonly found in pop.

Unlike in many countries where there are too many popular music groups to count, the popular music of North Korea is produced mainly by just two state-sanctioned bands: the Poch'ŏnbo Electronic Ensemble and the Wangjaesan Light Music Band. Some sources also count the Mansudae Art Troupe, although they do not focus exclusively on popular music per se. Following the introduction of pop music into other communist countries such as the Soviet Union and China, these bands were created to harness the more contemporary sounds and upbeat rhythms of pop to convey state-sanctioned themes to a new proletarian generation of North Koreans. Given the highly controlled nature of this music, there is little doubt that the Poch'ŏnbo and Wangjaesan ensembles are aligned with the North Korean state-run superculture. Even as "light music," it serves as a powerful political vehicle of state ideology.

What does this music sound like? Just a decade ago, about the only way to hear this music outside the DPRK was to tune into a North Korean channel on long distance shortwave radio. If you were lucky, you might pick up exuberantly synthesized, unabashedly upbeat music with unusually polished vocals (often a high soprano with a bright tone) and zingy instrumental fills.

ACTIVITY 6.4 *In Chapter 1, you heard amateur versions of a pair of reunification-themed songs: "Glad to Meet You" ("Pan'gapsŭmnida") and "Let's Meet Again" ("Dasi Mannapsida"). Do an internet search for online videos of these same songs.*

- *Compare the videos to the versions recorded by amateur singers on CD tracks 1 and 6.*
- *Analyze the imagery and the story portrayed in the videos. What kind of story are they trying to tell about themselves? How is this similar to or different from your perceptions of North Korea?*

Apart from familiar instruments such as the guitar or keyboard, this music may sound unlike any other kind of pop music that you have ever heard before. For one, the highly polished and strikingly uniform vocal sound immediately signals an institutional or supercultural association, as opposed to the casual, individual and more subcultural sounds that are normally associated with some pop vocalists in the West. Secondly, the heavily synthesized music will likely sound "dated" or even cheesy, but the fact is, North Koreans have very little desire to copy "the West" in this regard. Given their philosophy of self-reliance, the main concern of North Korean pop producers is to create a unique sound that will serve the needs of their people. In this way, the North Koreans may have inadvertently created one of the more intriguing pop music traditions in the world.

Since North Korea's socialist stance on art extends to the music of Poch'ŏnbo and Wangjaesan, many of the topics will be familiar from earlier discussion: (1) patriotic songs that praise the country, its revolutionary history, its policies and national heritage; (2) songs that glorify the leader; (3) songs about reunification; and (4) songs about labor, work and courtship. Examples in the first category abound and include such rousing songs as "We Like Our Country the Best" and "My Great Country."

In category two, numerous songs praise Kim Il-sung; an example is "Long Live General Kim Il-sung." However, as the DPRK began to have succession anxieties toward the end of Kim Il-sung's life, many light pop songs used metaphor to help establish his lineage and "rightful" place as the new leader (Howard 2006b: 159–62). For example, many songs in the early 1990s compared Kim Il-sung to the "sun" and Kim Jong-il to the "star" in songs such as "Oh My Homeland Bright Under the Sun and Star," and "With Sunlight and Starlight at Heart" (Howard 2006b: 160).

In the mid-1990s, North Korea was hit with an unfortunate combination of natural disasters (a drought followed by typhoons, floods and famine) that followed in the wake of Kim Il-sung's death in 1994. According to Keith Howard's analysis of popular music during this time, "ideology temporarily froze with Kim Il-sung's death" and "political music gave way to the more ephemeral" (2006b: 161). Here, the "ephemeral" included instrumental music, Korean folksongs and popular foreign instrumental pieces such as the "Hungarian Rhapsody" and even "Jingle Bells." The lack of a clear ideological direction in these songs reflected the instability of Kim Jong-il's initial transition to power. To bolster his authority, his supporters began to promote the status of his mother, Kim Jong-suk, as the "mother of the nation," thereby establishing a "trinity" of father, mother and son that would weaken any threat from Kim Il-sung's other descendants (from his second wife). Musically, the emphasis on the trinity was portrayed in several songs by the Poch'ŏnbo ensemble, playing a significant role in defining North Korean leadership in a new way (162). As North Korea prepares to bolster Kim Jong-il's rumored successor, it will be interesting to see how this transition will be reflected in the music.

As we saw in Chapter 1 and in Activity 6.4, songs about reunification are also common in the popular music repertoire, such as "We are One" and "Reunification Rainbow." Significantly, I have found that in recent years the topic of reunification is central to the ideology of North Koreans, whereas South Koreans are generally more wary and less idealistic about reunification. Most of the North Korean reunification songs tend to come across as surprisingly upbeat, considering the challenges that reunification involves (for instance, "Reunification Rainbow"), but some songs, such as "Let's Meet Again," possess a sense of poignancy in referring subtly to the gulf between the desire to "meet again" and the current state of separation.

Popular music has also helped to usher in more songs about love and courtship in the DPRK and is one of the few areas that can be seen as not so overtly political. Some of the most beloved songs in this category

---

ACTIVITY 6.5 *Find online videos of the songs listed in the paragraph that begins "Popular music has also helped. . . ." If you can pair with a person who has some knowledge of Korean, please do so. If not, see what you can glean from the images and music.*

- *View the videos, and write your own interpretation of the love story being depicted.*
- *What does this story say about courtship or gender relations in North Korea?*
- *Do you find this "story" to be dramatically different from the norms of courtship or gender relations in your own culture? Why or why not?*

are "Whistle" ("*Hwiparam*"), "Urban Girls Come to Get Married" ("*Dosi ch'ŏnyŏ sijip wayo*") and "Don't Ask My Name" ("*Nae irŭm mutchi masaeyo*"). Many of these songs are refreshingly lighthearted and fun, but it is important to remember that these songs represent state-sanctioned expressions of love and courtship and therefore imply an encroachment of the political into what is normally a personal domain.

Politicization of Popular Music in South Korea: T'ong Kit'a *and the Song Movement*

As North Korea was undergoing a musical revolution in the 1980s with the introduction of popular music, South Korea was undergoing a musical revolution of its own with the development of the countercultural phenomenon known as the "song movement" (*norae undong*). The North Korean songs were composed in support of a socialist state; the South Korean song movement was aimed squarely against the military regimes that had been in place since 1961 (Park Chung-hee 1961–1979, followed by Chun Doo-hwan 1980–1988). The song movement was part of a larger struggle to democratize the government and was seen as part of the cultural arm of the *minjung* movement (see Chapter 3).

This politicization of the South Korean popular music landscape did not happen overnight, especially given that the Korean government had no qualms about banning overtly political American songs by the likes of Paul Simon, John Lennon and Bob Dylan. Even so, Koreans were able to hear other songs by this new generation of artists and quickly gained exposure to new trends such as revivalist folk and roots-inspired music. As this exposure developed, bootleg copies circulated among Korean youths. Though they may not have always understood every word of these songs, many were drawn to the simple guitar-and-voice instrumentation of folk as well as to the more communal, sing-along quality that it elicited. By the late 1960s and early 1970s, the appeal of folk grew among young people and swelled into what became known as the *t'ong kit'a* boom. With *t'ong* meaning "box" and *kit'a* meaning "guitar," the term calls attention to the simple acoustic guitar instrumentation. *T'ong kit'a* music was the most important precursor to the song movement.

Unlike American sources of inspiration, *t'ong kit'a* lyrics were for the most part pretty benign and apolitical. This was most likely due to the harsh environment of censorship during the Park Chung-hee regime. The few artists who dared to perform or compose songs with lyrics that were critical of the social or political climate were penalized, and sometimes even put in jail. Therefore omission of political lyrics can be seen as a strategic move by artists who sought to appeal to the mainstream. A good example of the success of this strategy can be seen in the 1970s hit "Saturday Night" ("*T'oyoil pam*") by Kim Se-hwan.

Although *t'ong kit'a* may have fell short of being revolutionary in terms of lyrics, it was revolutionary in terms of its performance practices. The fact that *t'ong kit'a* became so popular in this era is astonishing given that it presented a completely different mode of engagement with popular music. For one, the most successful singers belonged to an entirely new breed of entertainer. Because of this, singers used a more "natural," untrained voice and a bare, down-to-earth performance style. In this way, *t'ong kit'a* was a compelling alternative to both slick American pop and the more theatrical and ornamented *trot* music style. According to Okon Hwang, another key to the appeal of *t'ong kit'a* was its participatory nature; in other words, it was music meant to be *sung* as much as listened to (Hwang 2006: 37). In fact, this participatory quality would later prove to be critical in the song movement as well.

Also striking about *t'ong kit'a* is that the major figures were almost all college-age students. Although they attended the nation's most prestigious universities (many of them were classmates at the same school), most were not professionally trained in music. One of the most influential members of this group was Kim Min-gi, who distinguished himself from his peers by courageously expressing powerful political statements in his music and performances. In addition, he was also an exceptional composer and lyricist, writing a body of songs that were trenchant in their social commentary but also pure in spirit and rich in nature-inspired figurative language. One of his most famous songs is "Morning Dew" ("*Ach'im Isŭl*"), which was released in 1971 and sung initially by Yang Hŭi-ŭn. In this poem (translated in Figure 6.1), the "long night" refers to Korea's history of colonization, conflict and military occupation, which contributes to a collective feeling of sorrow. Imagining this sorrow as something that forms like a "drop of morning dew" on "every blade of grass" accentuates how profoundly every Korean has been defined by this history. At the same time, the transience and fragility of morning dew also suggests that this is a history that can be overcome. In essence, "Morning Dew" is an eloquent song of hope acknowledging death and suffering but also suggesting the possibility of transformation.

Kin pam chisaeugo p'ulipmada
Maetch'in chinjuboda tŏ ko-un ach'im
isŭl ch'ŏrŏm
/ae ...am-e sŏlumi arari maetch'il ttae

...sane olla
...misorŭl pae-unda
cha..yang'ŭn myoji wi-ae bulgke ttŏ-
t'..rŭgo
han-najŭi tchinŭn tŏwinŭn na-ŭi
siryŏn-ilchira
Na ije kanora chŏ kŏch'in kwangya-e
Sŏrŏ-um modu pŏrigo na ijae kanora

Passing a long night without sleep,
pure drops of morning dew, more
precious than pearls,
glisten from every blade of grass
like beads of sorrow that form on my
soul.
As I climb up the hill in the morning
I study the small impressions of a smile.
The sun casts its red glow
over the cemetery
By midday, its heat will be my trial.

I go now, tossing away all of my grief,
as I pass through the wilderness, I go.

FIGURE 6.1 "Morning Dew" ("Ach'im Isŭl"). Music and lyrics by Kim Min-gi.

Although Kim Min-gi fits squarely with the t'ong kit'a generation of singers, his willingness to put his political beliefs on the line makes him more of a transitional figure who was equally important to the song movement. Even though the song movement did not begin to coalesce until 1980s, almost a decade after Kim first wrote "Morning Dew," his music was still considered highly relevant to those involved in it.

Building on t'ong kit'a performance practices, the song movement grew out of participatory sing-along gatherings organized by students and other community groups. In terms of creative production, the focus shifted from the individual artist to group-oriented collaboration. Although these groups began singing mostly t'ong kit'a songs, they soon came to view music as a vehicle for social change and began adapting their own lyrics to existing songs, or writing completely new ones. Given the continuing oppressive cultural policies of the military regime under Chun Doo-hwan, the song movement was largely an underground phenomenon. In addition, many of its members were avidly anticommercial and believed that mainstream popular music promotes an escapist, overly sentimental colonial mentality.

As student members of college singing circles began to graduate, some of the leading members saw a need to extend their activities beyond the college campus. Mun Sŭnghyŏn recruited some of the most promising former members of various college singing circles and created a music organization called Saepyŏk, or "Dawn." Their first album, "People Seeking Songs" (*"Noraerŭl ch'atnŭn saramdŭl"*) was produced by Kim Min-gi and released in 1984 to become a substantial hit. Its surprising success drew attention to the possibilities of fusing activism with song and was an early sign of things to come. As opposition to the military regime swelled in the 1980s, especially in the wake of the Kwangju Uprising (1980; recall the discussion in Chapter 3), the democratization movement became a mainstream phenomenon that the majority of Korean young people supported. This opened up a rare opportunity for song movement practitioners to take the spotlight, even if only for a passing moment in history.

One of the first to take advantage of this moment was a splinter group from *Saepyŏk*, who called themselves Noraerŭl Ch'atnŭn Saramdŭl ("People Seeking Songs," hereafter Noch'atsa for short), building on the success of the aforementioned album of the same name. By collaborating with a range of very talented artists, Noch'atsa recorded some of the most beloved songs of the movement, many of which became so popular that they were covered by numerous other artists and are still sung today in Korean karaoke establishments. They include (1) "Pine Tree, Pine Tree, Green Pine Tree" (*"Sora Sora Purŭrŭn Sora"*); (2) "In the Wilderness" (*"Kwangya-esŏ"*); and (3) "When That Day Comes" (*"Kŭnari omyŏn"*). The first two songs rank among the most popular songs from the movement of all time. In fact, more than a decade later, "Pine Tree, Pine Tree, Green Pine Tree" was even covered by the respected Korean rapper, MC Sniper (CD track 33).

As the song movement developed, groups such as Noch'atsa moved beyond the traditional solo guitar accompaniment of *t'ong kit'a* and experimented with incorporating various genres, styles and instruments. Joung Taechoon (regarded as a "brother" to those in the Noch'atsa family) experimented with fusing Western and Korean instrumentation in the song "Going Home to My Hometown" (*"Kohyangjip Kasae"*), recorded in 1988 (Figure 6.2). Here, Joung seamlessly weaves a simple *puk* drum accompaniment and solo *p'iri* with intricate guitar parts and soft keyboards in the verses. He creates further timbral interest and dynamic movement by playing with the tempo and adding *p'ansori*-style voices, bells and a small gong or *soe* part in the subsequent refrains and interludes (CD track 34). Lyrically, this song is not directly political, but

FIGURE 6.2 *Song movement (*norae undong*) performer/composer Joung Taechoon. (Photo courtesy of Joung Taechoon.)*

ACTIVITY 6.6 *Listen to the first 30 seconds of MC Sniper's version of "Pine Tree, Pine Tree, Green Pine Tree" (CD track 33). Note that the* cappella *introduction is sung much in the way song movement practitioners would have sung it at a college gathering. Follow along with the words printed below and reflect on the following:*

- *Many of the lyrics of the song movement are full of figurative language. In this context, circle the words or phrases that may serve as good examples of metaphor, imagery, metonymy, etc. Then analyze each example and make an interpretation of what the whole refrain might mean in the context of the struggles of the song movement.*

Sora sora purŭrŭn sora	*Pine tree, pine tree, green pine tree*
Saetparame ttŏlchimara	*Do not tremble in the easterly wind*
Ch'angsal-arae naega mukkinkot	*Beneath the bars where I am tied*
Sarasŏ mannarira	*Let us meet in order to live*

together with the melding of Korean instruments and timbres, Joung makes a compelling and hopeful statement about not forgetting the value and meaning of one's culture, home and family, especially amid rising urbanization.

As introduced in Chapter 1, the song "From Seoul to Pyongyang," by Kkottaji, is an intriguing example of a reunification song that pushes not only national boundaries but boundaries of genre as well (CD track 8). Written in the style of the *trot* (or *ppongtchak*), this song also demonstrates the tendency toward experimenting with multiple genres. Given the undeniable Japanese influences in *trot*, writing in this style was quite controversial in the song movement and elicited what became known as the *"ppongtchak* debate." What is interesting here is that genres can carry

ACTIVITY 6.7   *Listen to "Going Home to My Hometown"* *("Kohyangjip Kasae"), by Joung Taechoon (CD track 34).*

- *See if you can differentiate among the verses, chorus and instrumental interlude, and take note of their timings.*
- *Then make sure that you can identify the sounds of the bells, puk, p'iri and kkwaenggwari and take note of where they occur in the song.*
- *Then compare the voices in the recording. How would you characterize the lead male voice versus the second voice that comes in on the choruses?*
- *In terms of genre, how would you categorize this song?*

extremely loaded political associations. On the one hand, some critics felt that the nostalgic sentimentality of *trot* and its nonnative associations were inappropriate for a politically progressive movement that sought to revolutionize society and move beyond a colonial past. On the other hand, groups such as Kkottaji felt they could reach out to a crucial segment of the "people" (especially older people and the working class) by performing in the *trot* style.

The song movement was unique in that it was defined more by its commitment to a political sensibility than to a singular musical genre, sound or style. Even though the practitioners of the song movement did not see significant changes in all of the areas that they sang about, the politicization of popular music that was set in motion by the *t'ong kit'a* and song movements was still quite remarkable. In terms of democratizing the government, at no other time in Korean history have the political and musical aspirations of the people come together so successfully to bring about major change.

CULTURAL CONTINUITY IN KOREAN POPULAR MUSIC: INDEXING "TRADITION" IN KOREAN HIP-HOP

Decades after its inception in the Bronx, hip-hop continues to invigorate the popular music landscape in South Korea with its sounds, style, dance moves and transnational modes of musical production. Korean b-boy crews (break-dancers), such as the Gamblerz, T.I.P., Last for One, Expression and Extreme Crew, grabbed the international spotlight by winning top prizes in the prestigious Battle of the Year competition in the first decade of the 21st century. Since the onset of Korean hip-hop in the early 1990s with Seo Taiji and the Boys, Korean hip-hop artists have consistently strived to create cultural continuity in their work. They have done so by indexing, sampling or re-creating sounds that are heard as "traditional" or that otherwise represent a Korean or Asian cultural identity.

Despite the desire to localize hip-hop and incorporate traditional influences, this process has not come easily. This is because of fundamental differences in language, rhythm, sociocultural attitudes, popular market tendencies and censorship practices. Linguistically, Korean rappers have faced challenges in adapting the rich patterns of rhyming and rhythmic flow, so characteristic of rap, to a language that features a radically different approach to syntax, prosody and poetry. Korean hip-hop artists also have to work around some significant incompatibilities between Korean music and hip-hop. Kinesthetically, Korean break-dancers have collaborated with performers of traditional percussion band music and dance forms, such as *p'ungmul* and *samulnori* (see Chapter 3), to exploit some spectacular compatibilities in their respective footwork, rhythmic drive and powerful, acrobatic movements.

One of the main challenges in creating meaningful rhymes and intriguing patterns of emphasis in Korean rap is that there is very little precedent for this type of linguistic play in the Korean language. Korean poetry tends to be based on an underlying segmental and rhetorical structure (see the discussion of *sijo* in Chapter 4); it is not based on dynamic patterns of stressed and unstressed syllables as in iambic tetrameter or sequences of rhymed couplets. Despite this, some Korean rappers take inspiration from folk vernacular forms, such as *minyo* (folksong) lyrics, to create a unique flow in their raps. Text repetition or call-and-response, as heard in folksongs such as *"Ong haeya,"* can also create flow in rap and be catchy as well. In this way, Korean rappers incorporate text repetition into the bridge or refrain sections of their songs. Rappers have also made good use of folk vernacular syllables that are either percussive or onomatopoetic in nature. In a song called *"Aradiho,"* Drunken Tiger uses text repetition and creatively plays on the folk vernacular syllables and lyrics of the well-known *"Arirang"* folksongs (CD track 35; see also the lyrics in Figure 4.1, and refer to CD tracks 3 and 22).

Musically, differences in the rhythms of hip-hop and Korean music also pose a challenge for Korean hip-hop artists. Korean rhythms are both a lure and an obstacle for Korean hip-hop artists. This is due to the triplet underpinning of most Korean rhythms; it has not been easy to integrate Korean rhythms with hip-hop beats. For example, in an early attempt by Seo Taiji in the song *"Hwansang sok-ŭi kŭdae"* (literally, "You in the Illusion"), a *samulnori* sample is used to open up the track, only to transition quickly into a whimsical interlude punctuated by the wily voice of Bart Simpson, which is then followed by a driving techno beat. At best, you are left with a fleeting impression of "traditional" music being part of a larger pastiche. Perhaps the best attempt to exploit the potential compatibilities between Korean rhythmic traditions and hip-hop sensibilities was initiated by the Samul-Nori master himself, Kim Duk Soo. Not only are the rhythms of the *samulnori* style selected by Kim Duk Soo to coordinate with hip-hop beats, but the movements of the standing style (with its acrobatic turns and *sangmo* streamer play) also echo the movements of the b-boys, creating a spectacular synergy of kinesthesia in space (see video on the companion website). Because of its visual and sonic appeal, this is one of the most tangible examples of how Koreans have bridged the national and the transnational to create a truly "glocal," comprehensive artistic expression.

In terms of instrumentation and vocals, Korean hip-hop artists draw on a range of sounds that are easily coded as "Korean" but also fit well within the conventions and recent trends of hip-hop. The most common of these are the plucked sounds of the *kayagŭm* zither, the expressive and flexible bowed sounds of the *haegŭm* and the wailing flourishes of the *t'aep'yŏngso* conical double reed. Initially, these sounds were sampled, but as "crossover" has become more acceptable for Korean instrumentalists live studio recording is more common, resulting in more sophisticated arrangements and richer sound quality. Nice examples of this can be heard in Seo Taiji's use of the *t'aep'yŏngso* in *"Hayŏga,"* which can be found online, and MC Sniper's incorporation of the *kayagŭm* in the relatively well-known hit called "Korean Person" (*"Hangugin,"* CD track 36). *P'ansori*-style vocals have also been sampled into hip-hop songs; in *"Sŏsa"* ("Written Word") the hip-hop artist One Sun incorporates a *p'ansori* excerpt from the soundtrack of Im Kwon-taek's film *Sŏp'yŏnje* (see Chapter 4, CD track 37). However, because the compound rhythm is not compatible with hip-hop beats, he does not continue the sample beyond the introduction.

ACTIVITY 6.8   *Listen carefully to the Korean hip-hop examples in this section (CD tracks 33, 35, 36 and 37).*

- *Identify the Korean instruments or rapping techniques that can be heard in these tracks, and note their timings.*
- *Also take note of the sampling techniques, timbres, rhythms and vocal styles that are similar to American hip-hop practices.*
- *On the basis of these observations, do you think Korean hip-hop has developed its own distinct sound? Why or why not?*

In another interesting development, Korean hip-hop artists also create a sense of cultural continuity, not only by referencing so-called traditional Korean sounds but also by drawing on other *syncretic* and transnational genres such as *trot* and the song movement. For example, in the intro to "Pine Tree, Pine Tree, Green Pine Tree" ("*Sora, Sora Purŭrŭn Sora*") MC Sniper invokes the raw emotion of the song movement simply by having the tune sung by a ragged, solo male voice in his powerful cover version (CD track 33). In this way, creating cultural continuity cannot be understood solely as a nationalist or nativist impulse but must also be examined from a situated yet broader geopolitical perspective.

MOVING BEYOND "TRADITION" IN THE MUSIC OF JANG GOON

Although many accomplished artists have contributed to creating a sense of cultural continuity in their work, I would like to end this chapter by introducing one more performer into the mix; she goes by the name of Jang Goon. With a moniker that means the "General," Jang Goon projects a striking, alternative image of womanhood in modern-day South Korea (Figure 6.3). While on a path of training in *p'ansori*, Jang Goon decided she wanted to make Korean music more accessible to the wider public. With this in mind, she is unafraid to mix Korean roots music with the gamut of genres, including *trot*, pop, rock, punk, jazz, reggae, and ska. Because *p'ansori* training requires development of a wide palette of timbres in the voice, Jang Goon has been able to adapt her voice to almost any style. In her song "*Ninano*," from her 2007 album of the same name, she energetically combines pop and *minyo*-style

FIGURE 6.3 *Jang Goon performing on stage with the Korean-dub fusion group* Djangdan. *(Photo courtesy of Jang Goon.)*

vocals over a funky 4/4 ensemble groove. She then picks up a small gong (*soe*) and transitions seamlessly into a 6/8 Korean rhythm and melodic feel during the chorus and instrumental interlude (CD track 38). Recently, she has become more deeply involved in combining the "roots" musics of Jamaica and Korea and has joined the Korean reggae/ dub band Djangdan. What makes many of these unlikely experiments work is Jang Goon's effusive presence and fearless artistic spirit as a performer. Perhaps most important, the work of people like her remind us that Korean music need not be perceived only as "tradition." Instead, I believe it should be viewed as a living, breathing body of expression that will always represent the diverse and changing needs of the people, even in a closed and slowly changing society such as North Korea.

Glossary

∞

Aak   Ritual court music of Chinese structure and origin

Aerophone   Instruments whose primary sound-producing medium is vibrating air

Ajaeng   Zither with seven twisted silk strings, bowed with a rosined stick of forsythia wood in court music; the version used in *sanjo* has eight strings and is sometimes bowed with a horsehair bow

Aniri   Spoken narration or dialogue in the context of the story-singing *p'ansori* genre

Appoggiatura   In Korean music, an embellishing or "leaning" note that seeks to resolve to a more weighted or central tone

Arirang   Legendary mountain pass that is the subject of numerous Korean folksongs such as *"Arirang," "Chindo Arirang"* and *"Miryang Arirang"*

Ch'angga   Western-style song deriving from Japanese, American or European models of children's songs, hymns, anthems, folksongs and popular songs

Ch'anggŭk   Staged Korean musical theater form with multiple performers playing individual parts, drawing on the techniques and repertoire of *p'ansori*

Ch'angjak kugak   Newly composed music written for Korean instruments using Korean idioms

Ch'uimsae   Shouts of encouragement such as *"olshigu!"* that are interjected by performers and audience members during a performance

Ch'uk   Wooden box idiophone that is played by placing a stick into its center cavity; used in ritual court music

Chajinmori   Fast tempo, rhythmic cycle or movement in 12/8 meter, see Activity 3.4

Changdan   Rhythmic cycle or rhythmic grouping of accented and unaccented beats

Changgo   Two-headed hourglass drum played with a thin stick on the right head and a hand or wood-tipped mallet on the left

Chapsaek Archetypal character players who perform as part of a *p'ungmul* troupe; include the hunter, monk, aristocrat, grandmother and maiden

Chi Transverse flute with a raised mouthpiece, derived from China and used in Confucian ritual music

Chindo Ssikkim-kut Cleansing of the dead; rituals performed by shamans on Chindo Island

Ching Large gong

Chingo Large barrel drum with tacked-on heads, used in court ritual music

Chinyangjo Slow tempo, rhythmic cycle or movement in 18/8 meter, see Activity 3.4

Chŏk Vertically played flute in Confucian ritual music

Chŏlgo Large barrel drum suspended at a slight angle, played in court ritual music

Chŏllima undong "Galloping horse movement," a North Korean state ideology that emphasizes rapid economic development

Chordophone Instrument whose primary sound-producing medium is a vibrating string

Chungin Middle-class professionals, including merchants, craftpersons and technicians

Chungjungmori Moderate tempo, rhythmic cycle or movement in 12/8 meter, see Activity 3.4

Chungmori Moderately slow tempo, rhythmic cycle or movement in 12/8 meter, see Activity 3.4

Compound meter Meter in which each beat subdivides into three equal counts/pulses

Enka Nostalgic Japanese popular song genre

Erhu Two-string fretless bowed lute, played vertically

Glissandos A sustained slide up or down from one pitch to another

Grace note Ornamental note that "graces" or embellishes a pitch

Guqin Seven-string plucked Chinese zither, also referred to as the *qin*

Haegŭm Two-string fretless spiked lute that is played vertically with a bow threaded between the two strings, similar to the Chinese *erhu*

Hallyu Term for the "Korean wave" that references the popularity of Korean cultural products beyond South Korea's borders

Han Aesthetic trope of grief, suffering or longing

Han'gŭl Korean alphabetic writing system

Heterophony "Different voices"; musical texture of one melody performed almost simultaneously and somewhat differently by multiple musicians

Hun Globe-shaped clay ocarina played in Confucian ritual music

Hwimori Fast tempo, rhythmic cycle or movement in 4/4 meter, see Activity 3.4

Hyangak Native court music performed in a variety of contexts, including ceremonies, banquets and processionals

Idiophone Instrument whose vibrating body is the primary sound-producing medium

Ingan munhwajae "Human cultural treasure"; a person who has been appointed to transmit a genre designated for preservation as an Intangible Cultural Property; also known as a "holder" or *poyuja*

Juche North Korean philosophy of self-reliance, viewed by North Koreans as central to their continued survival as a socialist nation

Kagok Lyric art-song tradition set to the three-line *sijo* poetic form; pieces are arranged in suites and result in a more varied repertoire than that of *sijo-ch'ang*

Kasa Narrative lyric art-song tradition

Kayagŭm Twelve-string plucked zither with strings made of twisted silk; other versions have been made with more strings (of various materials), such as the North Korean 21-string *kayagŭm* and the South Korean 17-string *kayagŭm*

Kayo Korean popular song

Kisaeng Female courtesan or female entertainer

Kkwaenggwari Small gong, also called the *soe*

Komagaku Pieces of imperial court music imported from Korea and Manchuria

Kŏmungo Six-string zither played by striking or plucking the strings with a pencillike stick

Kugak (Gugak) "National music"; a South Korean term referring to Korean music performed on Korean instruments

Kŭm Seven-string zither identical to the Chinese *guqin*

Kut Shamanistic ritual gatherings, performances or ceremonies

Kutkŏri Moderately fast tempo, rhythmic cycle or movement in 12/8 meter, See Activity 3.4

Kwangdae Itinerant folk entertainers

Kyemyŏnjo Musical mode with a plaintive, sorrowful sound

Kyŏnggi minyo Folksongs from the central region of Korea in the environs of Kyŏnggi province

Madang Spatial, temporal and aesthetic concept referring respectively to an open courtyard or field, an occasion in time, or a shared space of embodied participation; see also *p'an*

Membranophone Instrument whose primary sound-producing medium is a vibrating membrane

Meter Regular grouping of beats

Minjok ŭmak "People's music"; North Korean national music that is a synthesis of European and North Korean instruments, aesthetics and forms

Minjung "People"; refers to the spirit and consciousness of the "common people" or working class

Minyo Folksong

Mode Generally, pitch material for melody bearing particular expressive qualities

Monophony "One voice"; musical texture of a single melodic line and nothing else

Mudang Ritual specialist or shaman who mediates between the human and spirit/cosmological realms; in Korea, the two main types are spirit-appointed and hereditary shamans

Nabal Valveless long-necked bugle used in *p'ungmul*

Namdo minyo Folksongs from the Southern provinces

Nodo Confucian ritual instrument consisting of two small barrel drums mounted on a pole that is rotated to activate two knotted ropes that hit the drumheads

Nogo Confucian ritual instrument consisting of two large barrel drums mounted at right angles to each other and played with a single mallet

Nong Subtle inflection of single tones within a melody

Nongak "Farmer's music"; refers to rural percussion band music and dance, also called *p'ungmul*

Norae undong "Song movement"; countercultural musical movement of the 1970s and 1980s, not limited to one style of popular music

Norae-kut "Song ceremony"; a rhythmic series within the Honam Chwado P'ilbong *p'ungmul* tradition that includes call-and-response singing

Noraebang "Song room"; a Korean-style karaoke establishment that caters to groups who sing in individual rooms

Ŏ Tiger-shaped wooden scraper with serrated spine

Ogwangdae "Five Entertainers"; used as a name to characterize some styles of mask dance drama such as Kosŏng *Ogwangdae*

Ostinato   Constantly recurring melodic, rhythmic or harmonic motive

Ryu   Traditional style, teaching group or school

P'an   Spatial, temporal and aesthetic concept referring respectively to an open field or marketplace, an occasion in time, or a shared space of embodied participation and entertainment; see also *madang*

P'an-kut   *P'ungmul* performance that takes place in the *p'an* for the purposes of entertainment

P'ansori   An oral narrative genre in which a single performer employs singing, narration, dialogue and dramatic gesture, accompanied by a solo *puk* drum

P'arŭm   Corresponds with the Chinese *bayin*, "eight sounds" philosophy of classifying instruments into the eight natural materials of bamboo, wood, metal, silk, skin, stone, gourd and clay

P'iri   Keyless cylindrical double-reed oboe

P'ungmul   Rural percussion band music and dance

P'yŏn'gyŏng   Set of 16 L-shaped stone chimes used in ritual court music

P'yŏnjong   Set of 16 elliptical bronze bells used in ritual court music

Pak   Wooden clapper instrument used in court music

Pallim   Dramatic gesture in *p'ansori*

Pangch'ang   Popular North Korean revolutionary opera songs that are sung off-stage and meant to draw the audience deeper into the drama

Panghyang   Set of 16 iron-slab chimes played in royal ancestral ritual music

Pentatonic   Systematic set of five pitches

Pip'a   Imported West Asian lute with a distinctive pear shape

Polyphonic   "Multiple voices"; musical texture of two or more melodic parts performed together

Poyuja   "Holder"; a person who has been appointed to transmit a genre designated for preservation as an Intangible Cultural Property

Ppongtchak   Dramatic and nostalgic popular song genre believed to be derived from Japanese *enka*; also called *trot*

Pu   Clay vessel that is played with a bundle of split bamboo, in Confucian ritual music

Puk   Two-headed barrel drum, with heads that are either strung with ropes or tacked on

Saenap   Conical double-reed instrument; the North Korean version is fitted with Western-style keys whereas the South Korean version remains keyless

Samulnori   Virtuosic, entertainment-oriented percussion genre derived from *p'ungmul*

Sanjo   "Scattered melodies"; an instrumental genre featuring a solo instrumentalist who plays through a series of rhythmic cycles or *changdan* with *changgo* accompaniment

Scale   Pitch set (and therefore intervals) presented in straight ascending or descending order

Shaman   Ritual specialist who mediates among the human, spirit and cosmological realms to maintain harmony, peace, abundance, good health, etc.

Sijo   Three-line poetic form

Sijo-ch'ang   Lyric art song genre sung to the *sijo* poetic form; each song is relatively slow in tempo and short in overall duration

Simple meter   Meter in which each beat subdivides into two equal counts/pulses

Sin minyo   "New folksongs"; a hybrid popular song genre emerging in the 1930s that drew upon Korean folksongs as well as foreign styles of popular music

Sinawi   Genre featuring multiple instrumentalists who improvise simultaneously through a series of rhythmic cycles or *changdan*; derives from shamanist ritual music and dance

So   Panpipe of 16 notched bamboo pipes arranged in a row from shortest to longest and held in a wooden frame; used in Confucian ritual music

Sŏdosori   Folksongs from the northwestern provinces

Soe   Small metal gong, another term for the *kkwaenggwari*

Sogo   Small handheld drum with two heads, played in a *p'ungmul* ensemble

Sogŭm   Small transverse flute

Sori   "Sound"; refers to singing, especially in *p'ansori*

Sŭl   Twenty-five-string zither imported from China, featuring a painted soundboard made of paulownia wood

T'ong kit'a   "Box guitar," a song genre that favors simple acoustic guitar accompaniment; popular with students in the 1960s and 1970s

T'aep'yŏngso   Conical double-reed with a metal bell, same as the South Korean *saenap*

T'ŭkchong   Single, elliptical bronze bell used in Confucian ritual music

T'ŭkgyŏng   Single stone-slab chime used in Confucian ritual music

Taegŭm   Large transverse flute possessing a membrane that vibrates when played

Taejung kayo   Popular song

Tala   Term for India's system for organizing measured musical time

Tan'ga   "Short song" used as a warm-up for a *p'ansori* performance

Tangak   Ensemble music of Chinese origin performed in a Koreanized style, mainly in a variety of nonritual court contexts

Tanso   Vertical flute

Tasŭrŭm   unmetered prelude

Through-composed   Structure in which musical content changes from beginning to end of a selection with little or no repetition

Tôgaku   Pieces of imperial court music from in and south and west of China

Trot   Dramatic and nostalgic popular song genre, believed to be derived from Japanese *enka*; also called *ppongtchak* and pronounced *t'ŭrot'ŭ*

Weighted scale   A set of pitches where individual tones carry different "weights" or characteristic ornamental tendencies

Yak   Vertically played flute, used in Confucian ritual music

Yang-ak   Music composed for Western instruments in a Western style

Yangban   Member of the elite, aristocratic class

Yŏnŭm   Ornamental connecting figures

Zheng   Twelve- or 13-string plucked Chinese zither, also called the *guzheng*

References

Abelmann, Nancy. 1996. *Echoes of the Past, Epics of Dissent: A South Korean Social Movement*. Berkeley: University of California Press.

Allenby, David. 2009. "Unsuk Chin: Interview About Cello and Sheng Concertos." http://www.boosey.com/cr/news/11843 (accessed on August 1, 2010).

Cho Chae-sŏn. 1992. *Aspects of Melodic Formation and Structural Analysis in Sujech'ŏn*. Seoul: Soo Shu Won Press.

Cho Hae-Joang. 2006. "Reading the 'Korean Wave' as a Sign of Global Shift." *Korea Journal* (Winter): 147–82.

Choi Chungmoo. 1995. "The Minjung Culture Movement and the Construction of Popular Culture in Korea." In *South Korea's Minjung Movement: The Culture and Politics of Dissidence*, ed. Kenneth M. Wells, 105–18. Honolulu: University of Hawai'i Press.

Choi Jai-Keun. 2007. *The Korean Church Under Japanese Colonialism*. Seoul: Jimoondang.

Cumings, Bruce. 1997. *Korea's Place in the Sun: A Modern History*. New York: Norton.

De Marinis, Marco. 1993. *The Semiotics of Performance*, trans. Aine O'Healy. Bloomington: Indiana University Press.

Dilling, Margaret Walker. 2001. "The Script, Sound and Sense of the Seoul Olympic Ceremonies." In *Contemporary Directions: Korean Folk Music Engaging the Twentieth Century and Beyond*, 173–234.

Finchum-Sung, Hilary. 2006. "New Folksongs: *Shin Minyo* of the 1930s." In *Korean Pop Music: Riding the Wave*, ed. Keith Howard, 10-20. Folkestone, UK: Global Oriental.

Gold, Lisa. 2004. *Music in Bali: Experiencing Music, Expressing Culture*. New York: Oxford University Press.

Griffiths, Paul. 2003. "An Introduction to the Music of Unsuk Chin." http://www.boosey.com/pages/cr/composer/composer_main.asp?composerid=2754&ttype=INTRODUCTION&ttitle=In%20Focus (accessed on August 1, 2010).

Hesselink, Nathan. 1996. "*Changdan* Revisited: Korean Rhythmic Patterns in Theory and Contemporary Performance Practice." In *Han'guk Ŭmak*

Yŏngu [Studies in Korean Music] 24: 143–155.

———. 2006. *P'ungmul: South Korean Drumming and Dance.* Chicago: University of Chicago Press.

Howard, Keith. 1995. *Korean Musical Instruments.* Hong Kong and New York: Oxford University Press.

———. 1999. "*Minyo* in Korea: Songs of the People and Songs for the People." *Asian Music* 30/2: 1–38.

———. 2002. "Contemporary Genres." In *The Garland Encyclopedia of World Music: East Asia,* ed. Robert C. Provine, Yosihiko Tokumaru, and J. Lawrence Witzleben, 951–74. New York and London: Routledge.

———. 2006a. *Creating Korean Music: Tradition, Innovation and the Discourse of Identity: Perspectives on Korean Music Volume 2.* Burlington, VT: Ashgate.

———. 2006b. "The People Defeated Will Never Be United: Pop Music and Ideology in North Korea." In *Korean Pop Music: Riding the Wave,* ed. Keith Howard, 154–67. Folkestone, UK: Global Oriental.

———, Chaesuk Lee and Nicholas Casswell. 2008. *Korean Kayagum Sanjo: A Traditional Instrumental Genre.* (SOAS Musicology Series.) Burlington, VT: Ashgate.

Hwang, Okon. 2006. "The Ascent and Politicization of Pop Music in Korea: From the 1960s to the 1980s." In *Korean Pop Music: Riding the Wave,* ed. Keith Howard, 34–47. Folkestone, UK: Global Oriental.

Jung, Eun-Young. 2007. "Transnational Cultural Traffic in Northeast Asia: The 'Presence' of Japan in Korea's Popular Music Culture." Ph.D. dissertation, University of Pittsburgh.

Kim Jee-Hyun. 2008. "East Meets West: Isang Yun's *Gagok* for Voice, Guitar and Percussion." Ph.D. dissertation, Arizona State University.

Kim Jong-Il. 1982. "On the *Juche* Idea." http://www1.korea-np.co.jp/pk/062nd_issue/98092410.htm (accessed on August 10, 2010).

———. 1995 [1971]. "The Revolutionary Opera *The Sea of Blood* Is a New Opera of a Type of Our Own." In *Kim Jong-il: Selected Works* (2), 263–68. Pyongyang, Korea: Foreign Languages Publishing House.

Kirshenblatt-Gimblett, Barbara. 1995. "Theorizing Heritage." *Ethnomusicology* 39/3: 367-380.

Lau, Frederick. 2007. *Music in China: Experiencing Music, Expressing Culture.* New York: Oxford University Press.

Lee Bo-hyung. 2002. "Korean Religious Music: Shamanic." In *The Garland Encyclopedia of World Music: East Asia,* ed. Robert C. Provine, Yosihiko Tokumaru, and J. Lawrence Witzleben, 875–78. New York and London: Routledge.

Lee, Byong won. 1987. *Buddhist Music of Korea.* Seoul: Jungeumsa.

Lee, Katherine. 2009. "P'ungmul, Politics, and Protest: Drumming During South Korea's Democratization Movement." Paper presented at the

Annual Meeting of the Society for Ethnomusicology, Mexico City.

Lee Young Mee. 2006. *Han'guk Taejung kayosa* [Korean Popular Song History]. Seoul: Minsok-won.

Maliangkay, Roald. 2006. "Supporting Our Boys: American Military Entertainment and Korean Pop Music in the 1950s and Early-1960s." In *Korean Pop Music: Riding the Wave*, ed. Keith Howard, 148–61. Folkestone, UK: Global Oriental.

McCann, David. 1988. *Form and Freedom in Korean Poetry.* Leiden: Brill.

Mitchell, Tony. 2001. *Global Noise: Rap and Hip Hop Outside the USA.* Middletown, CT: Wesleyan University Press.

Park, Chan E. 2003. *Voices from the Straw Mat: Toward an Ethnography of Korean Story Singing.* Honolulu: University of Hawai'i Press.

Park Hyun Ok. 2005. *Two Dreams in One Bed: Empire, Social Life, and the Origins of the North Korean Revolution in Manchuria.* Durham and London: Duke University Press.

Park Mikyung. 2003. "Korean Shaman Rituals Revisited: The Case of *Chindo Ssikkim-kut* (Cleansing Rituals)," *Ethnomusicology* 47.3 (Fall): 355–75.

Provine, Robert. 2002a. "Confucian Ritual Music in Korea: Aak." In *The Garland Encyclopedia of World Music—East Asia: China, Japan and Korea*, eds. Robert C. Provine, Yosihiko Tokumaru, and J. Lawrence Witzleben, 861–64.

———. 2002b. "Court Music and Chŏngak." In *The Garland Encyclopedia of World Music—East Asia: China, Japan and Korea*, eds. Robert C. Provine, Yosihiko Tokumaru, and J. Lawrence Witzleben, 865–70.

Seo, Maria. 2002. *Hanyang Kut: Korean Shaman Ritual Music from Seoul.* New York and London: Routledge.

Sŏn Sŏng-wŏn. 1993. *P'algunsho-esŏ Raepkkaji* [From the Eighth Army Shows to Rap]. Seoul: Arŭm Ch'ulp'ansa.

Sung, Sang-Yeon. 2006. "The Hanliu Phenomenon in Taiwan: TV Dramas and Teenage Pop." In *Korean Pop Music: Riding the Wave*, ed. Keith Howard, 168–75. Folkestone, UK: Global Oriental.

Wade, Bonnie C. 2004. *Music in Japan: Experiencing Music, Expressing Culture.* New York: Oxford University Press.

———. 2009. *Thinking Musically: Experiencing Music, Expressing Culture.* New York: Oxford University Press.

Yano, Christine Reiko. 1995. "Shaping Tears of a Nation: An Ethnography of Emotion in Japanese Popular Song." Ph.D. dissertation, University of Hawai'i.

Yi Hyŏn-ju. 2006. *Pukhan Ŭmakkwa Chuch'e Ch'ŏlhak* [North Korean Music and Juche Philosophy]. Seoul: Minsok-wŏn.

Resources

Reading

Ahn, Choong-sik. 2005. *The Story of Western Music in Korea: A Social History, 1885–1950.* Morgan Hill, CA: eBookstand Books.

Chae Hyun Kyung. 1996. *"Ch'angjak Kugak:* Making Korean Music Korean." Ph.D. dissertation, University of Michigan.

Clark, Donald N. 2000. *Culture and Customs of Korea.* Westport, CT and London: Greenwood Press.

Condit, Jonathan. 1978. "Uncovering Earlier Melodic Forms from Modern Performance: The *Kasa* Repertoire." *Asian Music* 9/2: 3–20.

———. 1984. *Music of the Korean Renaissance: Songs and Dances of the Fifteenth Century.* Cambridge: Cambridge University Press.

Cumings, Bruce. 2004. *North Korea: Another Country.* New York and London: New Press.

Dilling, Margaret Walker. 2007. *Stories Inside Stories: Music in the Making of the Korean Olympic Ceremonies.* Berkeley: Center for Korean Studies, Institute of East Asian Studies, University of California.

Hahn, Man-young. 1978. "Folk Songs of Korean Rural Life and Their Characteristics Based on the Rice Farming Songs." *Asian Music* 9/2: 21–28.

———. 1990. *Kugak: Studies in Korean Traditional Music,* translated and edited by Inok Paek and Keith Howard. Republic of Korea: Tamgu Dang.

Hahn, Myung-hee. 1998. *A Study of Musical Instruments in Korean Traditional Music.* Seoul: National Center for Korean Traditional Performing Arts, Ministry of Culture and Tourism.

Hesselink, Nathan. 1999. "Kim Inu's *'Pungmulgut* and Communal Spirit': Edited and Translated with an Introduction and Commentary." *Asian Music* 31/1: 1–34.

———. 2001. "'Dance Is Played with Your Heel': Dance as a Determinant of Rhythmic Construct in Korean Percussion Band Music/Dance." *Music and Culture* 4: 99–110.

———. 2004. *"Samul Nori* as Traditional: Preservation and Innovation in a South Korean Contemporary Percussion Genre." *Ethnomusicology* 48/3: 405–432.

————, ed. *Contemporary Directions: Korean Folk Music Engaging the Twentieth Century and Beyond.* Berkeley: Center for Korean Studies, Institute of East Asian Studies, University of California-Berkeley.

Howard, Keith. 1989. *Bands, Songs, and Shamanistic Rituals: Folk Music in Korean Society.* Seoul: Royal Asiatic Society, Korea Branch/Korean National Commission for UNESCO, by Seoul Computer Press.

————. 1999. *Korean Music: A Listening Guide.* Seoul: National Center for Korean Traditional Performing Arts, Ministry of Culture and Tourism.

————. 2006. *Preserving Korean Music: Intangible Cultural Properties as Icons of Identity: Perspectives on Korean Music Volume 1.* Aldershot, England, and Burlington, VT: Ashgate.

————, ed. 2006. *Korean Pop Music: Riding the Wave.* Folkestone, Kent: Global Oriental.

Hwang Byung-ki. 1978. "Aesthetic Characteristics of Korean Music in Theory and in Practice." *Asian Music* 9/2: 29–40.

Kendall, Laurel. 1985. *Shaman, Housewives and Other Restless Spirits: Women in Korean Ritual Life.* Honolulu: University of Hawai'i Press.

————. 1988. *The Life and Hard Times of a Korean Shaman: Of Tales and the Telling of Tales.* Honolulu: University of Hawai'i Press.

————. 2010. *Shamans, Nostalgias, and the IMF: South Korean Popular Religion in Motion.* Honolulu: University of Hawai'i Press.

————, ed. 2010. *Consuming Korean Tradition in Early and Late Modernity: Commodification, Tourism and Performance.* Honolulu: University of Hawai'i Press.

Killick, Andrew. 2010. *In Search of Korean Traditional Opera: Discourses of Ch'angguk.* Honolulu: University of Hawai'i Press.

Kim, Hee-sun. 2008. *Contemporary Kayagŭm Music in Korea: Tradition, Modernity and Identity.* Seoul: Minsokwon.

Kim Kyu-taik, ed. 1978. *Traditional Performing Arts of Korea.* Seoul: Korean National Commission for UNESCO.

Koo, John H., and Nahm, Andrew C. 1998. *An Introduction to Korean Culture.* Elizabeth, NJ: Hollym.

Lee Byong Won. 1977. "Structural Formulae of Melodies in the Two Sacred Buddhist Chant Styles of Korea." *Korean Studies* 1: 111–96.

————. 1980. "Korea." In *The New Grove Dictionary of Music and Musicians,* edited by Stanley Sadie, 192–208. London: Macmillan.

————. 1993. "Contemporary Korean Music Cultures." In *Korea Briefing,* edited by Donald N. Clark, 5–31. Boulder: Westview Press.

————. 1997. *Styles and Esthetics in Korean Traditional Music.* Seoul: National Center for Korean Traditional Performing Arts, Ministry of Culture and Sports.

————, and Yi Yong-shik. 2007. *Music of Korea, Korean Musicology Series, 1.* Seoul, Korea: National Center for Korean Traditional Performing Arts.

Lee Hye-ku. 1981. *Essays on Korean Traditional Music*, translated by Robert C. Provine. Seoul: Royal Asiatic Society, Korea Branch.

————. 1977. *An Introduction to Korean Music and Dance.* Seoul: Royal Asiatic Society.

Lee, Kang-sook. 1980. "Certain Experiences in Korean Music." In *Musics of Many Cultures: An Introduction*, edited by Elizabeth May. Berkeley: University of California Press.

Lee, Kang-sook. 1978. "An Essay on Korean Modes." *Asian Music*, 9/2: 41–47.

Lee, Peter H. 1981. *Anthology of Korean Literature: From Early Times to the Nineteenth Century.* Honolulu: University Press of Hawai'i.

Malm, William P. 1995. *Music Cultures of the Pacific, the Near East, and Asia.* Englewood Cliffs, NJ: Prentice-Hall.

Mills, Simon. 2005. *Healing Rhythms: The World of South Korea's East Coast Hereditary Shamans.* Aldershot, Hampshire, England, and Burlington, VT: Ashgate.

Morelli, Sarah. 2002. "Who Is a Dancing Hero? Rap, Hip-Hop and Dance in Korean Popular Culture." In *Global Noise: Rap and Hip-Hop Outside the USA*, edited by Tony Mitchell, 248–58. Middletown, CT: Wesleyan University Press.

National Academy of Arts. 1973. *Survey of Korean Arts: Traditional Music.* Seoul: National Academy of Arts.

National Academy of Arts. 1974. *Survey of Korean Arts: Folk Arts.* Seoul: National Academy of Arts.

Park Mikyung. 1985. "Music and Shamanism in Korea: A Study of Selected *Sskikkim-kut* Rituals for the Dead." Ph.D. dissertation, University of California, Los Angeles.

————. 2004. "Improvisation in the Music of Korean Shamans: A Case of Degeneration Based on Examples from Chindo Island." In *Yearbook for Traditional Music* 36: 65–89.

Pihl, Marshall R. 1994. *The Korean Singer of Tales.* Cambridge: Harvard University Press.

Pilzer, Joshua. 2003. "*Sŏdosori* (Northwestern Korean Lyric Song) on the Demilitarized Zone: A Study in Music and Teleological Judgment." *Ethnomusicology* 47/1: 68–92.

Pratt, Keith. 1987. *Korean Music: Its History and Performance.* London: Faber & Faber, in association with Jungeumsa.

Provine, Robert C. 1988. *Essays in Sino-Korean Musicology: Early Sources for Korean Ritual Music.* Seoul: Il Ji Sa.

———. 1992. "The Korean Courtyard Ensemble for Ritual Music." *Yearbook for Traditional Music* 24: 91–117.

———. 1993. "Korea." In *Ethnomusicology: Historical and Regional Studies*, ed. Helen Myers, New Grove Handbooks in Music, pp. 363–76. London: Macmillan.

———, J. Lawrence Witzleben, and Tokumaru Yosihiko, eds. 2002. *The Garland Encyclopedia of World Music. Volume 7: East Asia: China, Japan and Korea*. New York and London: Routledge.

Rockwell, Coralie. 1972. *Kagok: A Traditional Korean Vocal Form*. Providence, RI: Asian Music.

Sadie, Stanley, ed. 1984. *The New Grove Dictionary of Musical Instruments*. London: Macmillan Press.

So, Inhwa. 2002. *Theoretical Perspectives on Korean Traditional Music: An Introduction*. Seoul, Korea: National Center for Korean Traditional Performing Arts, Ministry of Culture and Tourism.

Song, Bang-song. 1971. *An Annotated Bibliography of Korean Music*. Providence: Asian Music.

———. 1977. "Ritual Tradition of Korea." *Asian Music* 8/2: 26–46.

———. 1978. "Korean Music: An Annotated Bibliography, Second Supplement." *Asian Music* 9/2: 65–112.

———. 1980. *Source Readings in Korean Music, Korean Traditional Music, 1*. Seoul: Korean National Commission for UNESCO.

———. 1986. *The Sanjo Tradition of Korean Kŏmun'go Music, Traditional Korean Music, 1*. Seoul: Jungeumsa.

———. 1993. *A Study of the History of Korean Music*. Korea: Youngnam University.

———. 2000. *Korean Music: Historical and Other Aspects*. Seoul: Jimoondang.

———. 2001. *Introduction to Korean Musicology*. Seoul: Minsokwon.

Song, Hye-jin. 2000. *A Stroll Through Korean Music History*. Seoul: National Center for Korean Traditional Performing Arts, Ministry of Culture and Tourism.

Song, Kyong-rin. 1994. *Listening to Korean Music*. Seoul: Samho.

Um Hae-kyung. 1992. "Making *P'ansori*: Korean Musical Drama." Ph. D. dissertation, Queen's University of Belfast.

Willoughby, Heather. 2000. "The Sound of *Han*." *Yearbook for Traditional Music* 32: 17–30.

Yi Tu-hyon. 1997. *Korean Performing Arts: Drama, Dance and Music Theater*. Seoul: Chipmundang (Korean studies series).

Yi Yong-shik. 2004. *Shaman Ritual Music in Korea*. Seoul: Jimoondang.

———. 2008. *Pansori*. Seoul: National Center for Korean Traditional Performing Arts.

Videography

The Beat, Beat, Beat of Korea Rak: Performing Arts. 2008. Korea Foundation. The film shows how contemporary Korean rhythms and performance practices are rooted in the itinerant entertainment troupes called *namsadang*.

Ch'unhyang. 2000. Im Kwon-taek, dir. Contains some scenes of sexuality in depicting the courtship between two young lovers. Use discretion, but for college-age and older this is a straightforward and appealing depiction of the story of Ch'unhyang.

Families of Korea. 2001. Mark Marquisee, dir. Master Communications. A documentary that follows two South Korean school children—one urban, one rural—over the course of one day. (Online teacher's guide available at http://www.familiesoftheworld.com/teachers.html.)

Great Tales in Asian Art. 1995. Long Branch, NJ: Kultur International Films. Includes a performance of a Korean folk tale from *t'alchum* (mask dance drama).

Hidden Korea. 2001. PBS Home Video. A general introduction to various aspects of Korean culture. (Online guide available at http://www.pbs.org/hiddenkorea/intro.htm.)

An Initiation "Kut" for a Korean Shaman. 1991. By Diana S. Lee, Laurel Kendall, Kim Asch, Jeanne Bascom and Elizabeth Thompson. Distributed by University of Hawai'i Press. A thirty-two-year-old woman tells of the events that led to her decision to become a shaman. Includes scenes from the two-day initiation.

The JVC Video Anthology of World Music and Dance: East Asia, Volumes I and II. 2005. Ichikawa Katsumori, prod. Nakagawa Kunihiko, dir. JVC, Victor Company of Japan, Smithsonian/Folkways Recordings. Distributed by Multicultural Media. Previously released on VHS. Includes examples of court music, drum dance, *salp'uri* dance, cymbal dance, *kayagŭm* with singing, *taegŭm*, mask dance drama, Buddhist chant, *sungmu* dance, *p'ansori*, puppetry, tightrope walking, *nongak*, and shaman ritual.

North Korea: Beyond the DMZ. 2003. J. T. Takagi & Hey Jung Park, dir. Third World Newsreel, 2003. Follows a Korean-American woman who goes to visit relatives in North Korea, giving a recent picture of life in North Korea.

Our Nation: A Korean Punk Rock Community. 2001. Produced and directed by Stephen Epstein and Timothy Tangherlini. Distributed by Filmakers Library. Documents how Korean youth use punk rock to find a voice in their rapidly changing culture.

The Pacific Century, Vol. 8: The Fight for Democracy. 1992. Burlington, VT. Annenberg/CPB Project. Looks at democratization in the 1980s in South Korea.

Sŏp'yŏnje. 1993. Im Kwon-taek, dir. A fictional story of a struggling "family" of *p'ansori* singers. Appreciation of the film requires some knowledge of Korean literature, history, culture and aesthetic concepts such as *han*.

A State of Mind. 2003. Daniel Gordon, dir. Kino International. Feature-length documentary that follows North Korean schoolgirls preparing to perform in the 2003 Mass Games. Supplementary materials connected to this video, including a videotaped interview and briefings by North Korea experts, are available at http://www.pbs.org/wnet/wideangle/shows/northkorea/index.html.

Discography

Because of the limited availability of Korean recordings outside South Korea, these discographies have been written to help navigate this material.

Howard, Keith. 1996. "A Compact Discography of Korean Traditional Music." *Korea Journal* 36/3: 115–132 and 36/4: 120–140.

Song Bang-song. 1977. "A Discography of Korean Music." *Asian Music* 8/2: 82–121.

In general, selections from Seoul Records, Samsung Entertainment, SKC, Oasis and Jigu Records can sometimes be found internationally. AkdangEban is a recent company whose impressive catalogue has just been made available in America. In addition, anything released in conjunction with the National Center for Korean Traditional Performing Arts (*Kungnip Kugakwŏn*, now the National Gugak Center) will be of high quality and can be found in many university libraries. International record companies that have released Korean music include JVC, Nonesuch, Lyrichord and Folkways. Looking for recordings by Korea's most prominent touring musicians can also be effective. These include the performer/composer Hwang Byung-ki, *p'ansori* singers Kim Sohŭi and An Suk-sŏn and the percussion group Samul-Nori. Korean composers with internationally distributed recordings include Ahn Eak-Tai, Isang Yun, Hi Kyung Kim and Unsuk Chin. For popular music and culture, YesAsia (www.yesasia.com) is a reliable site for buying Korean popular music CDs and DVDs of films, videos and television serials.

Online Sources of Korean Music

These websites feature programs, information and visual materials on Korean culture, history, art and music:

http://www.koreasociety.org/

http://www.lifeinkorea.com/Culture/index.cfm

http://www.clickkorea.org/

http://www.gugak.go.kr/eng/index.jsp

Index